Latin American
Spanish
PHRASEBOOK & DICTIONARY

Acknowledgments
Product Editor Tracy Whitmey
Book Designer Gwen Cotter
Production Support Chris Love
Language Writer Roberto Esposto
Cover Image Researcher Naomi Parker

Thanks
James Hardy, Kirsten Rawlings, Angela Tinson

Published by Lonely Planet Global Limited
CRN 554153

8th Edition – June 2017
ISBN 978 1 78657 555 5
Text © Lonely Planet 2017
Cover Image Jupiterimages/Getty©

Printed in China   10 9 8 7 6 5 4 3 2 1

Contact lonelyplanet.com/contact

Paper in this book is certified against the Forest Stewardship Council™ standards. FSC™ promotes environmentally responsible, socially beneficial and economically viable management of the world's forests.

MIX
Paper from
responsible source
FSC™ C02174

Look out for the following icons throughout the book:

'Shortcut' Phrase
Easy to remember alternative to the full phrase

Q&A Pair
'Question-and-answer' pair – we suggest a response to the question asked

Look For
Phrases you may see on signs, menus etc

Listen For
Phrases you may hear from officials, locals etc

Language Tip
An insight into the foreign language

Culture Tip
An insight into the local culture

How to read the phrases:
- Coloured words and phrases throughout the book are phonetic guides to help you pronounce the foreign language.
- Lists of phrases with tinted background are options you can choose to complete the phrase above them.

These abbreviations will help you choose the right words and phrases in this book:

f feminine	**m** masculine	**pol** polite
inf informal	**pl** plural	**sg** singular
lit literal		

See also p7 for the abbreviations of country-specific terms.

Contents

PAGE 6

About Latin American Spanish

Learn about Latin American Spanish, build your own sentences and pronounce words correctly.

PAGE 29

Travel Phrases

Ready-made phrases for every situation – buy a ticket, book a hotel and much more.

Basics — 29

Practical — 39

PAGE
189

📖 **Menu Decoder**
Dishes and ingredients explained –
order with confidence and try new foods.

PAGE
205

📖 **Two-Way Dictionary**
Quick reference vocabulary guide –
3500 words to help you communicate.

INTRO Latin American Spanish

español latinoamericano
es·pa·*nyol* la·tee·no·a·me·ree·*ka*·no

Who speaks Latin American Spanish?

WIDELY UNDERSTOOD
BELIZE
EQUATORIAL GUINEA
SPAIN

OFFICIAL LANGUAGE
MEXICO · GUATEMALA · HONDURAS
NICARAGUA · EL SALVADOR
COSTA RICA · PANAMA · CUBA
DOMINICAN REPUBLIC
PUERTO RICO · VENEZUELA
COLOMBIA · ECUADOR · PERU
CHILE · BOLIVIA · PARAGUAY
URUGUAY · ARGENTINA

Why Bother

With an entire continent of gregarious Spanish-speaking locals to chat with, you don't want to be limited to 'gringo lingo' – and you'll find that revving up your *eres* e·res (*r*'s) and grunting out your *jotas kho·*tas (*j*'s) is fun.

Distinctive Sounds

The strong and rolled r, and kh (pronounced as in the Scottish *loch*).

Spanish in the World

Over the last 500 years, Spanish in Latin America has evolved differently to the

300 MILLION
speak Latin American Spanish
as their first language

100 MILLION
speak Latin American Spanish
as their second language

Spanish spoken in Europe.
You'll recognise Spaniards by
the 'lisp' in their speech – eg
cerveza (beer) is ser·*ve*·sa
across Latin America but
ther·*ve*·tha in Spain.

Spanish in Latin America

There's no doubting the
richness of the language that
has lent itself to the 'magic
realism' of world-famous
authors such as Gabriel
García Márquez. Influenced
by indigenous languages,
Latin American Spanish
varies slightly from country
to country, especially when it
comes to vocabulary. In this
book country-specific terms

are indicated with abbreviations (see below).

Language Family

Romance (developed from
Vulgar Latin spoken by
Romans during the conquest
of the Iberian Peninsula from
the 3rd to the 1st century
BC). Close relatives include
Portuguese, Italian, French
and Romanian.

Must-Know Grammar

Spanish has a formal and
informal word for 'you'
(*Usted* oo·*ste* and *tú* too
respectively). The verbs have
a different ending for each
person, like the English 'I do'
vs 'he/she does'.

ABOUT **INTRODUCTION**

Abbreviations of country-specific terms used in this book

Arg	Argentina	**Cub**	Cuba	**Par**	Paraguay
Bol	Bolivia	**Ecu**	Ecuador	**Per**	Peru
CAm	Central	**Gua**	Guatemala	**Pue**	Puerto Rico
	America	**Hon**	Honduras	**Sal**	El Salvador
Chi	Chile	**Mex**	Mexico	**SAm**	South America
Cos	Costa Rica	**Nic**	Nicaragua	**Uru**	Uruguay
Col	Colombia	**Pan**	Panama	**Ven**	Venezuela

5 Phrases to Learn Before You Go

1 **Can you recommend private lodgings?**
¿Puede recomendar una casa particular?
pwe·de re·ko·men·dar oo·na ka·sa par·tee·koo·lar

Staying with locals will give you a true Cuban experience and an opportunity to sample hearty home-cooked dishes.

2 **I'd like the fixed-price menu, please.**
Quisiera el menú del día, por favor.
kee·sye·ra el me·noo del dee·a por fa·vor

Eateries in Guatemala and Mexico usually offer a fixed-price meal which may include up to four courses and is great value.

3 **Where can I get a shared taxi/minibus?**
¿Dónde se puede tomar un colectivo?
don·de se pwe·de to·mar oon ko·lek·tee·vo

Cheap transport options in Peru and other countries are shared taxis or minibuses – ask locally as there are no obvious stops.

4 **Where can we go salsa/tango dancing?**
¿Dónde podemos ir a bailar salsa/tango?
don·de po·de·mos eer a bai·lar sal·sa/tan·go

In dance-crazy Colombia and Argentina you won't be lacking in dance-hall options, but you may want a local recommendation.

5 **How do you say ... in your language?**
¿Cómo se dice ... en su lengua?
ko·mo se dee·se ... en su len·gwa

Among hundreds of indigenous languages in Latin America are Quechua, Aymara, Mayan languages, Náhuatl and Guaraní.

10 Phrases to Sound Like a Local

What's up?	**¿Qué más?** (Col)	ke mas
What's up?	**¿Qué bolá asere?** (Cub)	ke bo·*la* a·*se*·re
Cool!	**¡Chévere!** (Col/Ven)	*che*·ve·re
How cool!	**¡Qué chido!** (Mex)	ke *chee*·do
No problem.	**No hay drama.**	no ai *dra*·ma
Get on with it!	**¡Ponte las pilas!** (Arg)	*pon*·te las *pee*·las
It's messed up.	**Está en llama.** (Cub)	es·*ta* en *ya*·ma
Come off it!	**¡No manches!** (Mex)	no *man*·ches
No way!	**¡Ni hablar!** (Arg)	nee a·*blar*
Of course!	**¡Claro!**	*kla*·ro

ABOUT LATIN AMERICAN SPANISH

Pronunciation

Latin American Spanish pronunciation differs from the Castilian Spanish spoken in Spain. The most obvious difference is the lack of the lisping 'th' sound which is found in Castilian Spanish. Pronunciation in Latin America also varies to an extent from country to country and from region to region (see p12). In this book we've used pronunciation guides which will allow you to be understood in all parts of Latin America. If you read them as if they were English, you should get your meaning across.

Vowel Sounds

Vowels are pronounced crisply. There are four vowel sounds that roughly correspond to diphthongs (vowel-sound combinations) in English.

SYMBOL	ENGLISH EQUIVALENT	SPANISH EXAMPLE	TRANSLITERATION
a	father	agua	*a*·gwa
ai	aisle	bailar	bai·*lar*
ay	say	seis	says
e	red	bebé	be·*be*
ee	bee	día	*dee*·a
o	hot	ojo	*o*·kho
oo	moon	gusto	*goo*·sto
ow	cow	autobús	ow·to·*boos*
oy	boy	hoy	oy

Consonant Sounds

SYMBOL	ENGLISH EQUIVALENT	SPANISH EXAMPLE	TRANSLITERATION
b	big	barco	*bar*·ko
ch	chili	chica	*chee*·ka
d	dog	dinero	dee·*ne*·ro
f	fun	fiesta	*fye*·sta
g	go	gato	*ga*·to
k	kick	cabeza, queso	ka·*be*·sa, *ke*·so
kh	as in the Scottish 'loch'	jardín, gente	khar·*deen*, *khen*·te
l	loud	lago	*la*·go
m	man	mañana	ma·*nya*·na
n	no	nuevo	*nwe*·vo
ny	canyon	señora	se·*nyo*·ra
p	pig	padre	*pa*·dre
r	run (strongly rolled, especially at the start of a word and as *rr*)	mariposa, ritmo, burro	ma·ree·*po*·sa, *reet*·mo, *boo*·ro
s	so	semana, zarzuela, cinco	se·*ma*·na, sar·*swe*·la, *seen*·ko
t	tin	tienda	*tyen*·da
v	very soft 'v' (between 'v' and 'b')	severo	se·*ve*·ro
w	win	guardia	*gwar*·dya
y	yes	viaje, llamada	*vya*·khe, ya·*ma*·da

Regional Variations

As mentioned previously, pronunciation varies across Latin America so you may expect to hear some of these variations as part of local accents:

The letters *ll* are pronounced as the 'y' in 'yes' in much of Latin America. Where this is the case, the y sound drops out altogether before the vowel sounds e and ee. Be alert, though: in Argentina and Uruguay you'll hear it pronounced as 'sh', in Colombia and Venezuela as the 'dg' in 'judge', and elsewhere you may hear it pronounced like the 'lli' in 'million' or the 's' in 'measure'. You'll hear the same range of sounds for the letter *y*.

In some parts of Latin America s is reduced to just a slight 'h' sound when at the end of a syllable or a word, so *tos* tos (cough) may sound like to followed by a barely audible 'h'.

Throughout Latin America there's confusion between the sounds r and l and you may hear one substituted for the other in a random way.

Word Stress

Latin American Spanish has stress. This means you emphasise one syllable in a word over another. Rule of thumb: when a word ends in *n*, *s* or a vowel, the stress falls on the second-last syllable. Otherwise, the last syllable is stressed. If you see an accent mark over a syllable, it cancels out these rules and you just stress that syllable instead. You needn't worry about these rules though, as the stressed syllables are always italicised in our pronunciation guides.

Reading & Writing

The relationship between Spanish sounds and their spelling is quite straightforward and consistent. The rules in the table opposite will help you read any written Spanish you may come across.

~ SPELLBOUND ~

c	before *e* or *i* pronounced as the 's' in 'so';	cerveza, cita	ser·ve·sa, *see*·ta
	before *a*, *o* and *u* pronounced as the 'k' in 'kick'	carro, corto, cubo	*ka*·ro, *kor*·to, *koo*·bo
g	before *e* or *i* pronounced as the 'ch' in the Scottish *loch*;	gente, gitano	*khen*·te, khee·*ta*·no
	before *a*, *o* and *u* pronounced as the 'g' in 'go'	gato, gordo, guante	*ga*·to, *gor*·do, *gwan*·te
gue, gui, güi	as the 'g' in 'go' (the *u* is not pronounced unless there are two dots over the *u*)	guerra, guinda	*ge*·ra, *geen*·da
		güiski	*gwees*·kee
h	never pronounced	haber	a·*ber*
j	as the 'ch' in the Scottish *loch*	jardín	khar·*deen*
ll	generally as the 'y' in 'yes'	llave	*ya*·ve
ñ	as the 'ny' in 'canyon'	niño	*nee*·nyo
qu	as the 'k' in 'kick' (the *u* is not pronounced)	quince	*keen*·se
z	as the 's' in 'soup'	zorro	*so*·ro

ABOUT PRONUNCIATION

~ SPANISH ALPHABET ~

A a	a	**J j**	*kho*·ta	**R r**	*e*·re
B b	be *lar*·ga	**K k**	ka	**S s**	*e*·se
C c	se	**L l**	*e*·le	**T t**	te
D d	de	**M m**	*e*·me	**U u**	oo
E e	e	**N n**	*e*·ne	**V v**	be kor·*ta*
F f	*e*·fe	**Ñ ñ**	*e*·nye	**W w**	*do*·ble be
G g	khe	**O o**	o	**X x**	*e*·kees
H h	a·che	**P p**	pe	**Y y**	ee *grye*·ga
I i	ee la·*tee*·na	**Q q**	koo	**Z z**	*se*·ta

ABOUT LATIN AMERICAN SPANISH

Grammar

This chapter is designed to explain the main grammatical structures you need in order to make your own sentences. Look under each heading – listed in alphabetical order – for information on functions which these grammatical categories express in a sentence. For example, demonstratives are used for giving instructions, so you'll need them to tell the taxi driver where your hotel is, etc. A glossary of grammatical terms is included at the end of the chapter to help you.

Adjectives & Adverbs

Describing People/Things • Doing Things

Adjectives in Spanish have different endings depending on whether the noun they describe is masculine or feminine, and singular or plural (see **gender** and **plurals**).

~ ADJECTIVES ~

m sg	**fantastic hotel**	hotel fantástico	o·*tel* fan·*tas*·tee·ko
f sg	**fantastic meal**	comida fantástica	ko·*mee*·da fan·*tas*·tee·ka
m pl	**fantastic books**	libros fantásticos	*lee*·bros fan·*tas*·tee·kos
f pl	**fantastic cakes**	tortas fantásticas	*tor*·tas fan·*tas*·tee·kas

As the examples show, adjectives generally come after the noun in Spanish. However, adjectives of quantity (such as 'much', 'a lot', 'little/few'), and possessive adjectives ('my' and 'your') and demonstratives ('this' and 'that') always precede the noun. See also **demonstratives** and **possessives**.

many tourists	muchos turistas (lit: many-m-pl tourists)
	moo·chos too·*rees*·tas
my car	mi carro (lit: my-sg car)
	mee *ka*·ro

Most adverbs in Spanish are derived from adjectives by adding the ending -*mente* ·*men*·te to the singular feminine form of the adjective (ie the form ending in -*a*), just like you add the ending '-ly' to the adjective in English. In Spanish, adverbs are generally placed after the verb they refer to.

a slow train	un tren lento (lit: a-m-sg train slow-m-sg)
	oon tren *len*·to
to speak slowly	hablar lentamente (lit: to-speak slowly)
	ab·*lar* len·ta·*men*·te

Articles

Naming People/Things

Spanish has two words for 'a/an': *un* oon and *una* oo·na. The gender of the noun determines which one you use. *Un* and *una* also have plural forms: *unos* oo·nos and *unas* oo·nas (some).

~ INDEFINITE ARTICLES ~

m sg	**an egg**	un huevo	oon *we*·vo
m pl	**some eggs**	unos huevos	oo·nos *we*·vos
f sg	**a llama**	una llama	oo·na *ya*·ma
f pl	**some llamas**	unas llamas	oo·nas *ya*·mas

The articles *el* el and *la* la both mean 'the'. Whether you use *el* or *la* also depends on the gender of the noun. For the plural, use *los* los and *las* las for masculine and feminine respectively. See also **gender** and **plurals**.

~ DEFINITE ARTICLES ~

m sg	**the car**	el carro	el *ka*·ro
m pl	**the cars**	los carros	los *ka*·ros
f sg	**the shop**	la tienda	la *tyen*·da
f pl	**the shops**	las tiendas	las *tyen*·das

Be

Describing People/Things • Making Statements

Spanish has two words for the English verb 'be': *ser* ser and *estar* es·*tar*, which are used depending on the context.

~ USE OF *SER* (TO BE) ~

permanent characteristics of persons/things	Ángel is very nice.	Ángel es muy amable. *an*·khel es mooy a·*ma*·ble
occupation or nationality	Sarita is from Puerto Rico.	Sarita es de Puerto Rico. sa *ree*·ta es de *pwer*·to *ree*·ko
time and location of events	It's 3 o'clock.	Son las tres. son las tres
possession	Whose backpack is this?	¿De quién es esta mochila? de kyen es es·*ta* mo·*chee*·la

~ USE OF *ESTAR* (TO BE) ~

temporary characteristics of persons/things	The meal is cold.	La comida está fría. la ko·*mee*·da es·*ta* *free*·a
time and location of persons/things	We are in Buenos Aires.	Estamos en Buenos Aires. es·*ta*·mos en *bwe*·nos *ai*·res
a person's mood	I'm happy.	Estoy contento/a. m/f es·*toy* kon·*ten*·to/a

~ *SER* (TO BE) – PRESENT TENSE ~

I	am	yo	soy	yo	soy
you sg inf	**are**	tú*	eres*	too	e·res
you sg pol	**are**	Usted	es	oos·te	es
he/she	**is**	él/ella	es	el/e·ya	es
we	**are**	nosotros m nosotras f	somos	no·so·tros no·so·tras	so·mos
you pl	**are**	Ustedes	son	oos·te·des	son
they	**are**	ellos m ellas f	son	e·yos e·yas	son

* Note that *vos sos* is used instead of *tú eres* in Argentina, Uruguay and Central America (see **personal pronouns**).

~ *ESTAR* (TO BE) – PRESENT TENSE ~

I	am	yo	estoy	yo	es·toy
you sg inf	**are**	tú	estás	too	es·tas
you sg pol	**are**	Usted	está	oos·te	es·ta
he/she	**is**	él/ella	está	el/e·ya	es·ta
we	**are**	nosotros m nosotras f	estamos	no·so·tros no·so·tras	es·ta·mos
you pl	**are**	Ustedes	están	oos·te·des	es·tan
they	**are**	ellos m ellas f	están	e·yos e·yas	es·tan

Demonstratives

Giving Instructions • Indicating Location • Pointing Things Out

To point something out, the easiest phrases to use are *es* es (it is) or *eso es* e·so es (that is).

Eso es mi pasaporte.	*e·so es mee pa·sa·por·te* That is my passport. (lit: that is my-sg passport)

The Spanish words for 'this' and 'that' vary, depending on whether something or someone is close (this), away from you (that) or even further away in time or distance (that over there). They also take the gender and number of the noun they refer to. See also **gender** and **plurals**.

~ DEMONSTRATIVES ~

	m sg		m pl	
this (close)	éste	*es·te*	éstos	*es·tos*
that (away)	ése	*e·se*	ésos	*e·sos*
that (further away)	aquél	*a·kel*	aquéllos	*a·ke·yos*
	f sg		f pl	
this (close)	ésta	*es·ta*	éstas	*es·tas*
that (away)	ésa	*e·sa*	ésas	*e·sas*
that (further away)	aquélla	*a·ke·ya*	aquéllas	*a·ke·yas*

Diminutives

Naming People/Things

A fun feature of Latin American Spanish is the use of diminutives. These are formed by adding word endings such as *-ito/a* *·ee·to/a*, *-cito/a* *·see·to/a*, *-ico/a* *·ee·ko/a* and *-cillo/a* *·see·yo/a*.

They're often used to indicate the smallness of something – eg *gato ga·to* (cat) becomes *gatito* ga·*tee*·to (kitten) – but they're also a way of expressing how a speaker feels about something. They may indicate that a speaker finds something charming, eg saying *perrito* pe·*ree*·to instead of *perro pe*·ro (dog) is akin to saying 'doggy' instead of 'dog' in English. Many Spanish terms of endearment end in *-ito/a* or *-illo/a*, eg *palomita* pa·lo·*mee*·ta (darling) is a diminutive of *paloma* pa·*lo*·ma (dove). Diminutives are used a lot in talking to children too.

These endings can give a friendly tone to a conversation. For instance, *un momentito* oon mo·men·*tee*·to (just a moment) sounds more light-hearted than *un momento* oon mo·*men*·to.

Gender

Naming People/Things

In Spanish, all nouns – words which denote a thing, person or concept – are either masculine or feminine. The dictionary will tell you what gender a noun is, but here are some handy tips to help you determine gender:

» gender is masculine when talking about a man and feminine when talking about a woman
» words ending in *-o* or *-or* are often masculine
» words ending in *-a, -d, -z* or *-ión* are often feminine

In this book, masculine forms appear before the feminine forms. If you see a word ending in *-o/a*, it means the masculine form ends in *-o*, and the feminine form ends in *-a* (that is, you replace the *-o* ending with the *-a* ending to make it feminine). The same goes for the plural endings *-os/as*. If you see a word ending in (*a*) between brackets, eg *escritor(a)* es·kree·*tor*/ es·kree·*to*·ra, it means you have to add the 'a' in order to make that word feminine. In other cases we spell out the whole word. In this book, masculine and feminine forms are indicated with m and f respectively where needed.

See also **adjectives**, **articles** and **possessives**.

Have

Possessing

Possession can be indicated in various ways in Spanish (see also **possessives**). The easiest way is by using the verb *tener* te·*ner* (have). For negative forms with 'have', see **negatives**.

I have two brothers.	Tengo dos hermanos. (lit: I-have two brothers) *ten·go dos er·man·os*

~ *TENER* (TO HAVE) – PRESENT TENSE ~

I	**have**	yo	tengo	yo	*ten·go*
you sg inf	**have**	tú*	tienes*	too	*tye·nes*
you sg pol	**have**	Usted	tiene	oos·te	*tye·ne*
he/she	**has**	él/ella	tiene	el/e·ya	*tye·ne*
we	**have**	nosotros m nosotras f	tenemos	no·so·tros no·so·tras	*te·ne·mos*
you pl	**have**	Ustedes	tienen	oos·te·des	*tye·nen*
they	**have**	ellos m ellas f	tienen	e·yos e·yas	*tye·nen*

* Note that *vos tenés* is used instead of *tú tienes* in Argentina, Uruguay and Central America (see **personal pronouns**).

Negatives

Negating

To make a negative statement, just add the word *no* no (not) before the main verb of the sentence:

I don't live with my family.	No vivo con mi familia. (lit: not I-live with my family) no *vee·*vo kon mee fa·*mee·*lya

Contrary to English, Spanish uses double negatives:

I have nothing to declare.	No tengo nada que declarar. (lit: not I-have nothing that to-declare) no *ten·*go *na·*da ke dek·la·*rar*

Personal Pronouns

Making Statements • Naming People/Things

Personal pronouns ('I', 'you' etc) change form in Spanish
depending on whether they're the subject or the object of a
sentence. It's the same in English, which has 'I' and 'me' as the
subject and object pronouns (eg 'I see her' and 'She sees me').
The subject pronoun is usually omitted in Spanish because
the subject is obvious from the corresponding verb form (see
verbs).

I'm a student.	Soy estudiante. (lit: I-am student) soy es·too·*dyan*·te

~ SUBJECT PRONOUNS ~

I	yo	yo	**we**	nosotros m nosotras f	no·so·tros no·so·tras
you sg inf	tú/ vos	too/ vos	**you** pl	Ustedes	oos·*te*·des
you sg pol	Usted	oos·*te*			
he **she**	él ella	el *e*·ya	**they**	ellos m ellas f	*e*·yos *e*·yas

As the table shows, Latin American Spanish has two forms
for the singular 'you'. When talking to someone familiar to
you or younger than you, use the informal form *tú* too, rather
than the polite form *Usted* oos·*te*. The polite form should be
used when you're meeting someone for the first time, talking
to someone much older than you or when you're in a formal
situation (eg when talking to the police, customs officers etc).
In this phrasebook we have chosen the appropriate form for
the situation. Where both forms are used, they are indicated
by pol and inf. Note that in Latin American Spanish there's no
polite/informal distinction for the plural 'you' – you always use
Ustedes oos·*te*·des.

In many Latin American countries (particularly in Argentina, Chile, Paraguay, Uruguay and some Central American countries), you'll hear *vos* vos instead of *tú*. The form of the verb that goes with *vos* may differ slightly from the form of the verb that goes with *tú*. The *vos* verb form that you're likely to hear most is *sos* sos, from the verb *ser* ser (be): instead of *¿Eres de Australia?* e·res de ow·stra·lya (Are you from Australia?), you may hear *¿Sos de Australia?* sos de ow·stra·lya. In this book we've only used *tú* (and the verb form that goes with it). You'll be perfectly well understood if you use *tú*, just be aware that locals may use *vos* forms instead.

Plurals

Naming People/Things

In general, if the word ends in a vowel, you add -*s* for plural. If the noun ends in a consonant (or *y*), you add -*es*. In this book, singular and plural forms are shown with sg and pl respectively where needed.

~ SINGULAR ~			~ PLURAL ~		
bed	cama	*ka·ma*	**beds**	camas	*ka·mas*
woman	mujer	moo·*kher*	**women**	mujeres	moo·*khe·res*

Possessives

Possessing

A common way of indicating possession is by using a possessive adjective before the noun it describes. As with any other adjectives, possessive adjectives always agree with the noun in number (singular or plural) and gender (masculine or feminine). See also **gender** and **plurals**.

This is our daughter. Ésta es nuestra hija.
(lit: this-**f-sg** is our-**f-sg** daughter)
es·ta es nwes·tra ee·kha

~ POSSESSIVE ADJECTIVES ~

my	mi/ mis	mee/ mees	**our**	nuestro/ nuestros m nuestra/ nuestras f	nwes·tro/ nwes·tros nwes·tra/ nwes·tras
your sg inf	tu/ tus	too/ toos	**your** pl inf	vuestro/ vuestros m vuestra/ vuestras f	vwes·tro/ vwes·tros vwes·tra/ vwes·tras
your sg pol	su/ sus	soo/ soos	**your** pl pol	su/ sus	soo/ soos
his **her** **its**	su/ sus	soo/ soos	**their**	su/ sus	soo/ soos

ABOUT GRAMMAR

In the table above, the forms separated by a slash are used with a singular/plural noun.

In Spanish, ownership can also be expressed by using the word *de* de (of).

This is my friend's tent.	Esta es la carpa de mi amiga. (lit: this-f-sg is the-f-sg tent of my-sg friend-f) es·ta es la *kar*·pa de mee a·*mee*·ga

Another way to express possession is by using the verb *tener* te·*ner* (to have). For more information, see **have**.

Prepositions

Giving Instructions • Indicating Location • Pointing Things Out

Like English, Spanish uses prepositions to explain where things are in time or space. Common prepositions are listed in the table overleaf. For more prepositions, see the **dictionary**.

~ PREPOSITIONS ~

after	después de	des·*pwes* de	**from**	de	de
at (time)	a	a	**in (place)**	en	en
before	antes de	*an*·tes de	**to**	a	a

Questions

Asking Questions • Negating

To ask a 'yes/no' question, simply make a statement, but raise your intonation towards the end of the sentence, as you would in English. The inverted question mark in written Spanish prompts you to do so.

Do you have a car? ¿Tienes un carro?
(lit: you-have-**sg-inf** a-**m-sg** car)
tye·nes oon *ka*·ro

It's not impolite to answer questions with a simple *sí* see (yes) or *no* no (no) in Spanish, even when you'd like to say 'Yes, it is/does', or 'No, it isn't/doesn't'.

~ QUESTION WORDS ~

How?	¿Cómo?	*ko*·mo
How many?	¿Cuántos? **m pl** ¿Cuántas? **f pl**	*kwan*·tos *kwan*·tas
How much?	¿Cuánto?	*kwan*·to
What?	¿Qué?	ke
When?	¿Cuándo?	*kwan*·do
Where?	¿Dónde?	*don*·de
Which?	¿Cuál? **sg** ¿Cuáles? **pl**	kwal *kwa*·les
Who?	¿Quién? **sg** ¿Quiénes? **pl**	kyen *kye*·nes
Why?	¿Por qué?	por ke

Verbs

Doing Things • Making Statements

There are three verb categories in Spanish – verbs whose infinitive (dictionary form) ends in *-ar*, *-er* or *-ir*, eg *hablar* ab·*lar* (talk), *comer* ko·*mer* (eat), *vivir* vee·*veer* (live). Tenses are formed by adding various endings for each person to the verb stem (the part that remains after removing *-ar*, *-er* or *-ir* from the infinitive) or simply to the infinitive, and for most verbs these endings follow regular patterns. The verb endings for the present, past and future tenses are presented in the tables on the following pages. For negative forms of verbs, see **negatives**.

~ PRESENT TENSE ~

		hablar	comer	vivir
I	yo	hablo	como	vivo
you sg inf	tú	hablas	comes	vives
you sg pol	Usted	habla	come	vive
he **she**	él ella	habla	come	vive
we	nosotros m nosotras f	hablamos	comemos	vivimos
you pl	Ustedes	hablan	comen	viven
they	ellos m ellas f	hablan	comen	viven

See also **be** and **have** for present-tense forms of these two verbs, and **personal pronouns** for more information about the 'you' forms.

~ PAST TENSE ~

		hablar	comer	vivir
I	yo	hablé	comí	viví
you sg inf	tú	hablaste	comiste	viviste
you sg pol	Usted	habló	comió	vivió
he/she	él/ella	habló	comió	vivió
we	nosotros m nosotras f	hablamos	comimos	vivimos
you pl	Ustedes	hablaron	comieron	vivieron
they	ellos m ellas f	hablaron	comieron	vivieron

In the future tense, all three verb categories have the same endings added to the infinitive:

~ FUTURE TENSE ~

		hablar	comer	vivir
I	yo	hablaré	comeré	viviré
you sg inf	tú	hablarás	comerás	vivirás
you sg pol	Usted	hablará	comerá	vivirá
he/she	él/ella	hablará	comerá	vivirá
we	nosotros m nosotras f	hablaremos	comeremos	viviremos
you pl	Ustedes	hablarán	comerán	vivirán
they	ellos m ellas f	hablarán	comerán	vivirán

Word Order

Making Statements

Sentences in Spanish have a basic word order of subject–verb–object. The subject pronoun can be omitted because the subject is understood from the corresponding verb form (see **verbs**).

I study business.	Yo estudio comercio.
	(lit: I I-study business)
	yo es·*too*·dyo ko·*mer*·syo
	Estudio comercio.
	(lit: I-study business)
	es·*too*·dyo ko·*mer*·syo

CULTURE TIP   **Latin American Currencies**

Argentina, Chile, Colombia and Uruguay use *peso* *pe*·so (lit: weight). Cuba has two currencies: *peso convertible* *pe*·so kon·ver·*tee*·ble and Cuban *peso* (the latter is also called *moneda nacional* mo·*ne*·da na·syo·*nal*).

Bolivia	*boliviano*	bo·lee·*vya*·no
Costa Rica	*colón* (named after Christopher Columbus)	ko·*lon*
Ecuador	*dólar*	do·lar
Guatemala	*quetzal* (a native bird)	ke·*tsal*
Honduras	*lempira* (the name of an indigenous chief)	lem·*pee*·ra
Nicaragua	*córdoba* (in honour of a Spanish explorer)	kor·do·ba
Panama	*balboa* (named after a Spanish explorer); *dólar*	bal·*bo*·a; do·lar
Paraguay	*guaraní* (an Amerindian people)	gwa·ra·*nee*
Peru	*nuevo sol* (lit: new sun)	*nwe*·vo sol
Venezuela	*bolívar* (named after Simón Bolívar)	bo·*lee*·var

~ GLOSSARY ~

adjective	a word that describes something – 'he was the **greatest** mariachi of his time'
adverb	a word that explains how an action is done – 'he sang **beautifully**'
article	the words 'a', 'an' and 'the'
demonstrative	a word that means 'this' or 'that'
direct object	the thing or person in the sentence that has the action directed to it – 'and the crowd loved **him**'
gender	classification of *nouns* into classes (like masculine and feminine), requiring other words (eg *adjectives*) to belong to the same class
indirect object	the person or thing in the sentence that is the recipient of the action – 'the public yelled to **him**'
infinitive	dictionary form of a *verb* – 'to **play** more'
noun	a thing, person or idea – 'the **ensemble** was excited'
number	whether a word is singular or plural – 'and they performed more **songs**'
personal pronoun	a word that means 'I', 'you' etc
possessive adjective	a word that means 'my', 'your' etc
possessive pronoun	a word that means 'mine', 'yours' etc
preposition	a word like 'for' or 'before' in English
subject	the thing or person in the sentence that does the action – 'the **musicians** played for hours'
tense	form of a *verb* that tells you whether the action is in the present, past or future – eg 'run' (present), 'ran' (past), 'will run' (future)
verb	a word that tells you what action happened – 'and **went** home late'
verb stem	part of a *verb* that doesn't change – eg '**play**' in '**play**ing' and '**play**ed'

Basics

BASICS UNDERSTANDING

Understanding

KEY PHRASES

Do you speak English?	¿Habla/Hablas inglés? pol/inf	a·bla/a·blas een·gles
I don't understand.	No entiendo.	no en·tyen·do
What does ... mean?	¿Qué significa ...?	ke seeg·nee·fee·ka ...

Q Do you speak (English)?	¿Habla/Hablas (inglés)? pol/inf a·bla/a·blas (een·gles)
Q Does anyone speak (English)?	¿Hay alguien que hable (inglés)? ai al·gyen ke a·ble (een·gles)
A I speak Spanish/English.	Hablo castellano/inglés. a·blo kas·te·ya·no/een·gles
A I speak a little.	Hablo un poco. a·blo oon po·ko
Q Do you understand?	¿Me entiende/entiendes? pol/inf me en·tyen·de/en·tyen·des
A I (don't) understand.	(No) Entiendo. (no) en·tyen·do
What does ... mean?	¿Qué significa ...? ke seeg·nee·fee·ka ...
How do you write ...?	¿Cómo se escribe ...? ko·mo se es·kree·be ...
How do you pronounce this?	¿Cómo se pronuncia esto? ko·mo se pro·noon·sya es·to

LANGUAGE TIP **False Friends**
Beware of 'false friends' – words which look and/or sound like an English word but have a different meaning altogether.

embarazada f   em·ba·ra·*sa*·da   pregnant
(not 'embarrassed', which is *avergonzado/a* m/f
a·ver·gon·*sa*·do/a)

injuria f   een·*khoo*·rya   insult
(not 'injury', which is *herida* e·*ree*·da)

parientes m pl   pa·*ryen*·tes   relatives
(not 'parents', which is *padres* pa·dres)

I'd like to learn some of your (indigenous) language.	Me gustaría aprender un poco de su lengua (indígena). me goos·ta·*ree*·a a·pren·*der* oon po·ko de soo *len*·gwa (een·*dee*·khe·na)
Would you like me to teach you some English?	¿Le/te gustaría que le/te enseñe un poco de inglés? pol/inf le/te goos·ta·*ree*·a ke le/te en·*se*·nye oon po·ko de een·*gles*
Could you please repeat that?	¿Puede repetirlo, por favor? *pwe*·de re·pe·*teer*·lo por fa·*vor*
Could you please write it down?	¿Puede escribirlo, por favor? *pwe*·de es·kree·*beer*·lo por fa·*vor*
Could you please speak more slowly?	¿Puede hablar más despacio, por favor? *pwe*·de a·*blar* mas des·*pa*·syo por fa·*vor*

 Slowly, please!   ¡Despacio, por favor!   des·*pa*·syo por fa·*vor*

Numbers & Amounts

KEY PHRASES

How much?	¿Cuánto?	*kwan*·to
a little	un poco	oon *po*·ko
a lot	mucho	*moo*·cho

Cardinal Numbers

1	uno	*oo*·no
2	dos	dos
3	tres	tres
4	cuatro	*kwa*·tro
5	cinco	*seen*·ko
6	seis	says
7	siete	*sye*·te
8	ocho	*o*·cho
9	nueve	*nwe*·ve
10	diez	dyes
11	once	*on*·se
12	doce	*do*·se
13	trece	*tre*·se
14	catorce	ka·*tor*·se
15	quince	*keen*·se
16	dieciséis	dye·see·*says*
17	diecisiete	dye·see·*sye*·te
18	dieciocho	dye·see·*o*·cho

19	diecinueve	dye·see·*nwe*·ve
20	veinte	*vayn*·te
21	veintiuno	vayn·tee·*oo*·no
30	treinta	*trayn*·ta
40	cuarenta	kwa·*ren*·ta
50	cincuenta	seen·*kwen*·ta
60	sesenta	se·*sen*·ta
70	setenta	se·*ten*·ta
80	ochenta	o·*chen*·ta
90	noventa	no·*ven*·ta
100	cien	syen
200	doscientos	do·*syen*·tos
1000	mil	meel
1,000,000	un millón	oon mee·*yon*

Ordinal Numbers

1st	primero/a m/f	pree·*me*·ro/a
2nd	segundo/a m/f	se·*goon*·do/a
3rd	tercero/a m/f	ter·*se*·ro/a

Amounts

How much?	¿Cuánto/a? m/f	*kwan*·to/a
How many?	¿Cuántos? m pl	*kwan*·tos
	¿Cuántas? f pl	*kwan*·tas
a little	un poco	oon *po*·ko
a lot/much	mucho/a m/f	*moo*·cho/a
many	muchos/as m/f pl	*moo*·chos/as
some	algunos/as m/f pl	al·*goo*·nos/as

For other useful amounts, see **self-catering** (p182).

BASICS **NUMBERS & AMOUNTS**

Time & Dates

KEY PHRASES

What time is it?	¿Qué hora es?	ke *o*·ra es
At what time ...?	¿A qué hora ...?	a ke *o*·ra ...
What date?	¿Qué fecha?	ke *fe*·cha

Telling the Time

When telling the time in Spanish, 'It's ...' is expressed by *Son las ...* son las ... followed by a number. However, 'It's one o'clock' is *Es la una* es la *oo*·na, and 'It's midnight' and 'It's midday' are *Es el mediodía* es el me·dyo·*dee*·a and *Es la medianoche* es la me·dya·*no*·che respectively. Both the 12-hour and the 24-hour clocks are commonly used.

Q	**What time is it?**	¿Qué hora es? ke *o*·ra es
A	**It's one o'clock.**	Es la una. es la *oo*·na
A	**It's (10) o'clock.**	Son las (diez). son las (dyes)
A	**Quarter past (two).**	(Las dos) y cuarto. (las dos) ee *kwar*·to
A	**Twenty past (two).**	(Las dos) y veinte. (las dos) ee *vayn*·te
A	**Half past (two).**	(Las dos) y media. (las dos) ee *me*·dya
A	**Twenty to (three).**	(Las tres) menos veinte. (las tres) *me*·nos *vayn*·te
A	**Quarter to (three).**	(Las tres) menos cuarto. (las tres) *me*·nos *kwar*·to

It's early.	Es temprano.	es tem·*pra*·no
It's late.	Es tarde.	es *tar*·de
am	de la mañana	de la ma·*nya*·na
pm	de la tarde	de la *tar*·de
in the morning	por la mañana	por la ma·*nya*·na
in the afternoon	por la tarde	por la *tar*·de
in the evening	por la noche	por la *no*·che
at night	por la noche	por la *no*·che
midday	mediodía m	me·dyo·*dee*·a
midnight	medianoche f	me·dya·*no*·che
sunrise	amanecer m	a·ma·ne·*ser*
sunset	atardecer m	a·tar·de·*ser*
Q **At what time ...?**	¿A qué hora ...?	a ke *o*·ra ...
A **At one o'clock.**	A la una.	a la *oo*·na
A **At (six) o'clock.**	A las (seis).	a las (says)

The Calendar

Monday	lunes m	*loo*·nes
Tuesday	martes m	*mar*·tes
Wednesday	miércoles m	*myer*·ko·les
Thursday	jueves m	*khwe*·ves
Friday	viernes m	*vyer*·nes
Saturday	sábado m	*sa*·ba·do
Sunday	domingo m	do·*meen*·go

January	enero m	e·ne·ro
February	febrero m	fe·bre·ro
March	marzo m	mar·so
April	abril m	a·breel
May	mayo m	ma·yo
June	junio m	khoo·nyo
July	julio m	khoo·lyo
August	agosto m	a·gos·to
September	septiembre m	sep·tyem·bre
October	octubre m	ok·too·bre
November	noviembre m	no·vyem·bre
December	diciembre m	dee·syem·bre
What date?	¿Qué fecha?	ke fe·cha
Q **What's today's date?**	¿Qué día es hoy?	ke dee·a es oy
A **It's (18 October).**	Es (el dieciocho de octubre).	es (el dye·see·o·cho de ok·too·bre)
summer	verano m	ve·ra·no
autumn	otoño m	o·to·nyo
winter	invierno m	een·vyer·no
spring	primavera f	pree·ma·ve·ra

Present

now	ahora	a·o·ra
today	hoy	oy
this morning	esta mañana	es·ta ma·nya·na
this afternoon	esta tarde	es·ta tar·de
tonight	esta noche	es·ta no·che
this week	esta semana	es·ta se·ma·na

LANGUAGE TIP

Tongue Twisters
Tongue twisters are known as *trabalenguas*
tra·ba·*len*·gwas in Spanish. Try exercising your
tongue with these two:

**Comí chirimoyas, me enchirimoyé.
Ahora, para desenchirimoyarme,
¿cómo me desenchirimoyaré?**
ko·*mee* chee·ree·mo·yas me en·chee·ree·mo·*ye*
a·o·ra *pa*·ra des·en·chee·ree·mo·*yar*·me
ko·mo me des·en·chee·ree·mo·ya·*re*
I ate custard apples, I ate too many custard apples.
Now, to get un-custard-appled,
how shall I un-custard-apple myself?

**Poquito a poquito Paquito empaca poquitas
copitas en pocos paquetes.**
po·*kee*·to a po·*kee*·to pa·*kee*·to em·*pa*·ka po·*kee*·tas
ko·*pee*·tas en *po*·kos pa·*ke*·tes
Little by little Paquito is packing a few small
wineglasses in few boxes.

| this month | este mes | es·te mes |
| this year | este año | es·te *a*·nyo |

Past

yesterday	ayer	a·*yer*
day before yesterday	anteayer	an·te·a·*yer*
(three days) ago	hace (tres días)	*a*·se (tres *dee*·as)
since (May)	desde (mayo)	*des*·de (*ma*·yo)
last night	anoche	a·*no*·che
last week	la semana pasada	la se·*ma*·na pa·*sa*·da
last month	el mes pasado	el mes pa·*sa*·do

BASICS   TIME & DATES

last year	el año pasado	el *a*·nyo pa·*sa*·do
yesterday morning	ayer por la mañana	a·*yer* por la ma·*nya*·na
yesterday afternoon	ayer por la tarde	a·*yer* por la *tar*·de
yesterday evening	ayer por la noche	a·*yer* por la *no*·che

Future

tomorrow	mañana	ma·*nya*·na
day after tomorrow	pasado mañana	pa·*sa*·do ma·*nya*·na
in (six days)	dentro de (seis días)	*den*·tro de (says *dee*·as)
until (June)	hasta (junio)	*as*·ta (*khoo*·nyo)
next week	la semana que viene	la se·*ma*·na ke *vye*·ne
next month	el mes que viene	el mes ke *vye*·ne
next year	el año que viene	el *a*·nyo ke *vye*·ne
tomorrow morning	mañana por la mañana	ma·*nya*·na por la ma·*nya*·na
tomorrow afternoon	mañana por la tarde	ma·*nya*·na por la *tar*·de
tomorrow evening	mañana por la noche	ma·*nya*·na por la *no*·che

CULTURE TIP   **Donations to English**
Thanks to Columbus' discovery of the New World in 1492, a large corpus of words from indigenous American languages has entered English via Latin American Spanish, eg *barbecue, canoe, hammock, potato, tobacco, chocolate* ...

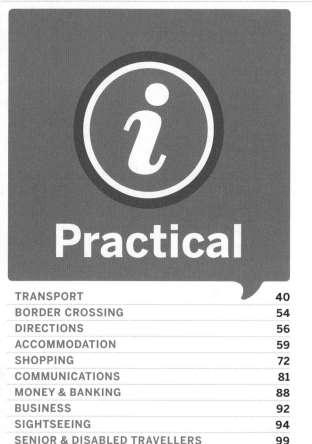
Practical

Transport

KEY PHRASES

When's the next bus?	¿A qué hora es el próximo autobús?	a ke *o*·ra es el *prok*·see·mo ow·to·*boos*
A ticket to ..., please.	Un boleto a ..., por favor.	oon bo·*le*·to a ... por fa·*vor*
Can you tell me when we get to ...?	¿Me puede decir cuándo lleguemos a ...?	me *pwe*·de de·*seer* kwan·do ye·*ge*·mos a ...
Please take me to this address.	Por favor, lléveme a esta dirección.	por fa·*vor* *ye*·ve·me a es·ta dee·rek·*syon*
I'd like to hire a car.	Quisiera alquilar un carro.	kee·*sye*·ra al·kee·*lar* oon *ka*·ro

Getting Around

Can we get there by public transport?	¿Podemos llegar allí en transporte público? po·*de*·mos ye·*gar* a·*yee* en trans·*por*·te *poo*·blee·ko
I'd prefer to walk there.	Prefiero caminar para ir allí. pre·*fye*·ro ka·mee·*nar* pa·ra eer a·*yee*
What time's the first/last bus?	¿A qué hora es el primer/ último autobús? a ke *o*·ra es el pree·*mer*/ *ool*·tee·mo ow·to·*boos*

What time's the next bus?	¿A qué hora es el próximo autobús?
	a ke *o·*ra es el *prok*·see·mo ow·to·*boos*

What time does the ... leave?	¿A qué hora sale ...?
	a ke *o·*ra *sa·*le ...

boat	el barco	el *bar·*ko
bus (city)	el autobús;	el ow·to·*boos;*
	la chiva (Col);	la *chee·*va;
	el colectivo (Arg);	el ko·lek·*tee·*vo;
	la guagua (Cub);	la *gwa·*gwa;
	el micro (Bol, Chi)	el *mee·*kro
bus (intercity)	el ómnibus;	el *om·*nee·boos;
	el micro (Arg)	el *mee·*kro
metro	el subterráneo;	el soob·te·*ra·*ne·o;
	el subte (Arg)	el *soob·*te
plane	el avión	el a·*vyon*
train	el tren	el tren
tram	el tranvía	el tran·*vee·*a

Could you give me a ride in your (pick-up)?	¿Me podría llevar en su (pick-up)?
	me po·*dree·*a ye·*var* en soo (*peek·*oop)

Are you waiting for more people?	¿Está esperando a más gente?
	es·*ta* es·pe·*ran·*do a mas *khen·*te

How much do I owe you?	¿Cuánto le debo?
	*kwan·*to le *de·*bo

Can you tell me when we get to (San Miguel)?	¿Me puede decir cuándo lleguemos a (San Miguel)?
	me *pwe·*de de·*seer kwan·*do ye·*ge·*mos a (san mee·*gel*)

PRACTICAL TRANSPORT

Está cancelado.	es·*ta* kan·se·*la*·do	It's cancelled.
Está completo.	es·*ta* kom·*ple*·to	It's full.
Está retrasado.	es·*ta* re·tra·*sa*·do	It's delayed.

I want to get off here.	Quiero bajarme aquí. *kye*·ro ba·*khar*·me a·*kee*
That's my seat.	Ése es mi asiento. *e*·se es mee a·*syen*·to
Is this seat free?	¿Está libre este asiento? es·*ta lee*·bre es·te a·*syen*·to

✂	**Is it free?**	¿Está libre?	es·*ta lee*·bre

For phrases about getting through customs and immigration, see **border crossing** (p54).

Buying Tickets

Where can I buy a ticket?	¿Dónde puedo comprar un boleto? *don*·de *pwe*·do kom·*prar* oon bo·*le*·to
Do I need to book?	¿Tengo que reservar? *ten*·go ke re·ser·*var*
Can I get a stand-by ticket?	¿Puede ponerme en la lista de espera? *pwe*·de po·*ner*·me en la *lees*·ta de es·*pe*·ra
How long does the trip take?	¿Cuánto se tarda? *kwan*·to se *tar*·da
Is it a direct route?	¿Es un viaje directo? es oon *vya*·khe dee·*rek*·to

Buying a Ticket

What time is the next ...?

¿A qué hora sale el próximo ...?
a ke *o*·ra *sa*·le el *prok*·see·mo ...

 boat
barco
bar·ko

 bus
autobús
ow·to·*boos*

 train
tren
tren

One ... ticket, please.

Un boleto ..., por favor.
oon bo·*le*·to ... por fa·*vor*

one-way
de ida
de *ee*·da

return
de ida y vuelta
de *ee*·da ee *vwel*·ta

I'd like a/an ... seat.

Quisiera un asiento ...
kee·*sye*·ra oon a·*syen*·to ...

aisle
de pasillo
de pa·*see*·yo

window
junto a la
ventana
khoon·to a la
ven·*ta*·na

Which platform does it depart from?

¿De cuál plataforma sale?
de kwal pla·ta·*for*·ma *sa*·le

What time do I have to check in?	¿A qué hora tengo que facturar mi equipaje? a ke *o*·ra *ten*·go ke fak·too·*rar* mee e·kee·*pa*·khe
I'd like to cancel my ticket, please.	Quisiera cancelar mi boleto, por favor. kee·*sye*·ra kan·se·*lar* mee bo·*le*·to por fa·*vor*
I'd like to change my ticket, please.	Quisiera cambiar mi boleto, por favor. kee·*sye*·ra kam·*byar* mee bo·*le*·to por fa·*vor*
I'd like to confirm my ticket, please.	Quisiera confirmar mi boleto, por favor. kee·*sye*·ra kon·feer·*mar* mee bo·*le*·to por fa·*vor*
A ... ticket to (Lima), please.	Un boleto ... a (Lima), por favor. oon bo·*le*·to ... a (*lee*·ma) por fa·*vor*

1st-class	de primera clase	de pree·*me*·ra *kla*·se
2nd-class	de segunda clase	de se·*goon*·da *kla*·se
child's	infantil	een·fan·*teel*
one-way	de ida	de *ee*·da
return	de ida y vuelta	de *ee*·da ee *vwel*·ta
student's	de estudiante	de es·too·*dyan*·te

I'd like an aisle seat.	Quisiera un asiento de pasillo. kee·*sye*·ra oon a·*syen*·to de pa·*see*·yo

I'd like a window seat.	Quisiera un asiento junto a la ventana. kee·*sye*·ra oon a·*syen*·to *khoon*·to a la ven·*ta*·na
I'd like a (non)smoking seat.	Quisiera un asiento de (no) fumadores. kee·*sye*·ra oon a·*syen*·to de (no) foo·ma·*do*·res
Is there (a) ...?	¿Hay ... ? ai ...

air-conditioning	aire acondicionado	*ai*·re a·kon·dee·syo·*na*·do
blanket	una frazada	*oo*·na fra·*sa*·da
toilet	baños	*ba*·nyos
video	vídeo	*vee*·de·o

Luggage

My luggage has been damaged.	Mi equipaje ha sido dañado. mee e·kee·*pa*·khe a *see*·do da·*nya*·do
My luggage has been lost/stolen.	Mi equipaje ha sido perdido/robado. mee e·kee·*pa*·khe a *see*·do per·*dee*·do/ro·*ba*·do
I'd like a luggage locker.	Quisiera un casillero de consigna. kee·*sye*·ra oon ka·see·*ye*·ro de kon·*seeg*·na
I'd like some coins/tokens.	Quisiera unas monedas/fichas. kee·*sye*·ra *oo*·nas mo·*ne*·das/*fee*·chas

Bus, Tram & Metro

Which bus goes to (the centre of town)?	¿Qué autobús va al (centro de la cuidad)? ke ow·to·*boos* va al (*sen*·tro de la syoo·*da*)
Which bus goes to (Cochabamba)?	¿Qué ómnibus va a (Cochabamba)? ke *om*·nee·boos va a (ko·cha·*bam*·ba)
Tram number (three).	El tranvía número (tres). el tran·*vee*·a *noo*·me·ro (tres)
How many stops to (the museum)?	¿Cuántas paradas hay hasta (el museo)? *kwan*·tas pa·*ra*·das ai *as*·ta (el moo·*se*·o)
Do you stop at (the market)?	¿Tiene parada en (el mercado)? *tye*·ne pa·*ra*·da en (el mer·*ka*·do)

Train

What station is this?	¿Cuál es esta estación? kwal es *es*·ta es·ta·*syon*

LANGUAGE TIP

Regionalisms

Throughout Latin America the general name for a bus station is *una estación de autobuses* *oo*·na es·ta·*syon* de ow·to·*boo*·ses, although in Argentina it's known as *una terminal de ómnibuses* *oo*·na ter·mee·*nal* de *om*·nee·boo·ses. In Venezuela and Colombia you'll hear the term *una terminal terrestre* *oo*·na ter·mee·*nal* te·*re*·stre (lit: land terminal) or *una terminal de pasajeros* *oo*·na ter·mee·*nal* de pa·sa·*khe*·ros (lit: passenger terminal).

What's the next station?	¿Cuál es la próxima estación? kwal es la *prok*·see·ma es·ta·*syon*
Does this train stop at (Veracruz)?	¿Para el tren en (Veracruz)? *pa*·ra el tren en (ve·ra·*kroos*)
Do I need to change trains?	¿Tengo que cambiar de tren? *ten*·go ke kam·*byar* de tren
Which carriage is 1st class?	¿Cuál es el coche de primera clase? kwal es el *ko*·che de pree·*me*·ra *kla*·se
Which carriage is for (Buenos Aires)?	¿Cuál es el coche para (Buenos Aires)? kwal es el *ko*·che *pa*·ra (*bwe*·nos *ai*·res)
Which carriage is for dining?	¿Cuál es el coche comedor? kwal es el *ko*·che ko·me·*dor*
This/That one.	Éste./Ése. *es*·te/*es*·e

Boat

Where do we get on the boat?	¿Dónde subimos al barco? *don*·de soo·*bee*·mos al *bar*·ko
Are there life jackets?	¿Hay chalecos salvavidas? ai cha·*le*·kos sal·va·*vee*·das
What's the sea like today?	¿Cómo está el mar hoy? *ko*·mo es·*ta* el mar oy
I feel seasick.	Estoy mareado/a. **m/f** es·*toy* ma·re·*a*·do/a
wharf	embarcadero **m** em·bar·ka·*de*·ro malecón **m** (**CAm, Per**) ma·le·*kon*

Taxi

I'd like a taxi at (9am).	Quisiera un taxi a las (nueve de la mañana). kee·sye·ra oon tak·see a las (nwe·ve de la ma·nya·na)
I'd like a taxi now/ tomorrow.	Quisiera un taxi ahora/ mañana. kee·sye·ra oon tak·see a·o·ra/ ma·nya·na
Is this taxi free?	¿Está libre este taxi? es·ta lee·bre es·te tak·see

✂ | **Is it free?** | ¿Está libre? | es·ta lee·bre

How much is it (to the airport)?	¿Cuánto cuesta ir (al aeropuerto)? kwan·to kwes·ta eer (al a·e·ro·pwer·to)

🔍 LOOK FOR

Acceso	ak·se·so	Entrance
Aparcamiento	a·par·ka·myen·to	Parking
Ceda el Paso	se·da el pa·so	Give Way
Dirección Única	dee·rek·syon oo·nee·ka	One Way
Pare	pa·re	Stop
Peaje	pe·a·khe	Toll
Peligro	pe·lee·gro	Danger
Prohibido Aparcar	pro·ee·bee·do a·par·kar	No Parking
Prohibido el Paso	pro·ee·bee·do el pa·so	No Entry
Salida de Autopista	sa·lee·da de ow·to·pees·ta	Exit Freeway

Please put the meter on.	Por favor, ponga el taxímetro.
	por fa·*vor* pon·ga el tak·*see*·me·tro
Please take me to (this address).	Por favor, lléveme a (esta dirección).
	por fa·*vor* ye·ve·me a (es·ta dee·rek·*syon*)
✂ **To ...**	A ... a ...
Please slow down.	Por favor vaya más despacio.
	por fa·*vor* va·ya mas des·*pa*·syo
Please wait here.	Por favor espere aquí.
	por fa·*vor* es·pe·re a·*kee*
Stop at the corner.	Pare en la esquina.
	pa·re en la es·*kee*·na
Stop here.	Pare aquí.
	pa·re a·*kee*

Quiero bajarme aquí.
kye·ro ba·*khar*·me a·*kee*
I want to get off here.

Car & Motorbike

I'd like to hire a/an ...
Quisiera alquilar ...
kee·*sye*·ra al·kee·*lar* ...

4WD	un todo terreno	oon *to*·do te·*re*·no
automatic	un carro automático	oon *ka*·ro ow·to·*ma*·tee·ko
car	un carro; un auto (SAm)	oon *ka*·ro; oon *ow*·to
manual	un carro manual	oon *ka*·ro man·*wal*
motorbike	una moto	*oo*·na *mo*·to

LANGUAGE TIP

Regionalisms
The word *gasolinera* ga·so·lee·*ne*·ra is the standard term for 'petrol/gas station', and will be understood throughout Latin America. You may also come across these country-specific terms:

Argentina	estación f de servicio	es·ta·*syon* de ser·*vee*·syo
Bolivia	surtidor m	soor·tee·*dor*
Central America, Colombia, Mexico	bomba f	*bom*·ba
Chile	bencinera f	ben·see·*ne*·ra
Peru	grifo m	*gree*·fo

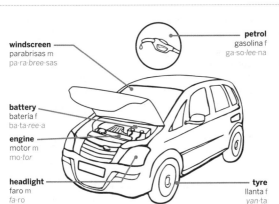

petrol
gasolina f
ga·so·lee·na

windscreen
parabrisas m
pa·ra·bree·sas

battery
batería f
ba·ta·ree·a

engine
motor m
mo·tor

headlight
faro m
fa·ro

tyre
llanta f
yan·ta

with air-conditioning	con aire acondicionado kon ai·re a·kon·dee·syo·na·do
with a driver	con un chofer kon oon cho·fer
How much for daily/ weekly hire?	¿Cuánto cuesta alquilar por día/semana? kwan·to kwes·ta al·kee·lar por dee·a/se·ma·na
What's the city speed limit?	¿Cuál es el límite de velocidad en la ciudad? kwal es el lee·mee·te de ve·lo·see·da en la syoo·da
What's the country speed limit?	¿Cuál es el límite de velocidad en el campo? kwal es el lee·mee·te de ve·lo·see·da en el kam·po

🔍 LOOK FOR

bencina (Chi)	ben·*see*·na	petrol/gas
con plomo	kon *plo*·mo	leaded (regular)
gasolina	ga·so·*lee*·na	petrol/gas
nafta (Arg)	*naf*·ta	petrol/gas
sin plomo	seen *plo*·mo	unleaded

Is this the road to (Tegucigalpa)?	¿Se va a (Tegucigalpa) por esta carretera? se va a (te·goo·see·*gal*·pa) por *es*·ta ka·re·*te*·ra
(How long) Can I park here?	¿(Por cuánto tiempo) Puedo aparcar aquí? (por *kwan*·to *tyem*·po) *pwe*·do a·par·*kar* a·*kee*
Where's a petrol/gas station?	¿Dónde hay una gasolinera? *don*·de ai oo·na ga·so·lee·*ne*·ra
Please fill it up.	Lleno, por favor. *ye*·no por fa·*vor*
I'd like (20) litres.	Quiero (veinte) litros. *kye*·ro (*vayn*·te) *lee*·tros
Where do I pay?	¿Dónde se paga? *don*·de se *pa*·ga
I need a mechanic.	Necesito un mecánico. ne·se·*see*·to oon me·*ka*·nee·ko
I had an accident.	Tuve un accidente. *too*·ve oon ak·see·*den*·te
The car has broken down (in Granada).	El carro se ha averiado (en Granada). el *ka*·ro se a a·ve·*rya*·do (en gra·*na*·da)

Bicycle

Can we get there by bike?	¿Podemos llegar allí en bicicleta? po·de·mos lye·gar a·yee en bee·see·kle·ta
I have a puncture.	Se me pinchó una rueda. se me peen·cho oo·na rwe·da
Where can I hire a bicycle?	¿Dónde se puede alquilar una bicicleta? don·de se pwe·de al·kee·lar oo·na bee·see·kle·ta
Where can I buy a second-hand bike?	¿Dónde se puede comprar una bicicleta de segunda mano? don·de se pwe·de kom·prar oo·na bee·see·kle·ta de se·goon·da ma·no
How much is it per day?	¿Cuánto cuesta por un día? kwan·to kwes·ta por oon dee·a
How much is it per hour?	¿Cuánto cuesta por hora? kwan·to kwes·ta por o·ra

 **LISTEN FOR**

¿De qué marca es?	de ke mar·ka es What make/model is it?
Tengo que pedir ese repuesto.	ten·go ke pe·deer e·se re·pwes·to I have to order that part.

PRACTICAL TRANSPORT

Border Crossing

KEY PHRASES

I'm here for ... days.	Estoy aquí por ... días.	es·*toy* a·*kee* por ... *dee*·as
I'm staying at ...	Me estoy alojando en ...	me es·*toy* a·lo·*khan*·do en ...
I have nothing to declare.	No tengo nada que declarar.	No *ten*·go *na*·da ke de·kla·*rar*

Border Crossing

I'm here in transit.	Estoy aquí en tránsito. es·*toy* a·*kee* en *tran*·see·to
I'm here on business/ holiday.	Estoy aquí de negocios/ vacaciones. es·*toy* a·*kee* de ne·*go*·syos/ va·ka·*syo*·nes
I'm here for (four) days.	Estoy aquí por (cuatro) días. es·*toy* a·*kee* por (*kwa*·tro) *dee*·as
I'm here for (two) weeks.	Estoy aquí por (dos) semanas. es·*toy* a·*kee* por (dos) se·*ma*·nas

🔊 LISTEN FOR

Su pasaporte, por favor.	soo pa·sa·*por*·te por fa·*vor* Your passport, please.
¿Está viajando solo/a? m/f	es·*ta* vya·*khan*·do so·lo/a Are you travelling on your own?

🔍 LOOK FOR

Aduana	a·*dwa*·na Customs
Artículos Libres **de Impuestos**	ar·*tee*·koo·los *lee*·bres de eem·*pwes*·tos Duty-Free Goods
Control de Pasaportes	kon·*trol* de pa·sa·*por*·tes Passport Control

I'm here for (three) **months.**	Estoy aquí por (tres) meses. es·*toy* a·*kee* por (tres) *me*·ses
I'm staying at ...	Me estoy alojando en ... me es·*toy* a·lo·*khan*·do en ...
I have a visa.	Tengo un visado. *ten*·go oon vee·*sa*·do
I have a study/work **permit.**	Tengo un permiso de estudios/trabajo. *ten*·go oon per·*mee*·so de es·*too*·dyos/tra·*ba*·kho

At Customs

I have nothing to declare.	No tengo nada que declarar. no *ten*·go *na*·da ke de·kla·*rar*
I have something to **declare.**	Tengo algo que declarar. *ten*·go *al*·go ke de·kla·*rar*
I didn't know I had to **declare it.**	No sabía que tenía que declararlo. no sa·*bee*·a ke te·*nee*·a ke de·kla·*rar*·lo
Do you have this form in **(English)?**	¿Tiene ese formulario en (inglés)? *tye*·ne *e*·se for·moo·*la*·ryo en (een·*gles*)

Directions

KEY PHRASES

Where's ...?	¿Dónde está ...?	*don*·de es·*ta* ...
What's the address?	¿Cuál es la dirección?	kwal es la dee·rek·*syon*
How far is it?	¿A cuánta distancia está?	a *kwan*·ta dees·*tan*·sya es·*ta*

Q Where's (the bank)?	¿Dónde está (el banco)? *don*·de es·*ta* (el *ban*·ko)
A It's ...	Está ... es·*ta* ...
I'm looking for (the public toilets).	Busco (los baños). *boos*·ko (los *ba*·nyos)
Which way's (the post office)?	¿Por dónde se va (a correos)? por *don*·de se va (a ko·*re*·os)
How can I get there?	¿Cómo puedo ir? *ko*·mo *pwe*·do eer
How far is it?	¿A cuánta distancia está? a *kwan*·ta dees·*tan*·sya es·*ta*
Can you show me (on the map)?	¿Me lo podría indicar (en el mapa)? me lo po·*dree*·a een·dee·*kar* (en el *ma*·pa)
What's the address?	¿Cuál es la dirección? kwal es la dee·rek·*syon*
It's (100) metres.	Está a (cien) metros. es·*ta* a (syen) *me*·tros
It's (two) kilometres.	Está a (dos) kilómetros. es·*ta* a (dos) kee·*lo*·me·tros
It's (five) minutes.	Está a (cinco) minutos. es·*ta* a (*seen*·ko) mee·*noo*·tos

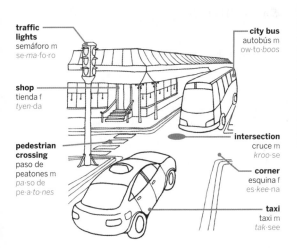

traffic lights
semáforo m
se·ma·fo·ro

shop
tienda f
tyen·da

pedestrian crossing
paso de peatones m
pa·so de
pe·a·to·nes

city bus
autobús m
ow·to·boos

intersection
cruce m
kroo·se

corner
esquina f
es·kee·na

taxi
taxi m
tak·see

🔍 **LOOK FOR**

Abierto	a·byer·to	Open
Caliente	ka·lyen·te	Hot
Cerrado	se·ra·do	Closed
Entrada	en·tra·da	Entry
Frío	free·o	Cold
Información	een·for·ma·syon	Information
No Tocar	no to·kar	Don't Touch
Prohibido Tomar Fotos	pro·ee·bee·do to·mar fo·tos	No Photography
Reservado	re·ser·va·do	Reserved
Salida	sa·lee·da	Exit

PRACTICAL DIRECTIONS

🔊 LISTEN FOR

acá (Arg)	a·*ka*	there
adelante de ...	a·de·*lan*·te de ...	in front of ...
ahí	a·*ee*	there
al lado de ...	al *la*·do de ...	next to ...
aquí	a·*kee*	here
cerca	*ser*·ka	near
detrás de ...	de·*tras* de ...	behind ...
frente a ...	*fren*·te a ...	opposite ...
lejos	*le*·khos	far away
todo derecho	*to*·do de·*re*·cho	straight ahead

by bus	en autobús en ow·to·*boos*
by taxi	en taxi en *tak*·see
by train	en tren en tren
on foot	a pie a pye
Turn left.	Doble a la izquierda. *do*·ble a la ees·*kyer*·da
Turn right.	Doble a la derecha. *do*·ble a la de·*re*·cha
Turn at the corner.	Doble en la esquina. *do*·ble en la es·*kee*·na
Turn at the traffic lights.	Doble en el semáforo. *do*·ble en el se·*ma*·fo·ro

Accommodation

KEY PHRASES

Where's a hotel?	¿Dónde hay un hotel?	*don*·de ai oon o·*tel*
Do you have a double room?	¿Tiene una habitación doble?	*tye*·ne *oo*·na a·bee·ta·*syon* do·ble
How much is it per night?	¿Cuánto cuesta por noche?	*kwan*·to *kwes*·ta por *no*·che
Is breakfast included?	¿El desayuno está incluído?	el de·sa·*yoo*·no es·*ta* een·kloo·ee·do
What time is checkout?	¿A qué hora hay que dejar libre la habitación?	a ke o·ra ai ke de·*khar lee*·bre la a·bee·ta·*syon*

Finding Accommodation

Can you recommend somewhere ...?	¿Puede recomendar algún sitio ...? *pwe*·de re·ko·men·*dar* al·*goon see*·tyo ...

cheap	barato	ba·*ra*·to
good	bueno	*bwe*·no
luxurious	de lujo	de *loo*·kho
nearby	cercano	ser·*ka*·no
romantic	romántico	ro·*man*·tee·ko

What's the address?	¿Cuál es la dirección? kwal es la dee·rek·*syon*

Where's a ...?	¿Dónde hay ...?
	don·de ai ...

bed and breakfast	una pensión con desayuno	*oo·na pen·syon kon de·sa·yoo·no*
cabin	una cabaña	*oo·na ka·ba·nya*
campsite	un terreno de cámping	*oon te·re·no de kam·peen*
guesthouse	una pensión; una casa de huéspedes; una hostería (Arg, Chi)	*oo·na pen·syon; oo·na ka·sa de wes·pe·des; oo·na os·te·ree·a*
hotel	un hotel	*oon o·tel*
youth hostel	un albergue juvenil	*oon al·ber·ge khoo·ve·neel*

For getting there, see **directions** (p56).

Booking Ahead & Checking In

Do you have a double room?	¿Tiene una habitación doble? *tye·ne oo·na a·bee·ta·syon do·ble*
Do you have a single room?	¿Tiene una habitación individual? *tye·ne oo·na a·bee·ta·syon een·dee·vee·dwal*
Do you have a twin room?	¿Tiene una habitación con dos camas? *tye·ne oo·na a·bee·ta·syon kon dos ka·mas*
How much is it per night?	¿Cuánto cuesta por noche? *kwan·to kwes·ta por no·che*

Finding a Room

Do you have a ... room?
¿Tiene una habitación ...?
tye·ne oo·na a·bee·ta·syon ...

double
doble
do·ble

single
individual
een·dee·vee·dwal

How much is it per ...?
¿Cuánto cuesta por ...?
kwan·to kwes·ta por ...

night
noche
no·che

person
persona
per·so·na

Is breakfast included?
¿El desayuno está incluído?
el de·sa·yoo·no es·ta een·kloo·ee·do

Can I see the room?
¿Puedo verla?
pwe·do ver·la

I'll take it.
La alquilo.
la al·kee·lo

I won't take it.
No la alquilo.
no la al·kee·lo

How much is it per person?	¿Cuánto cuesta por persona? *kwan·*to kwes·ta por per·*so·*na
How much is it per week?	¿Cuánto cuesta por semana? *kwan·*to kwes·ta por se·*ma·*na
Is breakfast included?	¿El desayuno está incluído? el de·sa·*yoo·*no es·*ta een·kloo·ee·do
I'd like to book a room, please.	Quisiera reservar una habitación. kee·*sye·*ra re·ser·*var* oo·na a·bee·ta·*syon*

✂ **Are there rooms?**	¿Hay cuartos disponibles?	ai *kwar·*tos dis·po·*nee·*bles

I have a reservation.	Tengo una reserva. *ten·*go oo·na re·*ser·*va
For (three) nights/weeks.	Para (tres) noches/semanas. *pa·*ra (tres) no·ches/ se·*ma·*nas
From (July 2) to (July 6).	Desde (el dos de julio) hasta (el seis de julio). *des·*de (el dos de k*hoo·*lyo) *as·*ta (el says de k*hoo·*lyo)
Can I see it?	¿Puedo verla? *pwe·*do ver·la

🔊 LISTEN FOR

¿Por cuántas noches?	por *kwan·*tas no·ches	For how many nights?
Lo siento, está completo.	lo *syen·*to es·*ta* kom·*ple·*to	I'm sorry, we're full.
La llave está en recepción.	la *ya·*ve es·*ta* en re·sep·*syon*	The key is at reception.

I'll take it.	La alquilo.
	la al·*kee*·lo

For methods of payment, see **money & banking** (p88).

Requests & Queries

When/Where is breakfast served?	¿Cuándo/Dónde se sirve el desayuno?
	kwan·do/*don*·de se *seer*·ve el de·sa·*yoo*·no
Please wake me at (seven).	Por favor, despiérteme a (las siete).
	por fa·*vor* des·*pyer*·te·me a (las *sye*·te)
Can I get another ...?	¿Puede darme otro/a ...? m/f
	pwe·de *dar*·me o·tro/a ...
Can I use the ...?	¿Puedo usar el/la ...? m/f
	pwe·do oo·*sar* el/la ...
Do you have a/an ...?	¿Hay ...?
	ai ...

elevator	ascensor m	a·sen·*sor*
kitchen	cocina f	ko·*see*·na
laundry	lavandería f	la·van·de·*ree*·a
message board	tablón m de anuncios;	ta·*blon* de a·*noon*·syos;
	pizarra f de anuncios (CAm);	pee·*sa*·ra de a·*noon*·syos;
	diario m	*dya*·ryo
	mural (Chi)	moo·*ral*
safe	caja f fuerte	*ka*·kha *fwer*·te
swimming pool	piscina f (SAm);	pee·*see*·na;
	pileta f (Arg)	pee·*le*·ta
telephone	teléfono m	te·*le*·fo·no

Do you arrange tours here?	¿Aquí organizan paseos guiados? a·*kee* or·ga·*nee*·san pa·*se*·os gee·*a*·dos
Do you change money here?	¿Aquí cambian dinero? a·*kee* *kam*·byan dee·*ne*·ro
Can I leave a message for someone?	¿Puedo dejar un mensaje para alguien? *pwe*·do de·*khar* oon men·*sa*·khe *pa*·ra al·gyen
Is there a message for me?	¿Hay algún mensaje para mí? ai al·*goon* men·*sa*·khe *pa*·ra mee
There's no need to change my sheets.	No hace falta cambiar mis sábanas. no *a*·se *fal*·ta kam·*byar* mees *sa*·ba·nas
The (bathroom) door is locked.	La puerta (del baño) está cerrada con llave. la *pwer*·ta (del *ba*·nyo) es·*ta* se·*ra*·da kon *ya*·ve

Complaints

The room is too ...	La habitación es demasiado ... la a·bee·ta·*syon* es de·ma·*sya*·do ...

cold	fría	*free*·a
dark	oscura	os·*koo*·ra
dirty	sucia	*soo*·sya
light/bright	luminosa	loo·mee·*no*·sa
noisy	ruidosa	rwee·*do*·sa
small	pequeña	pe·*ke*·nya

| **The ... doesn't work.** | No funciona ...
no foon·*syo*·na ... |

air- conditioning	el aire acondicionado	el *ai*·re a·kon·dee·*syo*·*na*·do
fan	el ventilador	el ven·tee·la·*dor*
heater	la estufa	la es·*too*·fa
toilet	el baño	el *ba*·nyo
window	la ventana	la ven·*ta*·na

The toilet smells.	El baño huele mal. el *ba*·nyo *we*·le mal
The room smells.	La habitación huele mal. la a·bee·ta·*syon we*·le mal
There's no hot water.	No hay agua caliente. no ai *a*·gwa ka·*lyen*·te
This ... isn't clean.	Este/a ... no está limpio/a. **m/f** *es*·te/a ... no es·*ta* leem·pyo/a
There's a mistake in the bill.	Hay un error en la cuenta. ai oon e·*ror* en la *kwen*·ta

Answering the Door

Who is it?	¿Quién es? kyen es
Just a moment.	Un momento. oon mo·*men*·to
Come in.	Adelante. a·de·*lan*·te
Come back later, please.	¿Puede volver más tarde, por favor? *pwe*·de vol·*ver* mas *tar*·de por fa·*vor*

Checking Out

What time is checkout?	¿A qué hora hay que dejar libre la habitación? *a ke o·ra ai ke de·khar lee·bre la a·bee·ta·syon*
Can I have a late checkout?	¿Puedo dejar libre la habitación más tarde? *pwe·do de·khar lee·bre la a·bee·ta·syon mas tar·de*
How much extra to stay until (six o'clock)?	¿Cuánto más cuesta quedarse hasta (las seis)? *kwan·to mas kwes·ta ke·dar·se as·ta (las says)*
Can I leave my luggage here?	¿Puedo dejar el equipaje aquí? *pwe·do de·khar el e·kee·pa·khe a·kee*
I'm leaving now.	Me voy ahora. *me voy a·o·ra*
Can you call a taxi for me (for 11 o'clock)?	¿Me puede pedir un taxi (para las once)? *me pwe·de pe·deer oon tak·see (pa·ra las on·se)*
Could I have my deposit, please?	¿Me puede dar mi depósito, por favor? *me pwe·de dar mee de·po·see·to por fa·vor*
Could I have my passport, please?	¿Me puede dar mi pasaporte, por favor? *me pwe·de dar mee pa·sa·por·te por fa·vor*
Could I have my valuables, please?	¿Me puede dar mis objetos de valor, por favor? *me pwe·de dar mees ob·khe·tos de va·lor por fa·vor*

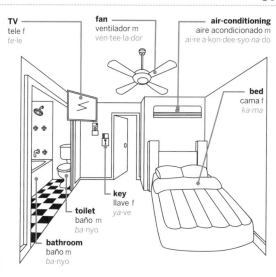

TV
tele f
te·le

fan
ventilador m
ven·tee·la·*dor*

air-conditioning
aire acondicionado m
*ai·*re a·kon·dee·syo·*na·*do

bed
cama f
*ka·*ma

key
llave f
*ya·*ve

toilet
baño m
*ba·*nyo

bathroom
baño m
*ba·*nyo

I'll be back in (three) days.	Volveré en (tres) días. vol·ve·*re* en (tres) *dee·*as
I'll be back on (Tuesday).	Volveré el (martes). vol·ve·*re* el (*mar·*tes)
I had a great stay, thank you.	Tuve una estancia muy agradable, gracias. *too·*ve *oo·*na es·*tan·*sya mooy a·gra·*da·*ble *gra·*syas
You've been terrific.	Fueron muy amables. *fwe·*ron mooy a·*ma·*bles
I'll recommend it to my friends.	Se lo recomendaré a mis amigos. se lo re·ko·men·da·*re* a mees a·*mee·*gos

Camping

Where's the nearest campsite?	¿Dónde está el terreno de cámping más cercano? *don·de es·ta el te·re·no de kam·peen mas ser·ka·no*
Where's the nearest shop?	¿Dónde está la tienda más cercana? *don·de es·ta la tyen·da mas ser·ka·na*
Where are the nearest showers?	Donde están las duchas más cercanas? *don·de es·tan las doo·chas mas ser·ka·nas*
Where are the nearest toilets?	Donde están los baños más cercanos? *don·de es·tan los ba·nyos mas ser·ka·nos*
Do you have ...?	¿Tiene ...? *tye·ne ...*

a site	lugar	loo·*gar*
electricity	electricidad	e·lek·tree·see·*da*
shower facilities	duchas	*doo*·chas
tents for hire	carpas para alquilar	*kar*·pas *pa*·ra al·kee·*lar*

How much is it per ...?	¿Cuánto vale por ...? *kwan·to va·le por ...*	

caravan	caravana	ka·ra·*va*·na
person	persona	per·*so*·na
tent	carpa	*kar*·pa
vehicle	vehículo	ve·ee·*koo*·lo

Who do I ask to stay here?	¿Con quién tengo que hablar para quedarme aquí? kon kyen *ten*·go ke a·*blar* *pa*·ra ke·*dar*·me a·*kee*
Can I camp here?	¿Se puede acampar aquí? se *pwe*·de a·kam·*par* a·*kee*
Can I park next to my tent?	¿Se puede estacionar al lado de mi carpa? se *pwe*·de es·ta·syo·*nar* al *la*·do de mee *kar*·pa
Is it coin-operated?	¿Funciona con monedas? foon·*syo*·na kon mo·*ne*·das
Is the water drinkable?	¿Se puede beber el agua? se *pwe*·de be·*ber* el *a*·gwa
Could I borrow (a mallet)?	¿Me podría prestar (un mazo)? me po·*dree*·a pres·*tar* (oon *ma*·so)

For more words related to camping, see the **dictionary**.

¿Se puede acampar aquí?
se *pwe*·de a·kam·*par* a·*kee*

Can I camp here?

Renting

I'm here about (the room) for rent.	Vengo por (la habitación) que anuncian para alquilar. *ven·go por (la a·bee·ta·syon) ke a·noon·syan pa·ra al·kee·lar*
Do you have a/an ... for rent?	¿Tiene ... para alquilar? *tye·ne ... pa·ra al·kee·lar*

apartment	un departamento	oon de·par·ta·men·to
cabin	una cabaña	oo·na ka·ba·nya
house	una casa	oo·na ka·sa
room	una habitación	oo·na a·bee·ta·syon
villa	un chalet	oon cha·le

Do I need to pay upfront?	¿Necesito pagar por adelantado? *ne·se·see·to pa·gar por a·de·lan·ta·do*
furnished	amueblado/a m/f *a·mwe·bla·do/a*
partly furnished	parcialmente amueblado/a m/f *par·syal·men·te a·mwe·bla·do/a*
unfurnished	sin amueblar *seen a·mwe·blar*

Staying with Locals

Can I stay at your place?	¿Me podría quedar en su/tu casa? pol/inf *me po·dree·a ke·dar en soo/too ka·sa*
Is there anything I can do to help?	¿Puedo ayudar en algo? *pwe·do a·yoo·dar en al·go*
I have my own mattress.	Tengo mi propio colchón. *ten·go mee pro·pyo kol·chon*
I have my own sleeping bag.	Tengo mi propia bolsa de dormir. *ten·go mee pro·pya bol·sa de dor·meer*
Can I ...?	¿Puedo ...? *pwe·do ...*

bring anything for the meal	traer algo para la comida	tra·er al·go pa·ra la ko·mee·da
do the dishes	lavar los platos	la·var los pla·tos
set/clear the table	poner/quitar la mesa	po·ner/kee·tar la me·sa
take out the rubbish	sacar la basura	sa·kar la ba·soo·ra

Thanks for your hospitality.	Gracias por su/tu hospitalidad. pol/inf *gra·syas por soo/too os·pee·ta·lee·da*

If you're dining with your hosts, see **eating out** (p166) for more phrases.

PRACTICAL SHOPPING

Shopping

KEY PHRASES

I'd like to buy ...	Quisiera comprar ...	kee·sye·ra kom·prar ...
Can I look at it?	¿Puedo verlo?	pwe·do ver·lo
Can I try it on?	¿Me lo puedo probar?	me lo pwe·do pro·bar
How much is it?	¿Cuánto cuesta esto?	kwan·to kwes·ta es·to
That's too expensive.	Es muy caro.	es mooy ka·ro

Looking For ...

Where's (a supermarket)?	¿Dónde hay (un supermercado)? don·de ai (oon soo·per·mer·ka·do)
Where can I buy (locally produced goods/souvenirs)?	¿Dónde puedo comprar (productos/recuerdos locales)? don·de pwe·do kom·prar (pro·dook·tos/re·kwer·dos lo·ka·les)

For asking and giving directions, see **directions** (p56), and for types of shops, see the **dictionary**.

Making a Purchase

I'd like to buy ...	Quisiera comprar ... kee·sye·ra kom·prar ...

I'm just looking.	Sólo estoy mirando. *so·lo es·toy mee·ran·do*
Can I look at it?	¿Puedo verlo? *pwe·do ver·lo*
How much is it?	¿Cuánto cuesta esto? *kwan·to kwes·ta es·to*

✂ **How much?** ¿Cuánto cuesta? *kwan·to kwes·ta*

Can you write down the price?	¿Puede escribir el precio? *pwe·de es·kree·beer el pre·syo*
Do you have any others?	¿Tiene otros? *tye·ne o·tros*
Does it have a guarantee?	¿Tiene garantía? *tye·ne ga·ran·tee·a*
It's faulty.	Es defectuoso. *es de·fek·two·so*
I don't like it.	No me gusta. *no me goos·ta*
Could I have a bag, please?	¿Podría darme una bolsa, por favor? *po·dree·a dar·me oo·na bol·sa por fa·vor*
Could I have it wrapped?	¿Me lo podría envolver? *me lo po·dree·a en·vol·ver*
Could I have a receipt, please?	¿Podría darme un recibo, por favor? *po·dree·a dar·me oon re·see·bo por fa·vor*

 Receipt, please. Un recibo, por favor. *oon re·see·bo por fa·vor*

PRACTICAL SHOPPING

I'd like my change, please.	Quisiera mi cambio, por favor. kee·*sye*·ra mee *kam*·byo por fa·*vor*
I'd like my money back, please.	Quisiera que me devuelva el dinero, por favor. kee·*sye*·ra ke me de·*vwel*·va el dee·*ne*·ro por fa·*vor*
I'd like to return this, please.	Quisiera devolver esto, por favor. kee·*sye*·ra de·vol·*ver* es·to por fa·*vor*

Bargaining

That's too expensive.	Es muy caro. es mooy *ka*·ro
Can you lower the price (a little)?	¿Podría bajar (un poco) el precio? po·*dree*·a ba·*khar* (oon *po*·ko) el *pre*·syo
Do you have something cheaper?	¿Tiene algo más barato? *tye*·ne *al*·go mas ba·*ra*·to
I'll give you ...	Le daré ... le da·*re* ...

Making a Purchase

I'd like to buy ...
Quisiera comprar ...
kee·sye·ra kom·prar ...

How much is it?
¿Cuánto cuesta esto?
kwan·to kwes·ta es·to

—— **OR** ——

Can you write down the price?
¿Puede escribir el precio?
pwe·de es·kree·beer el pre·syo

Do you accept credit cards?
¿Aceptan tarjetas de crédito?
a·sep·tan tar·khe·tas de kre·dee·to

Could I have a ..., please?
¿Podría darme ..., por favor?
po·dree·a dar·me ... por fa·vor

 receipt
un recibo
oon re·see·bo

 bag
una bolsa
oo·na bol·sa

🔊 LISTEN FOR

cazador m **de ofertas**	ka·sa·*dor* de o·*fer*·tas	bargain hunter
estafa f	es·*ta*·fa	rip-off
ganga f	*gan*·ga	bargain
saldos m pl	*sal*·dos	specials
venta f	*ven*·ta	sale

What's your final price?	¿Cuál es su precio final? kwal es soo *pre*·syo fee·*nal*

Books & Reading

Is there an English-language bookshop/section?	¿Hay alguna librería/sección en inglés? ai al·*goo*·na lee·bre·*ree*·a/sek·*syon* en een·*gles*
Is there a/an (English-language) entertainment guide?	¿Hay alguna guía de espectáculos (en inglés)? ai al·*goo*·na *gee*·a de es·pek·*ta*·koo·los (en een·*gles*)
Do you have a book by ...?	¿Tiene un libro de ...? *tye*·ne oon *lee*·bro de ...

Clothes

Can I try it on?	¿Me lo puedo probar? me lo *pwe*·do pro·*bar*
My size is (medium).	Uso la talla (mediana). *oo*·so la *ta*·ya (me·*dya*·na)
It doesn't fit.	No me queda bien. no me *ke*·da byen

For different types of clothing, see the **dictionary**, and for sizes, see **numbers & amounts** (p32).

Music & DVD

I'd like a CD/DVD.	Quisiera un cómpact/DVD. kee·*sye*·ra oon *kom*·pak/ de·ve·*de*
I'd like some headphones.	Quisiera unos auriculares. kee·*sye*·ra *oo*·nos ow·ree·koo·*la*·res
I heard a singer called ...	Escuché un/una cantante que se llama ... **m/f** es·koo·*che* oon/*oo*·na kan·*tan*·te ke se *ya*·ma ...
I heard a band called ...	Escuché un grupo que se llama ... es·koo·*che* oon *groo*·po ke se *ya*·ma ...

¿Tiene otros?
tye·ne *o*·tros
Do you have any others?

> **LANGUAGE TIP**
>
> **Regionalisms**
> In Latin America the common term for 'general store' is *una tienda* oo·na *tyen*·da. Look out for some of these regional variations:
>
> | | | |
> |---|---|---|
> | **Argentina** | un almacén | oon al·ma·*sen* |
> | **Bolivia, Central America, Colombia, Ecuador, Mexico, Peru** | una tienda de abarrrotes | oo·na *tyen*·da de a·ba·*ro*·tes |
> | **Central America** | una bodega | oo·na bo·*de*·ga |
> | **Chile, Costa Rica** | una pulpería | oo·na pool·pe·*ree*·a |
> | **Venezuela** | un abasto | oon a·*bas*·to |

What's his/her best recording?	¿Cuál es su mejor disco? kwal es soo me·*khor* dees·ko
Can I listen to this?	¿Puedo escuchar éste? *pwe*·do es·koo·*char* es·te
What region is this DVD for?	¿Para qué región es este DVD? *pa*·ra ke re·*khyon* es es·te de·ve·de

Photography

Can you print digital photos?	¿Se puede imprimir fotos digitales? se *pwe*·de eem·pree·*meer fo*·tos dee·khee·*ta*·les
Can you recharge the battery?	¿Se puede recargar la pila? se *pwe*·de re·kar·*gar* la *pee*·la
Can you transfer my photos to CD?	¿Se puede pasar las fotos a un CD? se *pwe*·de pa·*sar* las *fo*·tos a oon se·*de*

Do you have batteries for this camera?	¿Tiene pilas para esta cámara? *tye*·ne *pee*·las *pa*·ra es·ta *ka*·ma·ra
Do you have a memory card for this camera?	¿Tiene tarjeta de memoria para esta cámara? *tye*·ne tar·*khe*·ta de me·*mo*·rya *pa*·ra es·ta *ka*·ma·ra
Can you load my film?	¿Puede cargar el carrete? *pwe*·de kar·*gar* el ka·*re*·te
Can you develop this film?	¿Puede revelar este carrete? *pwe*·de re·ve·*lar* es·te ka·*re*·te
When will it be ready?	¿Cuándo estará listo? *kwan*·do es·ta·*ra* *lees*·to
I need ... film for this camera.	Necesito un carrete de película ... para esta cámara. ne·se·*see*·to oon ka·*re*·te de pe·*lee*·koo·la ... *pa*·ra es·ta *ka*·ma·ra

(400) speed	de sensibilidad (cuatrocientos)	de sen·see·bee·lee·*da* (*kwa*·tro·*syen*·tos)
B&W	en blanco y negro	en *blan*·ko ee *ne*·gro
colour	en color	en ko·*lor*
slide	para diapositivas	*pa*·ra dya·po·see·*tee*·vas

I'm not happy with these photos.	No estoy contento/a con estas fotos. **m/f** no es·*toy* kon·*ten*·to/a kon es·tas *fo*·tos

For more photographic equipment, see the **dictionary**.

CULTURE TIP

Market-Hopping

Mercados mer·*ka*·dos (markets) are a colourful feature of Latin American life. Smaller, open-air street markets are known as *ferias* *fe*·ryas. If it's vibrant folk art you're after, the place to visit is a *mercado de artesanía* mer·*ka*·do de ar·te·sa·*nee*·ya (craft market). Here are some souvenirs you can look for:

alpaca jumper	chompa f de alpaca	*chom*·pa de al·*pa*·ka
cigars	cigarros m pl	see·*ga*·ros
hammock	hamaca f	a·*ma*·ka
jewellery	joyería f	kho·ye·*ree*·a
leather bag	cartera f de cuero	kar·*te*·ra de *kwe*·ro
panpipes	zampoña f	sam·*po*·nya
Peruvian hat	chullo m	*choo*·yo
pottery	alfarería f	al·fa·re·*ree*·a
silverware	plata f	*pla*·ta
weaving	tejido m	te·*khee*·do
woodcarving	talla f de madera	*ta*·ya de ma·*de*·ra

Repairs

Can I have my backpack/ camera repaired here?	¿Puede reparar mi mochila/cámara aquí? *pwe*·de re·pa·*rar* mee mo·*chee*·la/*ka*·ma·ra a·*kee*
Can I pick it up later?	¿Puedo recogerlo más tarde? *pwe*·do re·ko·*kher*·lo mas *tar*·de
When will my glasses/ shoes be ready?	¿Cuándo estarán listos mis anteojos/zapatos? *kwan*·do es·ta·*ran* *lees*·tos mees an·te·o·khos/sa·*pa*·tos

Communications

KEY PHRASES

Where's the local internet cafe?	¿Dónde hay un cibercafé cercano?	*don*·de ai oon see·ber·ka·*fe* ser·*ka*·no
I'd like to check my email.	Quisiera revisar mi correo electrónico.	kee·*sye*·ra re·vee·*sar* mee ko·*re*·o e·lek·*tro*·nee·ko
I'd like to send a parcel.	Quisiera enviar un paquete.	kee·*sye*·ra en·*vyar* oon pa·*ke*·te
I want to make a call to ...	Quiero hacer una llamada a ...	*kye*·ro a·*ser* oo·na ya·*ma*·da a ...
I'd like a SIM card.	Quisiera comprar una tarjeta SIM.	kee·*sye*·ra kom·*prar* oo·na tar·*khe*·ta seem

The Internet

Where's the local internet cafe?	¿Dónde hay un cibercafé cercano? *don*·de ai oon see·ber·ka·*fe* ser·*ka*·no
Is there (wireless) internet access here?	¿Hay acceso al internet (inalámbrico) aquí? ai ak·*se*·so al een·ter·*net* (ee·na·*lam*·bree·ko) a·*kee*
Can I connect my laptop here?	¿Se puede enchufar mi portátil aquí? se *pwe*·de en·choo·*far* mee por·*ta*·teel a·*kee*

I'd like to ...	Quisiera ... kee·sye·ra ...	
check my email	revisar mi correo electrónico	re·vee·sar mee ko·re·o e·lek·tro·nee·ko
download my photos	descargar mis fotos	des·kar·gar mees fo·tos
use a printer	usar una impresora	oo·sar oo·na eem·pre·so·ra
use a scanner	usar un escáner	oo·sar oon es·ka·ner
use Skype	usar el Skype	oo·sar el es·kai·pe

How much per ...?	¿Cuánto cuesta por ...? kwan·to kwes·ta por ...	
(10) minutes	(diez) minutos	(dyes) mee·noo·tos
CD	cómpact	kom·pak
hour	hora	o·ra
page	página	pa·khee·na

Do you have headphones (with a microphone)?	¿Tiene audífonos (con micrófono)? tye·ne ow·dee·fo·nos (kon mee·kro·fo·no)
Do you have PCs/Macs?	¿Tiene PC/MacIntosh? tye·ne pe·se/ma·keen·tosh
Do you have a Zip drive?	¿Tiene unidad de Zip? tye·ne oo·nee·da de seep
How do I log on?	¿Cómo me conecto al sistema? ko·mo me ko·nek·to al sees·te·ma

I need help with the computer.	Necesito ayuda con la computadora. ne·se·*see*·to a·*yoo*·da kon la kom·poo·ta·*do*·ra
It's crashed.	Se ha quedado colgado. se a ke·*da*·do kol·*ga*·do
I've finished.	He terminado. e ter·mee·*na*·do

Mobile/Cell Phone

I'd like a/an ...	Quisiera ... kee·*sye*·ra ...

adaptor plug	un adaptador	oon a·dap·ta·*dor*
charger for my phone	un cargador para mi teléfono	oon kar·ga·*dor* *pa*·ra mee te·*le*·fo·no
mobile/cell phone for hire	un móvil para alquilar	oon *mo*·veel *pa*·ra al·kee·*lar*
prepaid mobile/ cell phone	un móvil pagado por adelantado	oon *mo*·veel pa·*ga*·do por a·de·lan·*ta*·do
SIM card for your network	una tarjeta SIM para su red	*oo*·na tar·*khe*·ta seem *pa*·ra soo re

What are the rates?	¿Cuáles son las tarifas? *kwa*·les son las ta·*ree*·fas

LISTEN FOR

(Treinta centavos) por (treinta) segundos.	(*trayn*·ta sen·*ta*·vos) por (*trayn*·ta) se·*goon*·dos (30c) per (30) seconds.

Phone

Where's the nearest public phone?	¿Dónde está la cabina telefónica más cercana? *don·de es·ta la ka·bee·na te·le·fo·nee·ka mas ser·ka·na*
I want to make a (reverse-charge/collect) call to ...	Quiero hacer una llamada (a cobro revertido) a ... *kye·ro a·ser oo·na ya·ma·da (a ko·bro re·ver·tee·do) a ...*
I want to buy a phone card.	Quiero comprar una tarjeta telefónica. *kye·ro kom·prar oo·na tar·khe·ta te·le·fo·nee·ka*
I want to speak for (three) minutes.	Quiero hablar por (tres) minutos. *kye·ro a·blar por (tres) mee·noo·tos*
How much does a (three)-minute call cost?	¿Cuánto cuesta una llamada de (tres) minutos? *kwan·to kwes·ta oo·na ya·ma·da de (tres) mee·noo·tos*
How much does each extra minute cost?	¿Cuánto cuesta cada minuto extra? *kwan·to kwes·ta ka·da mee·noo·to eks·tra*
Q What's your phone number?	¿Cuál es su número de teléfono? *kwal es soo noo·me·ro de te·le·fo·no*
A The number is ...	El número es ... *el noo·me·ro es ...*
What's the area/country code for ...?	¿Cuál es el prefijo de ...? *kwal es el pre·fee·kho de ...*

It's engaged.	Está ocupada. es·ta o·koo·pa·da
The connection's bad.	Es mala conexión. es ma·la ko·nek·syon
I've been cut off.	Me han cortado (la comunicación). me an kor·ta·do (la ko·moo·nee·ka·syon)
Hello. (making a call)	¡Hola! o·la
Hello. (answering a call)	¿Diga? dee·ga
It's ... (identifying yourself)	Habla ... a·bla ...
Can I speak to ...?	¿Está ...? es·ta ...
Can I leave a message?	¿Puedo dejar un mensaje? pwe·do de·khar oon men·sa·khe

PRACTICAL COMMUNICATIONS

🔊 LISTEN FOR

¿De parte de quién?	de par·te de kyen Who's calling?
¿Con quién quiere hablar?	kon kyen kye·re a·blar Who do you want to speak to?
Lo siento, pero ahora no está.	lo syen·to pe·ro a·o·ra no es·ta I'm sorry he's/she's not here.
Lo siento, tiene el número equivocado.	lo syen·to tye·ne el noo·me·ro e·kee·vo·ka·do Sorry, wrong number.
Sí, aquí está.	see a·kee es·ta Yes, he/she is here.

Please tell him/her I called.	Dile/Dila que llamé, por favor. m/f *dee·le/dee·la ke ya·me por fa·vor*
I'll call back later.	Ya llamaré más tarde. *ya ya·ma·re mas tar·de*
I don't have a contact number.	No tengo número de contacto. *no ten·go noo·me·ro de kon·tak·to*

Post Office

I want to send a letter.	Quisiera enviar una carta. *kee·sye·ra en·vyar oo·na kar·ta*
I want to send a postcard.	Quisiera enviar una postal. *kee·sye·ra en·vyar oo·na pos·tal*

 LOOK FOR

In Latin America dwellings may not be numbered and addresses are sometimes short descriptive passages. Be prepared to decipher an address such as this one:

Marirosa Ferrer Botero	Marirosa Ferrer Botero
la casa azul en	the blue house on
la esquina de	the corner of
Avenida de la Paz y	Avenida de la Paz and
Calle 12	12th Street
cerca de la farmacia	near the pharmacy
una manzana al norte	one block north
de la catedral	of the cathedral
Tegucigalpa	Tegucigalpa
Honduras	Honduras

🔊 LISTEN FOR

¿Adónde lo manda?	a·*don*·de lo *man*·da Where are you sending it?
¿Por correo urgente o normal?	por ko·*re*·o oor·*khen*·te o nor·*mal* By express or regular post?
correo m **aéreo**	ko·*re*·o a·*e*·re·o airmail
correo m **certificado**	ko·*re*·o ser·tee·fee·*ka*·do registered mail
declaración f **de aduana**	de·kla·ra·*syon* de a·*dwa*·na customs declaration
por vía terrestre	por *vee*·a te·*res*·tre by surface mail

I want to buy an envelope.	Quisiera comprar un sobre. kee·*sye*·ra kom·*prar* oon *so*·bre
I want to buy stamps.	Quisiera comprar unos sellos. kee·*sye*·ra kom·*prar* oo·nos *se*·yos
Please send it by airmail/ surface mail (to ...).	Por favor, mándelo por vía aérea/terrestre (a ...). por fa·*vor* *man*·de·lo por *vee*·a a·*e*·re·a/te·*res*·tre (a ...)
It contains ...	Contiene ... kon·*tye*·ne ...
Where's the poste restante section?	¿Dónde está la lista de correos? *don*·de es·*ta* la *lees*·ta de ko·*re*·os
Is there any mail for me?	¿Hay alguna carta para mí? ai al·*goo*·na *kar*·ta *pa*·ra mee

Money & Banking

KEY PHRASES

How much is it?	¿Cuánto cuesta?	*kwan*·to *kwes*·ta
What's the exchange rate?	¿Cuál es la tasa de cambio?	kwal es la *ta*·sa de *kam*·byo
Where's the nearest ATM?	¿Dónde está el cajero automático más cercano?	*don*·de es·*ta* el ka·*khe*·ro ow·to·*ma*·tee·ko mas ser·*ka*·no
I'd like to change money.	Me gustaría cambiar dinero.	me goos·ta·*ree*·ya kam·*byar* dee·*ne*·ro
Can I have smaller notes?	¿Me lo puede dar en billetes más pequeños?	me lo *pwe*·de dar en bee·*ye*·tes mas pe·*ke*·nyos

Paying the Bill

Q How much is it?	¿Cuánto cuesta? *kwan*·to *kwes*·ta	
A It's free.	Es gratis. es *gra*·tees	
A It's ... (pesos).	Cuesta ... (pesos). *kwes*·ta ... (*pe*·sos)	
Can you write down the price?	¿Puede escribir el precio? *pwe*·de es·kree·*beer* el *pre*·syo	

Do I need to pay upfront?	¿Hay que pagar por adelantado? ai ke pa·*gar* por a·de·lan·*ta*·do
Do you accept credit/debit cards?	¿Aceptan tarjetas de crédito/débito? a·*sep*·tan tar·*khe*·tas de *kre*·dee·to/*de*·bee·to
Do you accept travellers cheques?	¿Aceptan cheques de viajero? a·*sep*·tan *che*·kes de vya·*khe*·ro
I'd like a receipt, please.	Quisiera un recibo, por favor. kee·*sye*·ra oon re·*see*·bo por fa·*vor*
I'd like my change, please.	Quisiera mi cambio, por favor. kee·*sye*·ra mee *kam*·byo por fa·*vor*

PRACTICAL **MONEY & BANKING**

| There's a mistake in the bill. | Hay un error en la cuenta.
ai oon e·*ror* en la *kwen*·ta |
| I don't want to pay the full price. | No quiero pagar el precio íntegro.
no *kye*·ro pa·*gar* el *pre*·syo *een*·te·gro |

Banking

What time does the bank open?	¿A qué hora abre el banco? a ke *o*·ra *a*·bre el *ban*·ko
Where's the nearest ATM?	¿Dónde está el cajero automático más cercano? *don*·de es·*ta* el ka·*khe*·ro ow·to·*ma*·tee·ko mas ser·*ka*·no
Where's the nearest foreign exchange office?	¿Dónde está la oficina de cambio más cercana? *don*·de es·*ta* la o·fee·*see*·na de *kam*·byo mas ser·*ka*·na
Do you change money here?	¿Se cambia dinero aquí? se *kam*·bya dee·*ne*·ro a·*kee*
What's the exchange rate?	¿Cuál es la tasa de cambio? kwal es la *ta*·sa de *kam*·byo
What's the commission?	¿Cuál es la comisión? kwal es la ko·mee·*syon*
What's the charge for that?	¿Cuánto hay que pagar por eso? *kwan*·to ai ke pa·*gar* por e·so
The ATM took my card.	El cajero automático se ha tragado mi tarjeta. el ka·*khe*·ro ow·to·*ma*·tee·ko se a tra·*ga*·do mee tar·*khe*·ta
I've forgotten my PIN.	Me he olvidado del NPI. me e ol·vee·*da*·do del e·ne·pe·ee

Where can I ...?	¿Dónde puedo ...?
	don·de *pwe*·do ...
I'd like to ...	Me gustaría ...
	me goos·ta·*ree*·a ...

arrange a transfer	organizar una transferencia	or·ga·nee·*sar* *oo*·na trans·fe·*ren*·sya
cash a cheque	cobrar un cheque	ko·*brar* oon *che*·ke
change a travellers cheque	cambiar un cheque de viajero	kam·*byar* oon *che*·ke de vya·*khe*·ro
change money	cambiar dinero	kam·*byar* dee·*ne*·ro
get a cash advance	obtener un adelanto	ob·te·*ner* oon a·de·*lan*·to
use internet banking	usar la banca por internet	oo·*sar* la *ban*·ka por een·ter·*net*
withdraw money	sacar dinero	sa·*kar* dee·*ne*·ro

Can I use my credit card to withdraw money?	¿Puedo usar mi tarjeta de crédito para sacar dinero?
	pwe·do oo·*sar* mee tar·*khe*·ta de *kre*·dee·to *pa*·ra sa·*kar* dee·*ne*·ro
Can I have smaller notes?	¿Me lo puede dar en billetes más pequeños?
	me lo *pwe*·de dar en bee·*ye*·tes mas pe·*ke*·nyos
Has my money arrived yet?	¿Ya ha llegado mi dinero?
	ya a ye·*ga*·do mee dee·*ne*·ro
How long will it take to arrive?	¿Cuánto tiempo tardará en llegar?
	kwan·to *tyem*·po tar·da·*ra* en ye·*gar*

PRACTICAL MONEY & BANKING

Business

KEY PHRASES

I'm attending a conference.	Asisto a un congreso.	a·*sees*·to a oon kon·*gre*·so
I have an appointment with ...	Tengo una cita con ...	*ten*·go oo·na *see*·ta kon ...
Can I have your business card?	¿Me dará su tarjeta de visita?	me da·*ra* soo tar·*khe*·ta de vee·*see*·ta

---

Where's the business centre?
¿Dónde está el servicio secretarial?
don·de es·*ta* el ser·*vee*·syo se·kre·ta·*ryal*

Where's the conference?
¿Dónde está el congreso?
don·de es·*ta* el kon·*gre*·so

Where's the meeting?
¿Dónde está la reunión?
don·de es·*ta* la re·oo·*nyon*

I have an appointment with ...
Tengo una cita con ...
ten·go oo·na *see*·ta kon ...

I'm attending a ...
Asisto a ...
a·*sees*·to a ...

---

conference	un congreso	oon kon·*gre*·so
course	un curso	oon *koor*·so
meeting	una reunión	oo·na re·oo·*nyon*
trade fair	una feria de muestras	oo·na *fe*·rya de *mwes*·tras

I'm here with my colleagues.	Estoy aquí con mis colegas. es·*toy* a·*kee* kon mees ko·*le*·gas
I'm alone.	Estoy solo/a. **m/f** es·*toy* so·lo/a
I'm expecting a call.	Estoy esperando una llamada. es·*toy* es·pe·*ran*·do *oo*·na ya·*ma*·da
I need ...	Necesito ... ne·se·*see*·to ...

a computer	una computadora	*oo*·na kom·poo·ta·*do*·ra
a connection to the internet	una conexión al internet	*oo*·na ko·nek·*syon* al een·ter·*net*
an interpreter	un/una intérprete **m/f**	oon/*oo*·na een·*ter*·pre·te
more business cards	más tarjetas de visita	mas tar·*khe*·tas de vee·*see*·ta

🇶 **Can I have your business card?**	¿Me dará su tarjeta de visita? me da·*ra* soo tar·*khe*·ta de vee·*see*·ta
🇦 **Here's my business card.**	Aquí tiene mi tarjeta de visita. a·*kee* tye·ne mee tar·*khe*·ta de vee·*see*·ta
Let me introduce you to my colleague.	¿Puedo presentarle a mi colega? *pwe*·do pre·sen·*tar*·le a mee ko·*le*·ga
That went very well.	Eso salió muy bien. e·so sa·*lyo* mooy byen
Shall we go for a drink/ meal?	¿Vamos a tomar/comer algo? *va*·mos a to·*mar*/ko·*mer* al·go

Sightseeing

KEY PHRASES

I'd like a guide.	Quisiera un/una guía. m/f	kee·*sye*·ra oon/*oo*·na *gee*·a
Can I take photos?	¿Puedo sacar fotos?	*pwe*·do sa·*kar fo*·tos
When's the museum open?	¿A qué hora abre el museo?	a ke *o*·ra *a*·bre el moo·*se*·o
I'm interested in ...	Me interesa ...	me een·te·*re*·sa ...
When is the next tour?	¿A qué hora sale el próximo recorrido?	a ke *o*·ra *sa*·le el *prok*·see·mo re·ko·*ree*·do

I'd like to see ...	Me gustaría ver ... me goos·ta·*ree*·a ver ...
I'd like a/an ...	Quisiera ... kee·*sye*·ra ...

audio set	un equipo audio	oon e·*kee*·po *ow*·dyo
catalogue	un catálogo	oon ka·*ta*·lo·go
guide	un/una guía m/f	oon/*oo*·na *gee*·a
guidebook (in English)	una guía turística (en inglés)	*oo*·na *gee*·a too·*rees*·tee·ka (en een·*gles*)
(local) map	un mapa (de la zona)	oon *ma*·pa (de la *so*·na)

| Do you have information on ... sights? | ¿Tiene información sobre los lugares ... de interés? |
| | *tye·ne een·for·ma·syon so·bre los loo·ga·res ... de een·te·res* |

cultural	culturales	kool·too·*ra*·les
local	locales	lo·*ka*·les
religious	religiosos	re·lee·*khyo*·sos
unique	únicos	*oo*·nee·kos

| **What's that?** | ¿Qué es eso? |
| | ke es *e*·so |

| **Who made it?** | ¿Quién lo hizo? |
| | kyen lo *ee*·so |

| **How old is it?** | ¿De cuándo es? |
| | de *kwan*·do es |

| **Could you take a photograph of me?** | ¿Me puede sacar una foto? |
| | me *pwe*·de sa·*kar* oo·na *fo*·to |

| **Can I take photographs (of you)?** | ¿(Le/Te) Puedo sacar fotos? **pol/inf** |
| | (le/te) *pwe*·do sa·*kar* *fo*·tos |

| **I'll send you the photograph.** | Le/Te mandaré la foto. **pol/inf** |
| | le/te man·da·*re* la *fo*·to |

Getting In

| **What time does it open/ close?** | ¿A qué hora abre/cierra? |
| | a ke *o*·ra *a*·bre/*sye*·ra |

| **What's the admission charge?** | ¿Cuánto cuesta la entrada? |
| | *kwan*·to *kwes*·ta la en·*tra*·da |

Is there a discount for ...?	¿Hay descuentos para ...? ai des·*kwen*·tos *pa*·ra ...

children	niños	*nee*·nyos
groups	grupos	*groo*·pos
pensioners	pensionados; jubilados (Arg)	pen·syo·*na*·dos; khoo·bee·*la*·dos
students	estudiantes	es·too·*dyan*·tes

Galleries & Museums

When's the gallery open?	¿A qué hora abre la galería? a ke o·ra *a*·bre la ga·le·*ree*·a
When's the museum open?	¿A qué hora abre el museo? a ke o·ra *a*·bre el moo·*se*·o
Q What kind of art are you interested in?	¿Qué tipo de arte le/te interesa? pol/inf ke *tee*·po de *ar*·te le/te een·te·*re*·sa
A I'm interested in ... art.	Me interesa el arte ... me een·te·*re*·sa el *ar*·te ...
A I like the works of ...	Me gusta la obra de ... me *goos*·ta la o·bra de ...
Q What's in the collection?	¿Qué hay en la colección? ke ai en la ko·lek·*syon*
A It's an exhibition of (pottery).	Hay una exposición de (alfarería). ai *oo*·na ek·spo·see·*syon* de (al·fa·re·*ree*·a)

Q What do you think of ...?	¿Qué piensa/piensas de ...? pol/inf ke *pyen*·sa/*pyen*·sas de ...
A It reminds me of ...	Me recuerda ... me re·*kwer*·da ...
... art	arte ... *ar*·te ...

Aztec	azteca	as·*te*·ka
graphic	gráfico	*gra*·fee·ko
Inca	inca	*een*·ka
Mayan	maya	*ma*·ya
pre-Columbian	precolombino	pre·ko·lom·*bee*·no

Tours

Can you recommend a tour?	¿Puede recomendar algún recorrido? *pwe*·de re·ko·men·*dar* al·*goon* re·ko·*ree*·do
Can you recommend a boat trip?	¿Puede recomendar algún paseo en barca? *pwe*·de re·ko·men·*dar* al·*goon* pa·*se*·o en *bar*·ka

> ### *¿Qué es eso?*
> ke es *e*·so
> ***What's that?***

When's the next day trip?
¿Cuándo es la próxima excursión de un día?
kwan·do es la prok·see·ma eks·koor·syon de oon dee·a

When's the next tour?
¿Cuándo es el próximo recorrido?
kwan·do es el prok·see·mo re·ko·ree·do

Is ... included?
¿Incluye ...?
een·kloo·ye ...

accommodation	alojamiento	a·lo·kha·myen·to
equipment	equipo	e·kee·po
food	comida	ko·mee·da
transport	transporte	trans·por·te

Can we hire a (local) guide?
¿Podemos alquilar un guía (local)?
po·de·mos al·kee·lar oon gee·a (lo·kal)

How long is the tour?
¿Cuánto dura el recorrido?
kwan·to doo·ra el re·ko·ree·do

What time should I be back?
¿A qué hora tengo que volver?
a ke o·ra ten·go ke vol·ver

The guide will pay.
El guía va a pagar.
el gee·a va a pa·gar

I'm with them.
Voy con ellos.
voy kon e·yos

I've lost my group.
He perdido mi grupo.
e per·dee·do mee groo·po

Senior & Disabled Travellers

KEY PHRASES

I need assistance.	Necesito asistencia.	ne·se·*see*·to a·sees·*ten*·sya
Is there wheelchair access?	¿Hay acceso para silla de ruedas?	ai ak·*se*·so *pa*·ra *see*·ya de *rwe*·das
Are there toilets for people with a disablity?	¿Hay baños para discapacitados?	ai *ba*·nyos *pa*·ra dees·ka·pa·see·*ta*·dos

I have a disability.	Soy discapacitado/a. m/f soy dees·ka·pa·see·*ta*·do/a
I need assistance.	Necesito asistencia. ne·se·*see*·to a·sees·*ten*·sya
What services do you have for people with a disability?	¿Qué servicios tienen para discapacitados? ke ser·*vee*·syos *tye*·nen *pa*·ra dees·ka·pa·see·*ta*·dos
Is there wheelchair access?	¿Hay acceso para silla de ruedas? ai ak·*se*·so *pa*·ra *see*·ya de *rwe*·das
Is there a lift?	¿Hay ascensor? ai a·sen·*sor*
How many steps are there?	¿Cuántos escalones hay? *kwan*·tos es·ka·*lo*·nes ai

How wide is the entrance?	¿Cuánto es de ancha la entrada?
	kwan·to es de an·cha la en·tra·da
Are guide dogs permitted?	¿Se permite la entrada a los perros guía?
	se per·mee·te la en·tra·da a los pe·ros gee·a
Are there toilets for people with a disablity?	¿Hay baños para discapacitados?
	ai ba·nyos pa·ra dees·ka·pa·see·ta·dos
Is there somewhere I can sit down?	¿Hay algún sitio dónde me pueda sentar?
	ai al·goon see·tyo don·de me pwe·da sen·tar
Could you call me a taxi for the disabled, please?	¿Me podría llamar a un taxi para discapacitados?
	me po·dree·a ya·mar a oon tak·see pa·ra dees·ka·pa·see·ta·dos
Could you help me cross this street?	¿Me puede ayudar a cruzar la calle?
	me pwe·de a·yoo·dar a kroo·sar la ka·ye
disabled person	persona f discapacitada
	per·so·na dees·ka·pa·see·ta·da
guide dog	perro m guía
	pe·ro gee·a
ramp	rampa f
	ram·pa
space (to move around)	espacio m (para moverse)
	es·pa·syo (pa·ra mo·ver·se)
wheelchair	silla f de ruedas
	see·ya de rwe·das

Travel with Children

KEY PHRASES

Are children allowed?	¿Se admiten niños?	se ad·*mee*·ten *nee*·nyos
Is there a family discount?	¿Hay un descuento familiar?	ai oon des·*kwen*·to fa·mee·*lyar*
Is there a baby change room?	¿Hay una sala en la que pueda cambiarle el pañal al bebé?	ai *oo*·na *sa*·la en la ke *pwe*·da kam·*byar*·le el pa·*nyal* al be·*be*

Are children allowed?	¿Se admiten niños? se ad·*mee*·ten *nee*·nyos
Is this suitable for (two)-year-old children?	¿Es apto para niños de (dos) años? es *ap*·to *pa*·ra *nee*·nyos de (dos) *a*·nyos
I need a ...	Necesito ... ne·se·*see*·to ...

baby seat	un asiento de seguridad para bebés	oon a·*syen*·to de se·goo·ree·*da pa*·ra be·*bes*
booster seat	un asiento de seguridad para niños	oon a·*syen*·to de se·goo·ree·*da pa*·ra *nee*·nyos
potty	una bacinica; una pelela **(SAm)**	*oo*·na ba·see·*nee*·ka; *oo*·na pe·*le*·la
stroller	un cochecito	oon ko·che·*see*·to

Do you mind if I breastfeed here?	¿Le molesta que dé de pecho aquí?
	le mo·*les*·ta ke de de *pe*·cho a·*kee*

Is there a/an ...?	¿Hay ...?
	ai ...

baby change room	una sala en la que pueda cambiarle el pañal al bebé	*oo*·na *sa*·la en la ke *pwe*·da kam·*byar*·le el pa·*nyal* al be·*be*
(English-speaking) babysitter	niñera (de habla inglesa)	nee·*nye*·ra (de a·bla een·*gle*·sa)
child-minding service	servicio de cuidado de niños	ser·*vee*·syo de kwee·*da*·do de *nee*·nyos
children's menu	menú infantil	me·*noo* een·fan·*teel*
creche	guardería	gwar·de·*ree*·a
family discount	descuento familiar	des·*kwen*·to fa·mee·*lyar*
highchair	trona	*tro*·na
park	un parque	oon *par*·ke
playground nearby	un parque infantil cercano	oon *par*·ke een·fan·*teel* ser·*ka*·no
theme park	un parque de atracciones	oon *par*·ke de a·trak·*syo*·nes
toyshop	una juguetería	*oo*·na khoo·ge·te·*ree*·a

If your child is sick, see **health** (p156). For talking with children, see **meeting people** (p112).

Social

Meeting People

KEY PHRASES

My name is ...	Me llamo ...	me *ya*·mo ...
I'm from ...	Soy de ...	soy de ...
I work in ...	Trabajo en ...	tra·*ba*·kho en ...
I'm ... years old.	Tengo ... años.	*ten*·go ... *a*·nyos
And you?	¿Y Usted/tú? **pol/inf**	ee oos·*te*/too

Basics

Yes.	Sí. see
No.	No. no
Please.	Por favor. por fa·*vor*
Thank you (very much).	(Muchas) Gracias. (*moo*·chas) *gra*·syas
You're welcome.	De nada. de *na*·da Con mucho gusto. **(CAm)** kon *moo*·cho *goo*·sto
Sorry. (condolence)	Lo siento. lo *syen*·to
Sorry. (apology)	Perdón. per·*don*
Excuse me. (regret)	Perdón. per·*don*

| Excuse me. (attention/apology) | Disculpe. dees·*kool*·pe |
| | Con permiso. **(CAm)** kon per·*mee*·so |

Greetings

Hello./Hi.	Hola. o·la
	¿Qué hubo? **(Chi)** ke oo·bo
Good day.	Buen día. bwen *dee*·a
Good morning.	Buenos días. *bwe*·nos *dee*·as
Good afternoon. (until 8pm)	Buenas tardes. *bwe*·nas *tar*·des
Good evening/night.	Buenas noches. *bwe*·nas *no*·ches
See you later.	Hasta luego. *as*·ta *lwe*·go
Goodbye.	¡Adiós! a·*dyos*
Bye.	Chao./Chaucito. chow/chow·*see*·to
🇶 How are you?	¿Cómo está? **sg pol** *ko*·mo es·*ta*
	¿Cómo estás? **sg inf** *ko*·mo es·*tas*
	¿Cómo están? **pl** *ko*·mo es·*tan*
🇦 Fine, thank you. And you?	Bien, gracias. ¿Y Usted/tú? **pol/inf** byen *gra*·syas ee oos·*te*/too

SOCIAL   MEETING PEOPLE

Q What's your name?	¿Cómo se llama Usted? pol ko·mo se ya·ma oos·te ¿Cómo te llamas? inf ko·mo te ya·mas
A My name is ...	Me llamo ... me ya·mo ...
I'd like to introduce you to ...	Quisiera presentarle/te a ... pol/inf kee·sye·ra pre·sen·tar·le/te a ...
✂ This is ...	Éste/Ésta es ... m/f es·te/es·ta es ...
I'm pleased to meet you.	Mucho gusto. moo·cho goos·to

Titles & Addressing People

Women are mostly addressed as *Señora* se·nyo·ra regardless of age and marital status, although some older unmarried women may prefer to be called *Señorita* se·nyo·ree·ta. Men are usually addressed as *Señor* se·nyor. Professional titles are important and should be used before the surname when addressing someone directly.

Mr	Señor se·nyor
Ms/Mrs	Señora se·nyo·ra
Miss	Señorita se·nyo·ree·ta
Doctor (holder of a PhD or medical doctor)	Doctor(a) m/f dok·tor/dok·to·ra
Graduate	Licenciado/a m/f lee·sen·sya·do/a
Master (teacher or skilled musician/craftsman)	Maestro/a m/f ma·es·tro/a

Making Conversation

Do you live here?	¿Vive/Vives aquí? pol/inf _vee·ve/vee·ves a·kee_
Where are you going?	¿Adónde va/vas? pol/inf _a·don·de va/vas_
What are you doing?	¿Qué hace/haces? pol/inf _ke a·se/a·ses_
Are you waiting (for a bus)?	¿Está/Estás esperando (un autobús)? pol/inf _es·ta/es·tas es·pe·ran·do (oon ow·to·boos)_
Can I have a light?	¿Tiene/Tienes fuego? pol/inf _tye·ne/tye·nes fwe·go_
What's this called?	¿Cómo se llama esto? _ko·mo se ya·ma es·to_
What a beautiful baby!	¡Qué niño/a más lindo/a! m/f _ke nee·nyo/a mas leen·do/a_
That's (beautiful), isn't it?	Qué (precioso), ¿no? _ke (pre·syo·so) no_

SOCIAL

MEETING PEOPLE

LANGUAGE TIP

Polite & Informal

Spanish has two forms for the singular 'you'. With people you know well, your peers and children, use the informal form _tú_ too. For addressing strangers, older people or people you've just met, use the polite form _Usted_ oos·_te_. When your new-found friends feel it's time to switch to _tú_, they may say:

Let's use the 'tú' form.	Hablemos de tú.	_a·ble·mos de too_

See also **personal pronouns** in the **grammar** chapter (p21).

Q Do you like it here?

¿Le/Te gusta estar aquí? pol/inf
le/te *goos*·ta es·*tar* a·*kee*

A I love it here.

Me encanta estar aquí.
me en·*kan*·ta es·*tar* a·*kee*

Q How long are you here for?

¿Cuánto tiempo se va a quedar? pol
kwan·to *tyem*·po se va a ke·*dar*
¿Cuánto tiempo te vas a quedar? inf
kwan·to *tyem*·po te vas a ke·*dar*

A I'm here for (four) weeks/days.

Estoy aquí por (cuatro) semanas/días.
es·*toy* a·*kee* por (*kwa*·tro) se·*ma*·nas/*dee*·as

Q Are you here on holiday?

¿Está/Estás aquí de vacaciones? pol/inf
es·*ta*/es·*tas* a·*kee* de va·ka·*syo*·nes

A I'm here ...

Estoy aquí ...
es·*toy* a·*kee* ...

for a holiday	de vacaciones	de va·ka·*syo*·nes
on business	en viaje de negocios	en *vya*·khe de ne·*go*·syos
to study	estudiando	es·too·*dyan*·do
with my family	con mi familia	kon mee fa·*mee*·lya
with my partner	con mi pareja m&f	kon mee pa·*re*·kha

Nationalities

Q Where are you from?	¿De dónde es/eres? pol/inf de *don*·de es/*e*·res
A I'm from ...	Soy de ... soy de ...

Australia	Australia	ow·*stra*·lya
Germany	Alemania	a·le·*ma*·nya
Scotland	Escocia	es·*ko*·sya
the USA	los Estados Unidos	los es·*ta*·dos oo·*nee*·dos

For more countries, see the **dictionary**.

Age

Q How old are you?	¿Cuántos años tiene/ tienes? pol/inf *kwan*·tos *a*·nyos *tye*·ne/ *tye*·nes
A I'm ... years old.	Tengo ... años. *ten*·go ... *a*·nyos
Q How old is your daughter?	¿Cuántos años tiene su/tu hija? pol/inf *kwan*·tos *a*·nyos *tye*·ne soo/too *ee*·kha
Q How old is your son?	¿Cuántos años tiene su/tu hijo? pol/inf *kwan*·tos *a*·nyos *tye*·ne soo/too *ee*·kho
A He/She is ... years old.	Tiene ... años. *tye*·ne ... *a*·nyos
Too old!	¡Demasiado viejo/a! m/f de·ma·*sya*·do *vye*·kho/a

🔊 LISTEN FOR

¡De ningún modo!	de neen·*goon* mo·do	No way!
¡Eh, tú!	e too	Hey!
¡Escucha (esto)!	es·*koo*·cha (es·to)	Listen (to this)!
Está bien.	es·*ta* byen	It's OK.
Estoy bien.	es·*toy* byen	I'm OK.
Macanudo. (Arg)	ma·ka·*noo*·do	Sure.
¡Mira!	*mee*·ra	Look!
¡Qué bárbaro!	ke *bar*·ba·ro	How cool!
¿Qué onda?	ke *on*·da	What's up?
¿Qué pasa?	ke *pa*·sa	What's up?
¿Qué pasó?	ke pa·*so*	What happened?
Quizás.	kee·*sas*	Maybe.
¡Se pasa! (Arg)	se *pa*·sa	How cool!
Te estoy cargando. (Arg)	te es·*toy* kar·*gan*·do	Just joking.
Te estoy tomando el pelo.	te es·*toy* to·*man*·do el *pe*·lo	Just joking.

I'm younger than I look.	Soy más joven de lo que parezco. soy mas *kho*·ven de lo ke pa·*res*·ko

For your age, see **numbers & amounts** (p32).

Occupations & Studies

Q	What's your occupation?	¿A qué se dedica? pol a ke se de·*dee*·ka ¿A qué te dedicas? inf a ke te de·*dee*·kas
A	I work in education.	Trabajo en enseñanza. tra·*ba*·kho en en·se·*nyan*·sa

🅰 I work in hospitality.	Trabajo en hostelería.	tra·*ba*·kho en os·te·le·*ree*·a
🅰 I'm self-employed.	Soy trabajador/trabajadora autónomo/a. **m/f**	soy tra·ba·kha·*dor*/ tra·ba·kha·*do*·ra ow·*to*·no·mo/a
🅰 I'm retired.	Estoy jubilado/a. **m/f**	es·*toy* khoo·bee·*la*·do/a
🅰 I'm unemployed.	Estoy desempleado/a. **m/f**	es·*toy* des·em·ple·*a*·do/a
🇶 What are you studying?	¿Qué estudia/estudias? **pol/inf**	ke es·*too*·dya/es·*too*·dyas
🅰 I'm studying business.	Estudio negocios.	es·*too*·dyo ne·*go*·syos
🅰 I'm studying languages.	Estudio idiomas.	es·*too*·dyo ee·*dyo*·mas
🅰 I'm studying science.	Estudio ciencias.	es·*too*·dyo *syen*·syas

For more occupations and studies, see the **dictionary**.

Family

🇶 Do you have (a brother)?	¿Tiene/Tienes (un hermano)? **pol/inf**	*tye*·ne/*tye*·nes (oon er·*ma*·no)
🅰 I have (a partner).	Tengo (pareja).	*ten*·go (pa·*re*·kha)
🇶 Do you live with (your family)?	¿Vive/Vives con (su/tu familia)? **pol/inf**	*vee*·ve/*vee*·ves kon (soo/too fa·*mee*·lya)
🅰 I live with (my sister).	Vivo con (mi hermana).	*vee*·vo kon (mee er·*ma*·na)

❓ Are you married?	¿Está casado/a? **m/f pol**
	es·*ta* ka·*sa*·do/a
	¿Estás casado/a? **m/f inf**
	es·*tas* ka·*sa*·do/a
🅰 I live with someone.	Vivo con alguien.
	vee·vo kon *al*·gyen
🅰 I'm single.	Soy soltero/a. **m/f**
	soy sol·*te*·ro/a
🅰 I'm married.	Estoy casado/a. **m/f**
	es·*toy* ka·*sa*·do/a
🅰 I'm separated.	Estoy separado/a. **m/f**
	es·*toy* se·pa·*ra*·do/a

For more kinship terms, see the **dictionary**.

Talking with Children

When's your birthday?	¿Cuándo es tu cumpleaños?
	kwan·do es too
	koom·ple·*a*·nyos
What grade are you in?	¿En qué grado estás?
	en ke *gra*·do es·*tas*
Do you like school?	¿Te gusta el colegio?
	te *goos*·ta el ko·*le*·khyo
Do you like sport?	¿Te gusta el deporte?
	te *goos*·ta el de·*por*·te
What do you do after school?	¿Qué haces después del colegio?
	ke *a*·ses des·*pwes* del ko·*le*·khyo
Do you learn English?	¿Aprendes inglés?
	a·*pren*·des een·*gles*
Tell me how to play.	Dime cómo se juega.
	dee·me *ko*·mo se *khwe*·ga
Well done!	¡Muy bien!
	mooy byen

Farewells

Tomorrow is my last day here.	Mañana es mi último día aquí. ma·*nya*·na es mee *ool*·tee·mo *dee*·a a·*kee*
It's been great meeting you.	Me ha encantado conocerte. me a en·kan·*ta*·do ko·no·*ser*·te
I'll miss you.	Te voy a echar de menos. te voy a e·*char* de *me*·nos
Keep in touch!	¡Nos mantendremos en contacto! nos man·ten·*dre*·mos en kon·*tak*·to

Me encanta estar aquí.
me en·*kan*·ta es·*tar* a·*kee*
I love it here.

Q **What's your ...?**	¿Cuál es tu ...? kwal es too ...
A **Here's my ...**	Éste/Ésta es mi ... m/f es·te/es·ta es mee ...

address	dirección f	dee·rek·*syon*
email address	dirección f de email	dee·rek·*syon* de ee·mayl
mobile number	número m de móvil	*noo*·me·ro de *mo*·veel
phone number	número m de teléfono	*noo*·mero de te·*le*·fo·no

If you ever visit (Scotland) come and visit us.	Si algún día visitas (Escocia), ven a vernos. see al·*goon dee*·a vee·*see*·tas (es·ko·sya) ven a *ver*·nos
If you ever visit (the USA), you can stay with me.	Si algún día visitas (los Estados Unidos), te puedes quedar conmigo. see al·*goon dee*·a vee·*see*·tas (los es·*ta*·dos oo·*nee*·dos) te *pwe*·des ke·*dar* kon·*mee*·go

---

CULTURE TIP **Body Language**
Personal space boundaries vary from culture to culture, and in Latin America they're set closer than in Anglo-Saxon countries. You'll probably find that when you're talking with someone they stand closer to you than you're used to, and may touch you on the arm or shoulder. Acquaintances always greet with a *beso* be·so (kiss), and good friends often add an *abrazo* a·bra·so (hug). It's also fairly common to see people of the same sex walking down the street arm-in-arm.

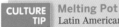
SOCIAL MEETING PEOPLE

CULTURE TIP Melting Pot
Latin American Spanish reflects the region's rich ethnic mix. One example of this are the words coined to refer to people with respect to their heritage. These terms aren't racially loaded labels, and people may use them to refer to themselves and their background.

criollo/a m/f   kree·o·yo/a
person born in Latin America of Spanish ancestry. On the Caribbean Coast, a person of mixed African and European ancestry.

ladino/a m/f   la·dee·no/a
Spanish-speaking person of mixed Indian and European ancestry

mestizo/a m/f   mes·tee·so/a
person of mixed ancestry (usually Spanish and Indian)

zambo/a m/f   sam·bo/a
person of mixed African and Indian ancestry

The term *indio/a* m/f *een*·dyo/a (Indian) can be offensive to indigenous people, so use *indígena* m&f een·*dee*·khe·na (indigenous person) instead.

I want to come and visit you.	Quiero venir a visitarte. *kye*·ro ve·*neer* a vee·see·*tar*·te
I'll send you copies of the photos.	Te enviaré copias de las fotos. te en·vya·*re ko*·pyas de las *fo*·tos

Interests

KEY PHRASES

What do you do in your spare time?	¿Qué te gusta hacer en tu tiempo libre?	ke te *goos*·ta a·*ser* en too *tyem*·po *lee*·bre
Do you like ...?	¿Te gusta/gustan ...? **sg/pl**	te *goos*·ta/*goos*·tan ...
I (don't) like ...	(No) Me gusta/gustan ... **sg/pl**	(no) me *goos*·ta/*goos*·tan ...

Common Interests

What do you do in your spare time?	¿Qué te gusta hacer en tu tiempo libre? ke te *goos*·ta a·*ser* en too *tyem*·po *lee*·bre
Q **Do you like ...?**	¿Te gusta/gustan ...? **sg/pl** te *goos*·ta/*goos*·tan ...
A **I (don't) like ...**	(No) Me gusta/gustan ... **sg/pl** (no) me *goos*·ta/*goos*·tan ...

board games	los juegos **pl** de tablero	los *khwe*·gos de ta·*ble*·ro
cooking	cocinar **sg**	ko·see·*nar*
films	el cine **sg**	el *see*·ne
travelling	viajar **sg**	vya·*khar*

For more hobbies and types of sports, see **sports** (p139), and the **dictionary**.

LANGUAGE TIP

Likes & Dislikes

In Spanish, in order to say you like something, you say *me gusta* me *goos*·ta (lit: me it-pleases). If what you're referring to is plural, use *me gustan* me *goos*·tan (lit: me they-please). If you're referring to an activity, eg cooking or travelling, use *me gusta* followed by the verb. You can negate any of these sentences by adding *no* no (not) to the beginning of the phrase.

I like this song.	Me gusta esta canción.
	me *goos*·ta es·ta kan·*syon*
I like soap operas.	Me gustan las telenovelas.
	me *goos*·tan las te·le·no·*ve*·las
I don't like dancing.	No me gusta bailar.
	no me *goos*·ta bai·*lar*

Music

Do you like to ...?	¿Te gusta ...?
	te *goos*·ta ...

dance	bailar	bai·*lar*
go to concerts	ir a conciertos	eer a kon·*syer*·tos
listen to music	escuchar	es·koo·*char*
	música	*moo*·see·ka
play an instrument	tocar un instrumento	to·*kar* oon een·stroo·*men*·to
sing	cantar	kan·*tar*

Which bands do you like?	¿Qué grupos te gustan?
	ke *groo*·pos te *goos*·tan

Which music do you like?	¿Qué música te gusta?
	ke *moo*·see·ka te *goos*·ta

... music	música ... *moo*·see·ka ...

classical	clásica	*kla*·see·ka
electronic	electrónica	e·lek·*tro*·nee·ka
traditional	folclórica	fol·*klo*·ree·ka
world	étnica	*et*·nee·ka

Planning to go to a concert? See **buying tickets** (p42) and **going out** (p126).

Cinema & Theatre

I feel like going to a ...	Tengo ganas de ir a ... *ten*·go *ga*·nas de eer a ...

ballet	un ballet	oon ba·*le*
comedy	una comedia	*oo*·na ko·*me*·dya
film	una película	*oo*·na pe·*lee*·koo·la
play	una obra de teatro	*oo*·na *o*·bra de te·*a*·tro

What's showing at the cinema (tonight)?	¿Qué película dan en el cine (esta noche)? ke pe·*lee*·koo·la dan en el *see*·ne (*es*·ta *no*·che)
Is it in English/Spanish?	¿Es en inglés/castellano? es en een·*gles*/kas·te·*ya*·no
Does it have (English) subtitles?	¿Tiene subtítulos (en inglés)? *tye*·ne soob·*tee*·too·los (en een·*gles*)
Are those seats taken?	¿Están libres estos asientos? es·*tan lee*·bres *es*·tos a·*syen*·tos

Have you seen ...?	¿Has visto ...? as *vees*·to ...
Q Who's in it?	¿Quién actúa? kyen ak·*too*·a
A It stars ...	Actúa ... ak·*too*·a ...
Q Did you like (the film)?	Te gustó (la película)? te goos·*to* (la pe·*lee*·koo·la)
A I thought it was crap.	Pienso que fue una porquería. *pyen*·so ke fwe *oo*·na por·ke·*ree*·a
A I thought it was excellent.	Pienso que fue excelente. *pyen*·so ke fwe ek·se·*len*·te
animated films	películas f pl de dibujos animados pe·*lee*·koo·las de dee·*boo*·khos a·nee·*ma*·dos
comedies	comedias f pl ko·*me*·dyas
documentaries	documentales m pl do·koo·men·*ta*·les
film noir	cine m negro *see*·ne *ne*·gro
horror movies	cine m de terror *see*·ne de te·*ror*
Latin American cinema	cine m latinoamericano *see*·ne la·tee·no·a·me·ree·*ka*·no
sci-fi	cine m de ciencia ficción *see*·ne de *syen*·sya feek·*syon*
short films	cortos m pl *kor*·tos
thrillers	cine m de suspenso *see*·ne de soos·*pen*·so

SOCIAL INTERESTS

Reading

❓ **What kind of books do you read?**	¿Qué tipo de libros lees? ke *tee*·po de *lee*·bros *le*·es
❓ **Have you read ...?**	¿Has leído a ...? as le·*ee*·do a ...
🅰 **I often read ...**	Suelo leer ... *swe*·lo le·*er* ...
🅰 **I'm reading ...**	Estoy leyendo ... es·*toy* le·*yen*·do ...
❓ **Which Latin American author do you recommend?**	¿Qué autor latinoamericano recomiendas? ke ow·*tor* la·tee·no·a·me·ree·*ka*·no re·ko·*myen*·das
🅰 **I'd recommend ...**	Recomiendo a ... re·ko·*myen*·do a ...
Where can I exchange books?	¿Dónde puedo cambiar libros? *don*·de *pwe*·do kam·*byar* *lee*·bros

For more on books, see **shopping** (p76).

Volunteering

I'd like to volunteer my skills.	Me gustaría ser voluntario. me goos·ta·*ree*·a ser vo·loon·*ta*·ryo
Are there any volunteer programs available in the area?	¿Hay programas para voluntarios en esta zona? ai pro·*gra*·mas *pa*·ra vo·loon·*ta*·ryos en *es*·ta *so*·na

Feelings & Opinions

KEY PHRASES

Are you ...?	¿Está/ Estás ...? pol/inf ¿Tiene/ Tienes ...? pol/inf	es·ta/ es·tas ... tye·ne/ tye·nes ...
I'm (not) ...	(No) Estoy ... (No) Tengo ...	(no) es·toy ... (no) ten·go ...
What did you think of it?	¿Qué pensó/ pensaste de eso? pol/inf	ke pen·so/ pen·sas·te de e·so
I thought it was OK.	Pienso que fue bien.	pyen·so ke fwe byen
How do people feel about ...?	¿Cómo se siente la gente con respecto a ...?	ko·mo se syen·te la khen·te kon res·pek·to a ...

Feelings

In Spanish feelings are described with either nouns or adjectives: the nouns use 'have' (eg 'I have hunger') and the adjectives use 'be' (as in English).

Are you (hungry)?	¿Tiene/Tienes (hambre)? pol/inf tye·ne/tye·nes (am·bre)
I'm (cold).	Tengo (frío). ten·go (free·o)
I'm not (hot).	No tengo (calor). no ten·go (ka·lor)

Are you (tired)?	¿Está (cansado/a)? m/f pol es·ta kan·sa·do/a
Are you (ready)?	¿Estás (listo/a)? m/f inf es·tas lis·to/a
I'm (annoyed).	Estoy (enojado/a). m/f es·toy (e·no·kha·do/a)
I'm not (embarrassed).	No estoy (avergonzado/a). m/f no es·toy (a·ver·gon·sa·do/a)
I'm a little (sad).	Estoy un poco (triste). es·toy oon po·ko (trees·te)
I'm quite (disappointed).	Estoy bastante (decepcionado/a). m/f es·toy bas·tan·te (de·sep·syo·na·do/a)

Opinions

Q Did you like it?	¿Le/Te gustó? pol/inf le/te goos·to
Q What did you think of it?	¿Qué pensó/pensaste de eso? pol/inf ke pen·so/pen·sas·te de e·so
A I thought it was ...	Pienso que fue ... pyen·so ke fwe ...
A It's ...	Es ... es ...

beautiful	bonito/a m/f	bo·nee·to/a
bizarre	raro/a m/f	ra·ro/a
crap	una porquería	oo·na por·ke·ree·ya
entertaining	entretenido/a m/f	en·tre·te·nee·do/a
excellent	fantástico/a m/f	fan·tas·tee·ko/a

Politics & Social Issues

Q Who do you vote for?
¿A quién vota/votas? pol/inf
a kyen *vo*·ta/*vo*·tas

A I support the ... party.
Apoyo al partido ...
a·*po*·yo al par·*tee*·do ...

communist	comunista	ko·moo·*nees*·ta
conservative	conservador	kon·ser·va·*dor*
green	verde	*ver*·de
labour	laborista	la·bo·*rees*·ta
liberal	progresista	pro·gre·*sees*·ta
social democratic	social-demócrata	so·*syal*·de·*mo*·kra·ta
socialist	socialista	so·sya·*lees*·ta

Es fantástico.
es fan·*tas*·tee·ko
It's excellent.

🔊 LISTEN FOR

¡Anda ya!	*an*·da ya	In your dreams!
¡Eso no es verdad!	*e*·so no es ver·*da*	That's not true!
¡Exactamente!	ek·sak·ta·*men*·te	Exactly!
¡Por supuesto!	por soo·*pwes*·to	Absolutely!
¡Qué interesante!	ke een·te·re·*san*·te	How interesting!

Q Do you agree with it?	¿Está/Estás de acuerdo con eso? **pol/inf** es·*ta*/es·*tas* de a·*kwer*·do kon *e*·so
A I (don't) agree with ...	(No) Estoy de acuerdo con ... (no) es·*toy* de a·*kwer*·do kon ...
How do people feel about ...?	¿Cómo se siente la gente con respecto a ...? *ko*·mo se *syen*·te la *khen*·te kon res·*pek*·to a ...
Are you in favour of ...?	¿Está/Estás a favor de ...? **pol/inf** es·*ta*/es·*tas* a fa·*vor* de ...
Are you against ...?	¿Está/Estás en contra de ...? **pol/inf** es·*ta*/es·*tas* en *kon*·tra de ...
drugs	drogas **f pl** *dro*·gas
immigration	inmigración **f** een·mee·gra·*syon*
the economy	economía **f** e·ko·no·*mee*·a
the environment	medio **m** ambiente *me*·dyo am·*byen*·te

CULTURE TIP **Latin American Place Names**
Many Latin American place names are linked to historical events. *Argentina* comes from the Latin *argentum* 'silver' allegedly because the first Europeans to arrive observed the indigenous people wearing silver jewellery. *Bolivia* is named after Simón Bolívar, the famous revolutionary general who helped liberate many Latin American countries from Spanish rule, then became Bolivia's first president. *Costa Rica* means 'rich coast' and was named by Christopher Columbus for the precious metals that the land was expected to yield. *Honduras* means 'depths' and was named by Columbus for the deep waters off the country's north coast. *Colombia* was named after Columbus, though not until the 19th century.

The Environment

Is there a/an (environmental) problem here?	¿Aquí hay un problema (con el medio ambiente)? a·*kee* ai oon pro·*ble*·ma (kon el *me*·dyo am·*byen*·te)
Is this a protected forest/ park?	¿Es este bosque/parque protegido? es *es*·te *bos*·ke/*par*·ke pro·te·*khee*·do
Is this a protected species?	¿Es esta especie protegida? es *es*·ta es·*pe*·sye pro·te·*khee*·da
Where can I recycle this?	¿Dónde puedo reciclar ésto? *don*·de *pwe*·do re·see·*klar* es·to
pollution	contaminación f kon·ta·mee·na·*syon*
water supply	suministro m de agua soo·mee·*nees*·tro de *a*·gwa

Going Out

KEY PHRASES

What's on tonight?	¿Qué hay esta noche?	ke ai es·ta no·che
Where are the clubs?	¿Dónde hay clubs nocturnos?	don·de ai kloobs nok·toor·nos
Would you like to go for a coffee?	¿Te/Les gustaría ir a tomar un café? sg/pl	te/les goos·ta·ree·a eer a to·mar oon ka·fe
What time shall we meet?	¿A qué hora quedamos?	a ke o·ra ke·da·mos
Where will we meet?	¿Dónde quedamos?	don·de ke·da·mos

Where to Go

What's there to do in the evenings?	¿Qué se puede hacer por las noches? ke se pwe·de a·ser por las no·ches
What's on ...?	¿Qué hay ...? ke ai ...

locally	en la zona	en la so·na
this weekend	este fin de semana	es·te feen de se·ma·na
today	hoy	oy
tonight	esta noche	es·ta no·che

Where are the ...?	¿Dónde hay ...? *don·de ai ...*	
clubs	clubs nocturnos	kloobs nok·*toor*·nos
gay venues	lugares gay	loo·*ga*·res gay
places to eat	lugares donde comer	loo·*ga*·res *don*·de ko·*mer*
pubs	bares	*ba*·res

Is there a local entertainment guide?	¿Hay una guía de espectáculos de la zona? ai *oo*·na *gee*·a de es·pek·*ta*·koo·los de la *so*·na
What's the cover charge?	¿Cuánto cuesta entrar? *kwan*·to *kwes*·ta en·*trar*
I feel like going to ...	Tengo ganas de ir ... *ten*·go *ga*·nas de eer ...

a bar	a un bar	a oon bar
a cafe	a una cafetería	a *oo*·na ka·fe·te·*ree*·a
a salsa dance club	a una salsoteca	a *oo*·na sal·so·*te*·ka
a tango club	a una milonga	a *oo*·na mee·*lon*·ga
the movies	al cine	al *see*·ne
the theatre	al teatro	al te·*a*·tro

Invitations

What are you doing this evening?	¿Qué haces/hacen esta noche? **sg/pl** ke *a*·ses/*a*·sen *es*·ta *no*·che

What are you doing this weekend?	¿Qué haces/hacen este fin de semana? sg/pl
	ke *a*·ses/*a*·sen es·te feen de se·*ma*·na
Would you like to go for a ...?	¿Te/Les gustaría ir a ...? sg/pl
	te/les goos·ta·*ree*·a eer a ...

coffee	tomar un café	to·*mar* oon ka·*fe*
drink	tomar unos tragos	to·*mar* oo·nos *tra*·gos
meal	comer	ko·*mer*
walk	pasear	pa·se·*ar*

I feel like going dancing.	Tengo ganas de ir a bailar.
	ten·go ga·nas de eer a bai·*lar*
Do you want to come to the concert with me?	¿Quieres/Quieren venir conmigo al concierto? sg/pl
	kye·res/*kye*·ren ve·*neer* kon·*mee*·go al kon·*syer*·to
Do you know a good restaurant?	¿Conoces/Conocen un buen restaurante? sg/pl
	ko·*no*·ses/ko·*no*·sen oon bwen res·tow·*ran*·te
We're having a party.	Vamos a dar una fiesta.
	va·mos a dar oo·na *fyes*·ta
You should come.	¿Por qué no vienes/vienen? sg/pl
	por ke no *vye*·nes/*vye*·nen

Responding to Invitations

Sure!	¡Por supuesto!
	por soo·*pwes*·to
Yes, I'd love to.	Me encantaría.
	me en·kan·ta·*ree*·a

LANGUAGE TIP

'Partying' Synonyms

Latin Americans know how to let down their hair and have a good time. Here are some expressions which all mean 'to go out drinking and partying', to help you get a slice of the action:

ir de copas	eer de *ko*·pas
ir de farra	eer de *fa*·ra
ir de fiesta	eer de *fyes*·ta
ir de juerga	eer de *khwer*·ga
ir de pachanga	eer de pa·*chan*·ga
ir de rumba	eer de *room*·ba

Yes, let's go.	Sí, vamos. see *va*·mos
No, I'm afraid I can't.	Lo siento pero no puedo. lo *syen*·to *pe*·ro no *pwe*·do
What about tomorrow?	¿Qué tal mañana? ke tal ma·*nya*·na
Sorry, I can't sing/dance.	Lo siento, no sé cantar/bailar. lo *syen*·to no se kan·*tar*/bai·*lar*

Arranging to Meet

Q **What time shall we meet?**	¿A qué hora quedamos? a ke *o*·ra ke·*da*·mos
A **Let's meet at (eight o'clock).**	Quedamos a las (ocho). ke·*da*·mos a las (*o*·cho)
Q **Where will we meet?**	¿Dónde quedamos? *don*·de ke·*da*·mos
A **Let's meet at the entrance.**	Quedamos en la entrada. ke·*da*·mos en la en·*tra*·da

I'll pick you up.	Paso a recogerte/ recogerles. **sg/pl** *pa·*so a re·ko·*kher·*te/ re·ko·*kher·*les
I'll be coming later.	Iré más tarde. ee·*re* mas *tar·*de
I'll see you then.	Nos vemos. nos *ve·*mos

CULTURE TIP Latin American Rhythms

música f **Andina**   *moo·see·ka* an·*dee·*na
Andean music incorporates the *quena ke·*na (reed flute), the
zampoña sam·*po·*nya (pan flute), the *caja ka·*kha (tambourine-
like drums) and the ukulele-like *charango* cha·*ran·*go.

música f **criolla**   *moo·see·ka* kree·o·ya
With its roots in Spain and Africa, the main instruments of Cre-
ole music are guitars and a *cajón* ka·*khon* (wooden box drum).

música f **de los**   *moo·see·ka* de los ya·nos
llanos
A Venezuelan and Colombian song style accompanied by a
*cuatro kwa·*tro (harp) and maracas.

reggae m   *re·*gay
The reggae influence is strongly felt along the Caribbean coast
of Central America.

salsa f   *sal·*sa
This immensely popular dance style originated in New York but
spread through the Caribbean in the 1960s.

tango m   *tan·*go
Argentina is the birthplace of this style. A visit to a *club de
tango* kloob de *tan·*go in Buenos Aires is an unforgettable
experience.

LANGUAGE TIP

Masculine or Feminine?

In this book, when you see an **m** it means masculine, so the article you use should be either *un* oon or *el* el. When you see an **f** it means feminine, so the article should be either *una* oo·na or *la* la.

Where an *-o* ending and an *-a* ending mark masculine and feminine forms respectively, we've used a slash. For example, the two forms of the word 'beautiful', *lindo* leen·do and *linda* leen·da, are written *lindo/a*.

Where the only difference between masculine and feminine forms is the addition of an *-a* ending for the feminine form, we've used brackets. Hence the two forms of the word 'doctor', *doctor* dok·tor and *doctora* dok·to·ra, are abbreviated to *doctor(a)*.

See also **gender** in the **grammar** chapter (p19).

If I'm not there by (nine), don't wait for me.	Si no estoy a las (nueve), no me esperes/esperen. **sg/pl** see no es·*toy* a las (*nwe*·ve) no me es·*pe*·res/es·*pe*·ren
Where will you be?	¿Dónde estarás/estarán? **sg/pl** *don*·de es·ta·*ras*/es·ta·*ran*
I'm looking forward to it.	Tengo muchas ganas de ir. *ten*·go *moo*·chas *ga*·nas de eer

Drugs

I don't take drugs.	No consumo ningún tipo de drogas. no kon·*soo*·mo neen·*goon* *tee*·po de *dro*·gas
I have ... occasionally.	Tomo ... de vez en cuando. *to*·mo ... de ves en *kwan*·do
Do you want to have a smoke?	¿Nos fumamos un porro? nos foo·*ma*·mos oon *po*·ro

Romance

KEY PHRASES

Would you like to do something?	¿Quieres hacer algo?	*kye*·res a·*ser al*·go
I love you.	Te quiero.	te *kye*·ro
Leave me alone!	¡Déjame en paz!	*de*·kha·me en pas

Asking Someone Out

Q Would you like to do something (tonight)?

¿Quieres hacer algo (esta noche)?
kye·res a·*ser al*·go (*es*·ta *no*·che)

A Yes, I'd love to.

Me encantaría.
me en·kan·ta·*ree*·a

A No, I'm afraid I can't.

Lo siento, pero no puedo.
lo *syen*·to *pe*·ro no *pwe*·do

Pick-up Lines

Would you like a drink?	¿Puedo ofrecerte una copa? *pwe*·do o·fre·*ser*·te oo·na *ko*·pa
Do you have a light?	¿Tienes fuego? *tye*·nes *fwe*·go
You have a beautiful laugh.	Tienes una risa preciosa. *tye*·nes oo·na *ree*·sa pre·*syo*·sa
You have beautiful eyes.	Tienes unos ojos preciosos. *tye*·nes oo·nos o·khos pre·*syo*·sos

What star sign are you?	¿Cuál es tu signo del horóscopo? kwal es too *seeg*·no del o·*ros*·ko·po
Shall we get some fresh air?	¿Vamos a tomar el aire? *va*·mos a to·*mar* el *ai*·re

Rejections

I have a boyfriend/ girlfriend.	Tengo novio/a. m/f *ten*·go *no*·vyo/a
Excuse me, I have to go now.	Lo siento, pero me tengo que ir. lo *syen*·to *pe*·ro me *ten*·go ke eer
I'm not interested.	No estoy interesado/a. m/f no es·*toy* een·te·re·*sa*·do/a
I'm busy.	Estoy ocupado/a. m/f es·*toy* o·koo·*pa*·do/a
Your ego is out of control.	Tu ego está fuera de control. too *e*·go es·*ta fwe*·ra de kon·*trol*
Leave me alone!	¡Déjame en paz! *de*·kha·me en pas
Piss off!	¡Andate a la mierda! *an*·da·te a la *myer*·da

Getting Closer

You're very nice.	Eres muy simpático/a. m/f *e*·res mooy seem·*pa*·tee·ko/a
You're very attractive.	Eres muy guapo/a. m/f *e*·res mooy *gwa*·po/a
I'm interested in you.	Me fascinas mucho. me fa·*see*·nas *moo*·cho

Q **Do you like me too?**	¿Me tienes algo de cariño también? me *tye*·nes *al*·go de ka·*ree*·nyo tam·*byen*
A **I like you very much.**	Me gustas mucho. me *goos*·tas *moo*·cho
Can I kiss you?	¿Te puedo besar? te *pwe*·do be·*sar*
Will you take me home?	¿Me acompañas a casa? me a·kom·*pa*·nyas a *ka*·sa
Do you want to come inside for a while?	¿Quieres entrar a tomar algo? *kye*·res en·*trar* a to·*mar* al·go

Sex

I want to make love to you.	Quiero hacerte el amor. *kye*·ro a·*ser*·te el a·*mor*
Do you have a condom?	¿Tienes un condón? *tye*·nes oon kon·*don*
I won't do it without protection.	No lo haré sin preservativos. no lo a·*re* seen pre·ser·va·*tee*·vos
I think we should stop now.	Pienso que deberíamos parar. *pyen*·so ke de·be·*ree*·a·mos pa·*rar*
Let's go to bed!	¡Vamos a la cama! *va*·mos a la *ka*·ma
Kiss me!	¡Bésame! *be*·sa·me
I want you.	Te deseo. te de·*se*·o
Take this off.	Saca esto. *sa*·ka *es*·to

LANGUAGE TIP

Risqué Expressions
To say you like something, use the expression *me gusta* me *goos*·ta (lit: me it-pleases). Beware of using it for people though – to say *me gustas* me *goos*·tas (lit: me you-please) has erotic overtones. A less risqué way of saying that you enjoy someone's company is *me caes bien* me *ka*·es byen, which equates to the English 'I like you'.

Touch me here.	Tócame aquí. *to*·ka·me a·*kee*
Q Do you like this?	¿Esto te gusta? *es*·to te *goos*·ta
A I (don't) like that.	Esto (no) me gusta. *es*·to (no) me *goos*·ta
Please stop!	¡Para! *pa*·ra
Please don't stop!	¡No pares! no *pa*·res
That was amazing.	Eso fue increíble. *e*·so fwe een·kre·*ee*·ble
Can I stay over?	¿Puedo quedarme? *pwe*·do ke·*dar*·me

Love

I'm in love with you.	Estoy enamorado/a de ti. **m/f** es·*toy* e·na·mo·*ra*·do/a de tee
Q Do you love me?	¿Me quieres? me *kye*·res
A I love you.	Te quiero. te *kye*·ro
I think we're good together.	Creo que estamos bien juntos. *kre*·o ke es·*ta*·mos byen *khoon*·tos

SOCIAL BELIEFS & CULTURE

Beliefs & Culture

What's your religion?	¿Cuál es su/tu religión? pol/inf	kwal es soo/too re·lee·*khyon*
I'm ...	Soy ...	soy ...
I'm sorry, it's against my beliefs.	Lo siento, eso va en contra de mis creencias.	lo *syen*·to e·so va en *kon*·tra de mees kre·*en*·syas

Religion

Q What's your religion?	¿Cuál es su/tu religión? pol/inf kwal es soo/too re·lee·*khyon*
A I'm (not) ...	(No) Soy ... (no) soy ...

an agnostic	agnóstico/a m/f	ag·*nos*·tee·ko/a
an atheist	ateo/a m/f	a·*te*·o/a
Buddhist	budista	boo·*dees*·ta
Catholic	católico/a m/f	ka·to·lee·ko/a
Christian	cristiano/a m/f	krees·*tya*·no/a
Hindu	hindú	een·*doo*
Jewish	judío/a m/f	khoo·*dee*·o/a
Muslim	musulmán m	moo·sool·*man*
	musulmana f	moo·sool·*ma*·na
practising	practicante	prak·tee·*kan*·te
religious	religioso/a m/f	re·lee·*khyo*·so/a

I (don't) believe in God.	(No) Creo en Dios.	(no) *kre*·o en dyos
I (don't) believe in fate.	(No) Creo en el destino.	(no) *kre*·o en el des·*tee*·no
I'd like to go to (the) ...	Quisiera ir ...	kee·*sye*·ra eer ...

church	a la iglesia	a la ee·*gle*·sya
mosque	a la mezquita	a la mes·*kee*·ta
synagogue	a la sinagoga	a la see·na·*go*·ga
temple	al templo	al *tem*·plo

Can I pray here?	¿Puedo rezar aquí?	*pwe*·do re·*sar* a·*kee*
Where can I attend mass?	¿Dónde puedo asistir a la misa?	*don*·de *pwe*·do a·sees·*teer* a la *mee*·sa

Cultural Differences

Is this a local custom?	¿Esto es una costumbre local?
	es·to es *oo*·na kos·*toom*·bre lo·*kal*
I'm not used to this.	No estoy acostumbrado/a a esto. **m/f**
	no es·*toy* a·kos·toom·*bra*·do/a a *es*·to
I'll try it.	Lo probaré.
	lo pro·ba·*re*
Sorry, I didn't mean to say/do anything wrong.	Lo siento, lo dije/hice sin querer.
	lo *syen*·to lo *dee*·khe/*ee*·se seen ke·*rer*

CULTURE TIP

Gringo Lingo

One word you might become well acquainted with is *gringo/a* m/f *green*·go/a. In Latin American Spanish this word has subtle nuances. It can simply be a neutral term meaning 'foreign' or 'foreigner', but it may be intended as pejorative in certain contexts. You'll notice this when it's combined with an unflattering word such as *pinche peen*·che (goddam) or said in an unfriendly tone of voice.

The term *gringo* can be used to refer to North Americans but also, in a broader sense, to visitors of European heritage. Blonde or fair-haired people are sometimes called *gringos* because they're marked out by their physical appearance. The word is thought to have originated from the Spanish word *griego grye*·go (Greek).

This is (very) different.	Esto es (muy) diferente. *es*·to es (mooy) dee·fe·*ren*·te
This is fun.	Esto es divertido. *es*·to es dee·ver·*tee*·do
This is interesting.	Esto es interesante. *es*·to es een·te·re·*san*·te
I don't mind watching, but I'd rather not join in.	No me importa mirar, pero prefiero no participar. no me eem·*por*·ta mee·*rar* *pe*·ro pre·*fye*·ro no par·tee·see·*par*
I'm sorry, it's against my beliefs.	Lo siento, eso va en contra de mis creencias. lo *syen*·to *e*·so va en *kon*·tra de mees kre·*en*·syas
I'm sorry, it's against my religion.	Lo siento, eso va en contra de mi religión. lo *syen*·to *e*·so va en *kon*·tra de mee re·lee·*khyon*

Sports

KEY PHRASES

Which sport do you play?	¿Qué deporte practicas?	ke de·por·te prak·tee·kas
Who's your favourite team?	¿Cuál es tu equipo favorito?	kwal es too e·kee·po fa·vo·ree·to
What's the score?	¿Cómo van?	ko·mo van

Sporting Interests

Q Do you like (sport)?
¿Te gustan (los deportes)?
te goos·tan (los de·por·tes)

A Yes, very much.
Sí, mucho.
see moo·cho

A Not really.
En realidad, no mucho.
en re·a·lee·da no moo·cho

A I like watching it.
Me gusta mirar.
me goos·ta mee·rar

Q Which sport do you play?
¿Qué deporte practicas?
ke de·por·te prak·tee·kas

A I play (tennis).
Practico (el tenis).
prak·tee·ko (el te·nees)

Who's your favourite athlete?
¿Quién es tu deportista favorito/a? m/f
kyen es too de·por·tees·ta fa·vo·ree·to/a

Who's your favourite team?
¿Cuál es tu equipo favorito?
kwal es too e·kee·po fa·vo·ree·to

Q Which sport do you follow?	¿A qué deporte eres aficionado/a? m/f a ke de·*por*·te e·res a·fee·syo·*na*·do/a
A I follow (cycling).	Soy aficionado/a al (ciclismo). m/f soy a·fee·syo·*na*·do/a al (see·*klees*·mo)

For more sports, see the **dictionary**.

Going to a Game

Would you like to go to a game?	¿Te gustaría ir a un partido? te goos·ta·*ree*·a eer a oon par·*tee*·do
Who are you supporting?	¿Con qué equipo vas? kon ke e·*kee*·po vas
Who's playing?	¿Quién juega? kyen *khwe*·ga
Who's winning?	¿Quién va ganando? kyen va ga·*nan*·do
How much time is left?	¿Cuánto tiempo queda? *kwan*·to *tyem*·po ke·da
Q What's the score?	¿Cómo van? *ko*·mo van
A It's a draw.	Empatados. em·pa·*ta*·dos
That was a bad/boring game!	¡Ese partido fue malo/aburrido! e·se par·*tee*·do fwe *ma*·lo/a·boo·*ree*·do
That was a great game!	¡Ese partido fue fabuloso/bárbaro! e·se par·*tee*·do fwe fa·boo·*lo*·so/*bar*·ba·ro

Playing Sport

Q Do you want to play?	¿Quieres jugar? *kye·*res khoo·*gar*
Q Can I join in?	¿Puedo jugar? *pwe·*do khoo·*gar*
A Yes, that'd be great.	Sí, me encantaría. see me en·kan·ta·*ree·*a
A Not at the moment, thanks.	Ahora mismo no, gracias. a·*o·*ra *mees·*mo no *gra·*syas
A I have an injury.	Tengo una lesion. *ten·*go *oo·*na le·*syon*
Thanks for the game.	Gracias por el partido. *gra·*syas por el par·*tee·*do
You're a good player.	Juegas bien. *khwe·*gas byen
Where's the nearest gym?	¿Dónde está el gimnasio más cercano? *don·*de es·*ta* el kheem·*na·*syo mas ser·*ka·*no

¿Con qué equipo vas?
kon ke e·*kee·*po vas
Who are you supporting?

SOCIAL SPORTS

¡Qué atajada!	ke a·ta·*kha*·da	What a save!
¡Qué cabezazo!	ke ka·be·*sa*·so	What a header!
¡Qué chute!	ke *choo*·te	What a kick/shot!
¡Qué golazo!	ke go·*la*·so	What a goal!
¡Qué pase!	ke *pa*·se	What a pass!
¡Qué tiro!	ke *tee*·ro	What a hit!

Where's the best place to jog around here?	¿Cuál es el mejor sitio para hacer footing por aquí? kwal es el me·*khor see*·tyo *pa*·ra a·*ser* foo·teen por a·*kee*
Where's the nearest swimming pool?	¿Dónde está la piscina más cercana? *don*·de es·*ta* la pee·*see*·na mas ser·*ka*·na ¿Dónde está la pileta más cercana? **(Arg)** *don*·de es·*ta* la pee·*le*·ta mas ser·*ka*·na
Where's the nearest tennis court?	¿Dónde está la cancha de tenis más cercana? *don*·de es·*ta* la *kan*·cha de *te*·nees mas ser·*ka*·na
Do I have to be a member to attend?	¿Hay que ser socio/a para entrar? **m/f** ai ke ser *so*·syo/a *pa*·ra en·*trar*

| **What's the charge per ...?** | ¿Cúanto cobran por ...? |
| | *kwan·to ko·bran por ...* |

day	día	*dee·a*
game	partido	*par·tee·do*
hour	hora	*o·ra*
visit	visita	*vee·see·ta*

| **Can I hire a ...?** | ¿Es posible alquilar una ...? |
| | *es po·see·ble al·kee·lar oo·na ...* |

ball	pelota	*pe·lo·ta*
bicycle	bicicleta	*bee·see·kle·ta*
court	cancha	*kan·cha*
racquet	raqueta	*ra·ke·ta*

| **Is there a women-only session?** | ¿Hay alguna sesión sólo para mujeres? |
| | *ai al·goo·na se·syon so·lo pa·ra moo·khe·res* |

| **Where are the changing rooms?** | ¿Dónde están los vestuarios? |
| | *don·de es·tan los ves·twa·ryos* |

| **Can I have a locker?** | ¿Puedo usar una lócker? |
| | *pwe·do oo·sar oo·na lo·ker* |

SOCIAL SPORTS

🔊 **LISTEN FOR**

| ¡Pásamelo! | *pa·sa·me·lo* | Kick/Pass it to me! |
| Mi/Tu punto. | *mee/too poon·to* | My/Your point. |

🔊 LISTEN FOR

amonestación f	a·mo·ne·sta·*syon*	warning
arquero/a m/f (Arg)	ar·*ke*·ro/a	goalkeeper
delantero/a m/f	de·lan·*te*·ro/a	striker
jugador m	khoo·ga·*dor*	player
jugadora f	khoo·ga·*do*·ra	player
marcar	mar·*kar*	score (a goal)
portero/a m/f	por·*te*·ro/a	goalkeeper
saque m	*sa*·ke	kickoff
saque m **de banda**	*sa*·ke de *ban*·da	throw-in
tarjeta f **roja/ amarilla**	tar·*khe*·ta ro·*kha*/ a·ma·*ree*·ya	red/yellow card
tiro m **libre**	*tee*·ro *lee*·bre	free kick

Football/Soccer

Which team is at the top of the league?	¿Qué equipo está en primera posición en la tabla de clasificaciones? ke e·*kee*·po es·*ta* en pree·*me*·ra po·see·*syon* en la *ta*·bla de kla·see·fee·ka·*syo*·nes
Who plays for ...?	¿Quién juega para el ...? kyen *khwe*·ga *pa*·ra el ...
He's a great (player).	Es un (jugador) bárbaro. es oon (khoo·ga·*dor*) *bar*·ba·ro
He played brilliantly in the match against (Brazil).	Jugó fenomenal en el partido contra (Brasil). khoo·*go* fe·no·me·*nal* en el par·*tee*·do *kon*·tra (bra·*seel*)
What a terrible team!	¡Qué equipo más malo! ke e·*kee*·po mas *ma*·lo

Outdoors

KEY PHRASES

Where can I buy supplies?	¿Dónde se puede comprar víveres?	*don*·de se *pwe*·de kom·*prar vee*·ve·res
Do we need a guide?	¿Se necesita un guía?	se ne·se·*see*·ta oon *gee*·a
Is it safe?	¿Es seguro?	es se·*goo*·ro
I'm lost.	Estoy perdido/a. m/f	es·*toy* per·*dee*·do/a
What's the weather like?	¿Qué tiempo hace?	ke *tyem*·po *a*·se

Hiking & Mountaineering

Where can I ...?	¿Dónde se puede ...? *don*·de se *pwe*·de ...	

buy supplies	comprar víveres	kom·*prar vee*·ve·res
find someone who knows this area	encontrar a alguien que conozca el área	en·kon·*trar* a *al*·gyen ke ko·*nos*·ka el *a*·re·a
get a map	obtener un mapa	ob·te·*ner* oon *ma*·pa
hire hiking gear	alquilar equipo para ir de excursión	al·kee·*lar* e·*kee*·po *pa*·ra eer de eks·koor·*syon*
hire mountain-eering gear	alquilar equipo de alpinismo	al·kee·*lar* e·*kee*·po de al·pee·*nees*·mo

How long is the trail?	¿Cómo es de largo el camino? *ko·mo es de lar·go el ka·mee·no*
How high is the climb?	¿A qué altura se escala? *a ke al·too·ra se es·ka·la*
Is the path open?	¿Está la ruta abierta? *es·ta la roo·ta a·byer·ta*
Is it safe?	¿Es seguro? *es se·goo·ro*
Is there a hut there?	¿Hay una cabaña allí? *ai oo·na ka·ba·nya a·yee*
When does it get dark?	¿A qué hora oscurece? *a ke o·ra os·koo·re·se*
Do we need a guide?	¿Se necesita un guía? *se ne·se·see·ta oon gee·a*
Are there guided treks/climbs?	¿Se organizan excursiones/escaladas guiadas? *se or·ga·nee·san eks·koor·syo·nes/es·ka·la·das gee·a·das*
Do we need to take bedding?	¿Se necesita llevar algo en que dormir? *se ne·se·see·ta ye·var al·go en ke dor·meer*
Do we need to take food/water?	¿Se necesita llevar comida/agua? *se ne·se·see·ta ye·var ko·mee·da/a·gwa*
Is the track (well) marked?	¿Es (bien) marcado el sendero? *es (byen) mar·ka·do el sen·de·ro*
Is the track scenic?	¿Es pintoresco el sendero? *es peen·to·res·ko el sen·de·ro*

🔊 LISTEN FOR

Cuidado con la corriente.	kwee·*da*·do kon la ko·*ryen*·te	Be careful of the undertow.
¡Es peligroso!	es pe·lee·*gro*·so	It's dangerous!
altura f	al·*too*·ra	altitude
escarpado/a m/f	es·kar·*pa*·do/a	steep
refugio m **de montaña**	re·*foo*·khyo de mon·*ta*·nya	mountain hut
subir de hielo	soo·*beer* de *ye*·lo	ice-climbing

Which is the easiest/ shortest route?	¿Cuál es el camino más fácil/corto? kwal es el ka·*mee*·no mas *fa*·seel/*kor*·to
Where have you come from?	¿De dónde vienes? de *don*·de *vye*·nes
How long did it take?	¿Cuánto has tardado? *kwan*·to as tar·*da*·do
Does this path go to ...?	¿Este camino va a ...? *es*·te ka·*mee*·no va a ...
Where's the nearest village?	¿Dónde está el pueblo más cercano? *don*·de es·*ta* el *pwe*·blo mas ser·*ka*·no
Where are we on this map?	¿Dónde estamos aquí en el mapa? *don*·de es·*ta*·mos a·*kee* en el *ma*·pa
I'm lost.	Estoy perdido/a. m/f es·*toy* per·*dee*·do/a
Is the water OK to drink?	¿Se puede beber el agua? se *pwe*·de be·*ber* el *a*·gwa

SOCIAL OUTDOORS

At the Beach

Where's the nearest beach?	¿Dónde está la playa más cercana? *don·de es·ta la pla·ya mas ser·ka·na*
Where's the nicest beach?	¿Dónde está la playa más bonita? *don·de es·ta la pla·ya mas bo·nee·ta*
Where's the nudist beach?	¿Dónde está la playa nudista? *don·de es·ta la pla·ya noo·dees·ta*
Are there any reefs?	¿Hay arrecifes? *ai a·re·see·fes*
Are there any rips?	¿Hay corrientes? *ai ko·ryen·tes*
Are there any water hazards?	¿Hay peligros en el agua? *ai pe·lee·gros en el a·gwa*
Is it safe to dive/swim here?	¿Es seguro bucear/nadar aquí? *es se·goo·ro boo·se·ar/na·dar a·kee*
What time is high/low tide?	¿A qué hora es la marea alta/baja? *a ke o·ra es la ma·re·a al·ta/ba·kha*
Where are the showers/ toilets?	¿Dónde hay duchas/baños? *don·de ai doo·chas/ba·nyos*

 LOOK FOR

Prohibido Nadar	pro·ee·bee·do na·dar	No Swimming

Weather

Q What's the weather like?	¿Qué tiempo hace?	ke *tyem*·po *a*·se
A It's raining.	Llueve.	*ywe*·ve
A It's snowing.	Nieva.	*nye*·va
A It's ...	Hace ...	*a*·se ...

cold	frío	*free*·o
freezing	un frío que pela	oon *free*·o ke *pe*·la
hot	calor	ka·*lor*
sunny	sol	sol
warm	calor	ka·*lor*
windy	viento	*vyen*·to

Q Will it be (cold) tomorrow?	¿Mañana hará (frío)?	ma·*nya*·na a·*ra* (*free*·o)
A It will rain (tomorrow).	(Mañana) Lloverá.	(ma·*nya*·na) yo·ve·*ra*
A It will snow (tomorrow).	(Mañana) Nevará.	(ma·*nya*·na) ne·va·*ra*
Where can I buy a rain jacket?	¿Dónde puedo comprar un impermeable?	*don*·de *pwe*·do kom·*prar* oon eem·per·me·*a*·ble
Where can I buy an umbrella?	¿Dónde puedo comprar un paraguas?	*don*·de *pwe*·do kom·*prar* oon pa·*ra*·gwas

Where can I buy sunblock?	¿Dónde puedo comprar crema solar? *don·de pwe·do kom·prar kre·ma so·lar*
dry season	época f seca *e·po·ka se·ka*
rainy season	época f de lluvias *e·po·ka de yoo·vyas*

Flora & Fauna

What ... is that?	¿Qué ... es ése/ésa? m/f *ke ... es e·se/e·sa*

animal	animal m	*a·nee·mal*
flower	flor f	flor
plant	planta f	*plan·ta*
tree	árbol m	*ar·bol*

Is it ...?	¿Es ...? *es ...*

common	común	*ko·moon*
dangerous	peligroso/a m/f	*pe·lee·gro·so/a*
poisonous	venenoso/a m/f	*ve·ne·no·so/a*
protected	protegido/a m/f	*pro·te·khee·do/a*

Is it endangered?	¿Está en peligro de extinción? *es·ta en pe·lee·gro de ek·steen·syon*
What's it used for?	¿Para qué se usa? *pa·ra ke se oo·sa*
Can you eat it?	¿Se puede comerlo? *se pwe·de ko·mer·lo*

For names of plants and animals, see the **dictionary**.

Safe Travel

Emergencies

KEY PHRASES

Help!	¡Socorro!	so·ko·ro
There's been an accident.	Ha habido un accidente.	a a·bee·do oon ak·see·den·te
It's an emergency.	Es una emergencia.	es oo·na e·mer·khen·sya

Help!	¡Socorro! so·ko·ro
Stop!	¡Pare! pa·re
Go away!	¡Váyase! va·ya·se
Thief!	¡Ladrón! la·dron
Fire!	¡Fuego! fwe·go
Watch out!	¡Cuidado! kwee·da·do
Call the police!	¡Llame a la policía! ya·me a la po·lee·see·a
Call a doctor!	¡Llame a un médico! ya·me a oon me·dee·ko
Call an ambulance!	¡Llame a una ambulancia! ya·me a oo·na am·boo·lan·sya
There's been an accident.	Ha habido un accidente. a a·bee·do oon ak·see·den·te

🔍 LOOK FOR

Comisaría de Policía	ko·me·sa·*ree*·a de po·lee·*see*·a	Police Station
Policía	po·lee·*see*·a	Police
Urgencias	oor·*khen*·syas	Casualty

It's an emergency.	Es una emergencia. es *oo*·na e·mer·*khen*·sya
Could you help me, please?	¿Me puede ayudar, por favor? me *pwe*·de a·yoo·*dar* por fa·*vor*
I have to use the telephone.	Necesito usar el teléfono. ne·se·*see*·to oo·*sar* el te·*le*·fo·no
I'm lost.	Estoy perdido/a. m/f es·*toy* per·*dee*·do/a
Where are the toilets?	¿Dónde están los baños? *don*·de es·*tan* los *ba*·nyos
Is it safe ...?	¿Es seguro ...? es se·*goo*·ro ...

at night	por la noche	por la *no*·che
for foreigners	para los extranjeros	*pa*·ra los ek·stran·*khe*·ros
for gay travellers	para viajeros gay	*pa*·ra vya·*khe*·ros gay
for women travellers	para viajeras	*pa*·ra vya·*khe*·ras

Police

KEY PHRASES

Where's the police station?	¿Dónde está la comisaría?	*don·*de es·*ta* la ko·mee·sa·*ree·*a
I want to contact my embassy/ consulate.	Quiero ponerme en contacto con mi embajada/ consulado.	*kye·*ro po·*ner·*me en kon·*tak·*to kon mee em·ba·*kha·*da/ kon·soo·*la·*do
My bag was stolen.	Mi bolso fue robado.	mee *bol·*so fwe ro·*ba·*do

Where's the police station?	¿Dónde está la comisaría? *don·*de es·*ta* la ko·mee·sa·*ree·*a
I want to report an offence.	Quiero denunciar un delito. *kye·*ro de·noon·*syar* oon de·*lee·*to
(My bag) was stolen.	(Mi bolso) fue robado. (mee *bol·*so) fwe ro·*ba·*do
I've lost (my wallet).	He perdido (mi cartera). e per·*dee·*do (mee kar·*te·*ra)
I've been robbed.	Me han robado. me an ro·*ba·*do
I've been raped.	He sido violado/a. **m/f** e *see·*do vyo·*la·*do/a
I have a prescription for this drug.	Tengo receta para este medicamento. *ten·*go re·*se·*ta *pa·*ra es·*te* me·dee·ka·*men·*to

This drug is for personal use.	Esta droga es para uso personal. *es*·ta *dro*·ga es *pa*·ra oo·so per·so·*nal*
Can I call a lawyer?	¿Puedo llamar a un abogado? *pwe*·do ya·*mar* a oon a·bo·*ga*·do
I need a lawyer who speaks English.	Necesito un abogado que hable inglés. ne·se·*see*·to oon a·bo·*ga*·do ke *a*·ble een·*gles*
I want to contact my embassy/consulate.	Quiero ponerme en contacto con mi embajada/consulado. *kye*·ro po·*ner*·me en kon·*tak*·to kon mee em·ba·*kha*·da/kon·soo·*la*·do
What am I accused of?	¿De qué me acusan? de ke me a·*koo*·san
I'm innocent.	Soy inocente. soy ee·no·*sen*·te

◀)) **LISTEN FOR**

alterar el orden público	al·te·*rar* el *or*·den *poo*·blee·ko	disturbing the peace
asalto m	a·*sal*·to	assault
exceso m **de velocidad**	ek·*se*·so de ve·lo·*see*·da	speeding
hurto m **en tiendas**	*oor*·to en *tyen*·das	shoplifting
posesión f **(de sustancias ilegales)**	po·se·*syon* (de soos·*tan*·syas ee·le·*ga*·les)	possession (of illegal substances)
robo m	*ro*·bo	theft
violación f	vyo·la·*syon*	rape

Health

KEY PHRASES

Where's the nearest hospital?	¿Dónde está el hospital más cercano?	*don*·de es·*ta* el os·pee·*tal* mas ser·*ka*·no
I'm sick.	Estoy enfermo/a. m/f	es·*toy* en·*fer*·mo/a
I need a doctor.	Necesito un médico.	ne·se·*see*·to oon *me*·dee·ko
I'm on medication for ...	Estoy bajo medicación para ...	es·*toy ba*·kho me·dee·ka·*syon pa*·ra ...
I'm allergic to ...	Soy alérgico/a a ... m/f	soy a·*ler*·khee·ko/a a ...

Doctor

Where's the nearest ...?	¿Dónde está ... más cercano/a? m/f *don*·de es·*ta* ... mas ser·*ka*·no/a

(night) chemist	la farmacia f (de guardia); la droguería f (de guardia) (Col)	la far·*ma*·sya (de *gwar*·dya); la dro·ge·*ree*·a (de *gwar*·dya)
dentist	el dentista m	el den·*tees*·ta
doctor	el médico m	el *me*·dee·ko
hospital	el hospital m	el os·pee·*tal*
optometrist	el oculista m	el o·koo·*lees*·ta

I need a doctor (who speaks English).	Necesito un médico (que hable inglés). ne·se·*see*·to *me*·dee·ko (ke *a*·ble een·*gles*)
Could I see a female doctor?	¿Puede examinarme una médica? *pwe*·de ek·sa·mee·*nar*·me *oo*·na *me*·dee·ka
Can the doctor come here?	¿Puede visitarme el médico? *pwe*·de vee·see·*tar*·me el *me*·dee·ko
I've been vaccinated against ...	Estoy vacunado/a contra ... **m/f** es·*toy* va·koo·*na*·do/a *kon*·tra ...

(yellow) fever	la fiebre (amarilla)	la *fye*·bre (a·ma·*ree*·ya)
hepatitis A/B/C	la hepatitis A/B/C	la e·pa·*tee*·tees a/be/se
tetanus	el tétano	el *te*·ta·no
typhoid	la tifus	la *tee*·foos

I need new glasses.	Necesito anteojos nuevos. ne·se·*see*·to an·te·o·khos *nwe*·vos
I need new contact lenses.	Necesito lentes de contacto nuevas. ne·se·*see*·to *len*·tes de kon·*tak*·to *nwe*·vas
I've run out of my medication.	Se me terminaron los medicamentos. se me ter·mee·*na*·ron los me·dee·ka·*men*·tos

🔊 LISTEN FOR

¿Dónde le duele?	*don*·de le *dwe*·le	
	Where does it hurt?	
¿Tiene fiebre?	*tye*·ne *fye*·bre	
	Do you have a temperature?	
¿Desde cuándo se siente así?	*des*·de *kwan*·do se *syen*·te a·*see*	
	How long have you been like this?	
¿Ha tenido esto antes?	a te·*nee*·do *es*·to *an*·tes	
	Have you had this before?	

Can I have a receipt for my insurance?	¿Puede darme un recibo para mi seguro médico? *pwe*·de *dar*·me oon re·*see*·bo *pa*·ra mee se·*goo*·ro *me*·dee·ko

Symptoms & Conditions

I'm sick.	Estoy enfermo/a. **m/f** es·*toy* en·*fer*·mo/a
It hurts here.	Me duele aquí. me *dwe*·le a·*kee*
I've been injured.	He sido herido. e *see*·do e·*ree*·do
I've been vomiting.	He estado vomitando. e es·*ta*·do vo·mee·*tan*·do
I'm dehydrated.	Estoy deshidratado/a. **m/f** es·*toy* des·ee·dra·*ta*·do/a
I can't sleep.	No puedo dormir. no *pwe*·do dor·*meer*
I feel hot and cold.	Tengo escalofríos. *ten*·go es·ka·lo·*free*·os
I feel breathless.	Tengo falta de aliento. *ten*·go *fal*·ta de a·*lyen*·to

I feel ...	Me siento ...
	me *syen*·to ...

dizzy	mareado/a m/f	ma·re·*a*·do/a
nauseous	con nauseas	kon *now*·se·as
shivery	destemplado/a m/f	des·tem·*pla*·do/a
weak	débil	*de*·beel

I'm asthmatic.	Soy asmático/a. m/f
	soy as·*ma*·tee·ko/a

I'm diabetic.	Soy diabético/a. m/f
	soy dya·*be*·tee·ko/a

I'm epileptic	Soy epiléptico/a. m/f
	soy e·pee·*lep*·tee·ko/a

I have (a fever).	Tengo (fiebre).
	ten·go (*fye*·bre)

I have a cold.	Estoy resfriado/a. m/f
	es·*toy* res·free·*a*·do/a
	Tengo un resfrío. (SAm)
	ten·go oon res·*free*·o

I've (recently) had ...	(Hace poco) He tenido ...
	(*a*·se *po*·ko) e te·*nee*·do ...

LISTEN FOR

¿Tiene Usted alergias?	*tye*·ne oos·*te* a·*ler*·khyas
	Are you allergic to anything?
¿Se encuentra bajo medicación?	se en·*kwen*·tra *ba*·kho me·dee·ka·*syon*
	Are you on medication?
¿Usted bebe/fuma?	oos·*te* be·be/*foo*·ma
	Do you drink/smoke?
¿Usted toma drogas?	oos·*te* *to*·ma *dro*·gas
	Do you take drugs?

I'm on medication for ...	Estoy bajo medicación para ... es·*toy ba*·kho me·dee·ka·*syon pa*·ra ...

For more symptoms and conditions, see the **dictionary**.

Women's Health

(I think) I'm pregnant.	(Creo que) Estoy embarazada. (*kre*·o ke) es·*toy* em·ba·ra·*sa*·da
I'm on the Pill.	Tomo la píldora. *to*·mo la *peel*·do·ra
I haven't had my period for (five) weeks.	Hace (cinco) semanas que no me viene la regla. *a*·se (*seen*·ko) se·*ma*·nas ke no me *vye*·ne la *re*·gla
I've noticed a lump here.	Me he fijado que tengo un bulto aquí. me e fee·*kha*·do ke *ten*·go oon *bool*·to a·*kee*
I need contraception.	Quisiera usar algún método anticonceptivo. kee·*sye*·ra oo·*sar* al·*goon* me·to·do an·tee·kon·sep·*tee*·vo
I need the morning-after pill.	Quisiera tomar la píldora del día siguiente. kee·*sye*·ra to·*mar* la *peel*·do·ra del *dee*·a see·*gyen*·te
I need a pregnancy test.	Quisiera una prueba de embarazo. kee·*sye*·ra oo·na *prwe*·ba de em·ba·*ra*·so

🔊 LISTEN FOR

¿Es usted sexualmente activa?	es oos·*te* sek·swal·*men*·te ak·*tee*·va Are you sexually active?
¿Usa anticonceptivos?	oo·sa an·tee·kon·sep·*tee*·vos Are you using contraception?
¿Tiene la menstruación?	*tye*·ne la mens·trwa·*syon* Are you menstruating?
¿Cuándo le vino la regla por última vez?	*kwan*·do le *vee*·no la *re*·gla por *ool*·tee·ma ves When did you last have your period?
¿Está embarazada?	es·*ta* em·ba·ra·*sa*·da Are you pregnant?
Está embarazada.	es·*ta* em·ba·ra·*sa*·da You're pregnant.

Allergies

I'm allergic to (anti-inflammatories).	Soy alérgico/a a (los antiinflamatorios). **m/f** soy a·*ler*·khee·ko/a a (los an·teen·fla·ma·*to*·ryos)
I have hay fever.	Tengo alergia al polen. *ten*·go a·*ler*·khya al *po*·len
I have a skin allergy.	Tengo una alergia en la piel. *ten*·go oo·na a·*ler*·khya en la pyel
I think it's the medication I'm on.	Me parece que son los medicamentos que estoy tomando. me pa·*re*·se ke son los me·dee·ka·*men*·tos ke es·*toy* to·*man*·do

For food-related allergies, see **vegetarian & special meals** (p186).

Parts of the Body

My (knee) hurts.	Me duele (la rodilla). me *dwe*·le (la ro·*dee*·ya)
I can't move (my ankle).	No puedo mover (el tobillo). no *pwe*·do mo·*ver* (el to·*bee*·yo)
I have a cramp (in my foot).	Tengo calambres (en el pie). *ten*·go ka·*lam*·bres (en el pye)
(My arm) is swollen.	Se me hinchó (el brazo). se me een·*cho* (el *bra*·so)

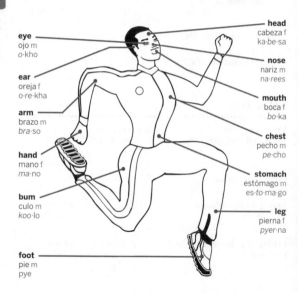

eye
ojo m
o·kho

ear
oreja f
o·*re*·kha

arm
brazo m
bra·so

hand
mano f
ma·no

bum
culo m
koo·lo

foot
pie m
pye

head
cabeza f
ka·*be*·sa

nose
nariz m
na·*rees*

mouth
boca f
bo·ka

chest
pecho m
pe·cho

stomach
estómago m
es·*to*·ma·go

leg
pierna f
pyer·na

Chemist

I need something for (diarrhoea).	Necesito algo para (diarrea). ne·se·*see*·to al·go *pa*·ra (dee·a·*re*·a)
Do I need a prescription for (antihistamines)?	¿Necesito receta para (antihistamínicos)? ne·se·*see*·to re·se·ta *pa*·ra (an·tee·ees·ta·*mee*·nee·kos)
I have a prescription.	Tengo receta médica. *ten*·go re·se·ta *me*·dee·ka
This is my usual medicine.	Éste es mi medicamento habitual. *es*·te es mee me·dee·ka·*men*·to a·bee·*twal*
How many times a day?	¿Cuántas veces al día? *kwan*·tas *ve*·ses al *dee*·a
Will it make me drowsy?	¿Me producirá somnolencia? me pro·doo·see·*ra* som·no·*len*·sya

🔊 LISTEN FOR

¿Ha tomado esto antes?	a to·*ma*·do es·to *an*·tes Have you taken this before?
Debe terminar el tratamiento.	*de*·be ter·mee·*nar* el tra·ta·*myen*·to You must complete the course.
Dos veces al día (con la comida).	dos *ve*·ses al *dee*·a (kon la ko·*mee*·da) Twice a day (with food).
Estará listo en (veinte minutos).	es·ta·*ra* *lees*·to en (*vayn*·te mee·*noo*·tos) It'll be ready in (20 minutes).

Dentist

I have a broken tooth.	Se me ha roto un diente. se me a *ro*·to oon *dyen*·te
I have a cavity.	Tengo una caries. *ten*·go oo·na ka·ryes
I have a toothache.	Me duele una muela. me *dwe*·le oo·na *mwe*·la
I've lost a filling.	Se me ha caído un empaste. se me a ka·*ee*·do oon em·*pas*·te
I need a filling.	Necesito un empaste. ne·se·*see*·to oon em·*pas*·te
My dentures are broken.	Se me han roto los dientes postizos. se me an *ro*·to los *dyen*·tes pos·*tee*·sos
My gums hurt.	Me duelen las encías. me *dwe*·len las en·*see*·as
I don't want it extracted.	No quiero que me lo arranque. no *kye*·ro ke me lo a·*ran*·ke
I need an anaesthetic.	Necesito anestesia. ne·se·*see*·to a·nes·te·sya

LISTEN FOR

Abra.	*a*·bra	Open wide.
Enjuague.	en·*khwa*·ge	Rinse.
Muerda esto.	*mwer*·da es·to	Bite down on this.

SAFE TRAVEL

HEALTH

Food

Eating Out

KEY PHRASES

Can you recommend a restaurant?	¿Puede recomendar un restaurante?	pwe·de re·ko·men·dar oon res·tow·ran·te
A table for two people, please.	Una mesa para dos, por favor.	oo·na me·sa pa·ra dos por fa·vor
I'd like the menu, please.	Quisiera el menú, por favor.	kee·sye·ra el me·noo por fa·vor
I'd like a beer, please.	Quisiera una cerveza, por favor.	kee·sye·ra oo·na ser·ve·sa por fa·vor
Please bring the bill.	Por favor nos trae la cuenta.	por fa·vor nos tra·e la kwen·ta

Basics

breakfast	desayuno m de·sa·yoo·no
lunch	almuerzo m al·mwer·so
dinner	cena f se·na
snack	tentempié m ten·tem·pye
eat	comer ko·mer
drink	beber be·ber

Finding a Place to Eat

Can you recommend a cafe?	¿Puede recomendar una cafetería? *pwe·*de re·ko·men·*dar oo·*na ka·fe·te·*ree·*a
Can you recommend a restaurant?	¿Puede recomendar un restaurante? *pwe·*de re·ko·men·*dar* oon res·tow·*ran·*te
Where would you go for (a) ...?	¿Adónde se va para ...? a·*don·*de se va *pa·*ra ...

business lunch	una comida de negocios	*oo·*na ko·*mee·*da de ne·*go·*syos
celebration	festejar	fes·te·*khar*
cheap meal	comer una comida barata	ko·*mer oo·*na ko·*mee·*da ba·*ra·*ta
local specialities	comer comida típica	ko·*mer* ko·*mee·*da *tee·pee·*ka

I'd like to reserve a table for (eight) o'clock.	Quisiera reservar una mesa para las (ocho). kee·*sye·*ra re·ser·*var oo·*na *me·*sa *pa·*ra las (o·cho)
I'd like to reserve a table for (two) people.	Quisiera reservar una mesa para (dos) personas. kee·*sye·*ra re·ser·*var oo·*na *me·*sa *pa·*ra (dos) per·*so·*nas

✂	**For two, please.**	Para dos, por favor.	*pa·*ra dos por fa·*vor*

CULTURE TIP Eateries

In Latin America there's no shortage of eateries where you can snack on the run or dine out at. Here are some of the typical establishments you may come across:

bar m — bar
many offer cheap light meals

chifa f — *chee·fa*
term for Chinese restaurant in various countries

churrasquería f — *choo·ras·ke·ree·a*
restaurant serving mainly barbecued meat

fuente f **de soda** — *fwen·te de so·da*
(lit: fountain of soda) cafe-style establishment serving snacks in addition to ice creams and soft drinks

lonchería f — *lon·che·ree·a*
cheap snack bar or diner

parrillada f — *pa·ree·ya·da*
Argentine steakhouse – a carnivore's delight

restaurante m **chino** — *res·tow·ran·te chee·no*
popular and cheap Chinese restaurant serving bowls of *tallarines* ta·ya·*ree*·nes (noodles) with chopped meat

Are you still serving food?	¿Siguen sirviendo comida? *see·gen seer·vyen·do ko·mee·da*
How long is the wait?	¿Cuánto hay que esperar? *kwan·to ai ke es·pe·rar*

FOOD **EATING OUT**

Hemos cerrado.	e·mos se·ra·do We're closed.
Estamos llenos.	es·ta·mos ye·nos We're fully booked.
No tenemos mesas.	no te·ne·mos me·sas We have no tables.
¿Dónde le gustaría sentarse?	don·de le goos·ta·ree·a sen·tar·se Where would you like to sit?

At the Restaurant

I'd like a/the ..., please.	Quisiera ..., por favor. kee·sye·ra ... por fa·vor	

drink list	la lista de bebidas	la lees·ta de be·bee·das
menu	el menú	el me·noo
(non)smoking section	(no) fumadores	(no) foo·ma·do·res
table for (two)	una mesa para (two)	oo·na me·sa pa·ra (dos)

✂ | **Menu, please.** | El menú, por favor. | el me·noo por fa·vor |

Do you have children's meals?	¿Tienen comidas para niños? tye·nen ko·mee·das pa·ra nee·nyos
Do you have a menu in English?	¿Tienen un menú en inglés? tye·nen oon me·noo en een·gles

🔊 LISTEN FOR

¿En qué le puedo servir?	en ke le *pwe*·do ser·*veer* What can I get for you?
¿Cómo lo quiere preparado?	*ko*·mo lo *kye*·re pre·pa·*ra*·do How would you like that cooked?
Recomiendo ...	re·ko·*myen*·do ... I suggest the ...
Aquí tiene.	a·*kee tye*·ne Here you go!
¡Que aproveche!	ke a·pro·*ve*·che Enjoy your meal.

Is it self-serve?	¿Es de autoservicio? es de ow·to·ser·*vee*·syo
What would you recommend?	¿Qué me recomienda? ke me re·ko·*myen*·da
I'll have what they're having.	Tomaré lo mismo que ellos. to·ma·*re* lo *mees*·mo ke e·yos
I'd like a local speciality.	Quisiera un plato típico. kee·*sye*·ra oon *pla*·to *tee*·pee·ko
What's in that dish?	¿De qué es ese plato? de ke es e·se *pla*·to
Does it take long to prepare?	¿Se tarda mucho en prepararlo? se *tar*·da *moo*·cho en pre·pa·*rar*·lo
Are these complimentary?	¿Éstos son gratis? *es*·tos son *gra*·tees

Eating Out

Can I see the menu, please?
¿Puedo ver el menú, por favor?
pwe·do ver el me·*noo* por fa·*vor*

What would you recommend for ...?
¿Qué recomienda para ...?
ke re·ko·*myen*·da *pa*·ra ...

the main meal
el plato principal
el *pla*·to preen·see·*pal*

dessert
el postre
el *pos*·tre

drinks
beber
be·*ber*

Can you bring me some ..., please?
Por favor me trae ...
por fa·*vor* me *tra*·e ...

I'd like the bill, please.
Quisiera la cuenta, por favor.
kee·*sye*·ra la *kwen*·ta por fa·*vor*

Requests

Is there any (tomato sauce)?	¿Hay (salsa de tomate)?	ai (*sal*·sa de to·*ma*·te)
Please bring a ...	Por favor nos trae ...	por fa·*vor* nos *tra*·e ...

cloth	un trapo	oon *tra*·po
glass	un vaso	oon *va*·so
serviette	una servilleta	oo·na ser·vee·*ye*·ta
wineglass	una copa de vino	*oo*·na *ko*·pa de *vee*·no

I'd like it ...	Lo quisiera ...	lo kee·*sye*·ra ...
I don't want it ...	No lo quiero ...	no lo *kye*·ro ...

boiled	hervido	er·*vee*·do
deep-fried	frito en aceite abundante	*free*·to en a·*say*·te a·boon·*dan*·te
fried	frito	*free*·to
grilled	a la parilla	a la pa·*ree*·ya
medium	no muy hecho	no mooy e·cho
rare	vuelta y vuelta	*vwel*·ta ee *vwel*·ta
reheated	recalentado	re·ka·len·*ta*·do
steamed	al vapor	al va·*por*
well done	muy hecho	mooy e·cho
with the dressing on the side	con el aliño aparte	kon el a·*lee*·nyo a·*par*·te
without (chilli)	sin (chile)	seen (*chee*·le)

LOOK FOR

Abrebocas	a·bre·*bo*·kas	Appetisers
Sopas	*so*·pas	Soups
De Entrada	de en·*tra*·da	Starters
Ensaladas	en·sa·*la*·das	Salads
Comidas Ligeras	ko·*mee*·das lee·*khe*·ras	Light Meals
Segundos Platos	se·*goon*·dos *pla*·tos	Main Courses
Postres	*pos*·tres	Desserts
Bebidas	be·*bee*·das	Drinks
Aperitivos	a·pe·ree·*tee*·vos	Aperitifs
Licores	lee·*ko*·res	Spirits
Cervezas	ser·*ve*·sas	Beers
Gaseosas	ga·se·o·sas	Soft Drinks
Vinos Blancos	*vee*·nos *blan*·kos	White Wines
Vinos de la Casa	*vee*·nos de la *ka*·sa	House Wines
Vinos del Lugar	*vee*·nos del loo·*gar*	Local Wines
Vinos Espumosos	*vee*·nos es·poo·*mo*·sos	Sparkling Wines
Vinos Rosados	*vee*·nos ro·*sa*·dos	Roses
Vinos Tintos	*vee*·nos *teen*·tos	Red Wines
Vinos Dulces	*vee*·nos *dool*·ses	Dessert Wine
Digestivos	dee·khes·*tee*·vos	Digestifs

For more words you might see on a menu, see the **menu decoder** (p189).

FOOD   **EATING OUT**

Compliments & Complaints

That was delicious!	¡Estaba buenísimo! es·ta·ba bwe·nee·see·mo
My compliments to the chef.	Felicitaciones al cocinero. fe·lee·see·ta·syo·nes al ko·see·ne·ro
I'm full.	Estoy satisfecho/a. m/f es·toy sa·tees·fe·cho/a
I love this dish.	Me encanta este plato. me en·kan·ta es·te pla·to
I love the local cuisine.	Me encanta la comida típica de la zona. me en·kan·ta la ko·mee·da tee·pee·ka de la so·na
This is ...	Esto está ... es·to es·ta ...

burnt	quemado	ke·ma·do
cold	frío	free·o
hot	caliente	ka·lyen·te
(too) spicy	(demasiado) picante	(de·ma·sya·do) pee·kan·te
superb	exquisito	ek·skee·see·to

Paying the Bill

Please bring the bill.	Por favor nos trae la cuenta. por fa·vor nos tra·e la kwen·ta

✂	**Bill, please.**	La cuenta, por favor. la kwen·ta por fa·vor

> **LANGUAGE TIP**
>
> **Regionalisms**
> The main meal of the day in Latin America is lunch, known as *el almuerzo* el al·*mwer*·so or *la comida* la ko·*mee*·da. Many restaurants in Latin America provide a set menu for lunch, usually consisting of soup, a main course and a drink. This cheap and popular option goes under the following guises:
>
> | | | |
> |---|---|---|
> | **Argentina, Central America, Chile** | almuerzo m completo; comida f corrida | al·*mwer*·so kom·*ple*·to; ko·*mee*·da ko·*ree*·da |
> | **Colombia** | almuerzo m corriente | al·*mwer*·so ko·*ryen*·te |
> | **Costa Rica** | casado m | ka·*sa*·do |
> | **Guatemala, Mexico, Peru** | menú m (del día) | me·*noo* (del *dee*·a) |

Is service included in the bill?	¿La cuenta incluye el servicio? la *kwen*·ta een·*kloo*·ye el ser·*vee*·syo
There's a mistake in the bill.	Hay un error en la cuenta. ai oon e·*ror* en la *kwen*·ta

Nonalcoholic Drinks

Latin Americans drink prodigious quantities of sweet, fizzy drinks. The general term for 'soft drink' is *gaseosa* ga·se·*o*·sa, but in Chile they are *bebidas* be·*bee*·das, in Panama *refrescos* re·*fres*·kos or *sodas* so·das, and in Ecuador *colas* ko·las.

boiled water	agua f hervida a·gwa er·*vee*·da
coffee (without sugar)	café m (sin azúcar) ka·*fe* (seen a·*soo*·kar)

(orange) juice	jugo m (de naranja) *khoo*·go (de na·*ran*·kha)
lemonade	limonada f lee·mo·*na*·da
milk	leche f *le*·che
(fruit) milkshake	licuado m (de frutas) lee·*kwa*·do (de *froo*·tas)
tea (with milk)	té m (con leche) te (kon *le*·che)
sparkling mineral water	agua f mineral con gas *a*·gwa mee·ne·*ral* kon gas
still mineral water	agua f mineral sin gas *a*·gwa mee·ne·*ral* seen gas

LANGUAGE TIP **Regionalisms**

Visitors to Latin America who are expecting out-of-this-world coffee might be surprised to learn that the best beans are shipped overseas to earn export dollars. It's still a popular drink though, and here's some vocabulary to help you order what you want:

black coffee	un café negro; un café tinto (Col)	oon ka·*fe ne*·gro; oon ka·*fe teen*·to
coffee with milk	un café con leche; un cortado (Arg)	oon ka·*fe* kon *le*·che; oon kor·*ta*·do
instant coffee	un nescafé	oon nes·ka·*fe*
milk coffee	un café con leche; un perico (Col)	oon ka·*fe* kon *le*·che; oon pe·*ree*·ko
small cup of coffee	un cafecito; un café chico (Arg)	oon ka·fe·*see*·to; oon ka·*fe chee*·ko

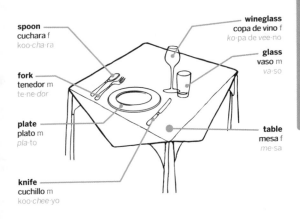

spoon
cuchara f
koo·cha·ra

fork
tenedor m
te·ne·dor

plate
plato m
pla·to

knife
cuchillo m
koo·chee·yo

wineglass
copa de vino f
ko·pa de vee·no

glass
vaso m
va·so

table
mesa f
me·sa

Alcoholic Drinks

brandy	coñac m ko·nyak
champagne	champán m cham·pan
cocktail	combinado m kom·bee·na·do
draught beer	cerveza f de baril ser·ve·sa de ba·reel

a shot of ...	un trago de ... oon *tra*·go de ...	
gin	ginebra	khee·*ne*·bra
pisco (grape brandy)	pisco	*pees*·ko
rum	ron	ron
tequila	tequila	te·*kee*·la
vodka	vodka	*vod*·ka
whisky	güisqui	*gwees*·kee

a bottle/glass of ... wine	una botella/copa de vino ... *oo*·na bo·*te*·ya/*ko*·pa de *vee*·no ...	
dessert	dulce	*dool*·se
red	tinto	*teen*·to
rose	rosado	ro·*sa*·do
sparkling	espumoso	es·poo·*mo*·so
white	blanco	*blan*·ko

a ... of beer	... de cerveza ... de ser·*ve*·sa	
glass	un vaso	oon *va*·so
jug	una jarra; un chop (SAm)	*oo*·na *kha*·ra; oon chop
large bottle	una litrona	*oo*·na lee·*tro*·na
pint	una pinta	*oo*·na *peen*·ta
small bottle	un botellín	oon bo·te·*yeen*

In the Bar

Excuse me!	¡Oiga! *oy*·ga
I'm next.	¡Ahora voy yo! a·*o*·ra voy yo
🇶 **What would you like?**	¿Qué quiere/quieres tomar? pol/inf ke *kye*·re/*kye*·res to·*mar*
🇦 **I'll have a glass of red wine.**	Para mí, una copa de vino tinto. *pa*·ra mee *oo*·na *ko*·pa de *vee*·no *teen*·to
🇦 **I'd like a beer, please.**	Quisiera una cerveza, por favor. kee·*sye*·ra *oo*·na ser·*ve*·sa por fa·*vor*
Same again, please.	Otra de lo mismo. o·tra de lo *mees*·mo
No ice, thanks.	Sin hielo, gracias. seen *ye*·lo *gra*·syas
I'd like it straight, please.	Solo, por favor. *so*·lo por fa·*vor*
I'll buy you a drink.	Le/Te invito a una copa. pol/inf le/te een·*vee*·to a *oo*·na *ko*·pa
It's my round.	Es mi ronda. es mee *ron*·da
You can get the next one.	La próxima la pagas tú. inf la *prok*·see·ma la *pa*·gas too
Do you serve meals here?	¿Sirven comidas aquí? *seer*·ven ko·*mee*·das a·*kee*

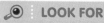

LOOK FOR

Baños	*ba*·nyos	Toilets
Caballeros	ka·ba·*ye*·ros	Men
Damas	*da*·mas	Women
Hombres	*om*·bres	Men
Mujeres	moo·*khe*·res	Women
Señoras	se·*nyo*·ras	Women
Servicios	ser·*vee*·syos	Toilets
Varones	va·*ro*·nes	Men

Drinking Up

Cheers!	¡Salud! sa·*loo*
This is hitting the spot.	Me lo estoy pasando muy bien. me lo es·*toy* pa·*san*·do mooy byen
Thanks, but I don't feel like it.	Lo siento, pero no me apetece. lo *syen*·to *pe*·ro no me a·pe·*te*·se
I don't drink alcohol.	No bebo alcohol. no *be*·bo al·*kol*
I'm feeling drunk.	Esto me está subiendo mucho. *es*·to me es·*ta* soo·*byen*·do *moo*·cho
I think I've had one too many.	Creo que he tomado una de más. *kre*·o ke e to·*ma*·do *oo*·na de mas
I'm pissed.	Estoy borracho/a. **m/f** es·*toy* bo·*ra*·cho/a

Self-Catering

What's the local speciality?	¿Cuál es la especialidad de la zona?	kwal es la es·pe·sya·lee·da de la so·na
Where can I find the ... section?	¿Dónde está la sección de ...?	don·de es·ta la sek·syon de ...
I'd like some ...	Déme unos/unas ... m/f	de·me oo·nos/oo·nas ...

Buying Food

What's the local speciality?	¿Cuál es la especialidad de la zona? kwal es la es·pe·sya·lee·da de la so·na
Do you sell locally produced food?	¿Vende productos locales? ven·de pro·dook·tos lo·ka·les
Do you sell organic produce?	¿Vende productos orgánicos? ven·de pro·dook·tos or·ga·nee·kos
What's that?	¿Qué es eso? ke es e·so
What's that called?	¿Cómo se llama eso? ko·mo se ya·ma e·so
Can I taste it?	¿Puedo probarlo/a? m/f pwe·do pro·bar·lo/a
Do you have other kinds?	¿Tiene otros tipos? tye·ne ot·ros tee·pos

How much is (a kilo of cheese)?	¿Cuánto vale (un kilo de queso)?
	kwan·to *va*·le (oon *kee*·lo de *ke*·so)

Do you have anything cheaper?	¿Tiene algo más barato?
	tye·ne *al*·go mas ba·*ra*·to

I'd like ...	Déme ...
	de·me ...

(200) grams	(doscientos) gramos	(do·*syen*·tos) *gra*·mos
a bottle	una botella	*oo*·na bo·*te*·ya
a dozen	una docena	*oo*·na do·*se*·na
a jar	una jarra	*oo*·na *kha*·ra
a kilo	un kilo	oon *kee*·lo
(two) kilos	(dos) kilos	(dos) *kee*·los
a packet	un paquete	oon pa·*ke*·te
a piece	un trozo	oon *tro*·so
(three) pieces	(tres) trozos	(tres) *tro*·sos
a slice	una loncha	*oo*·na *lon*·cha
(six) slices	(seis) lonchas	(says) *lon*·chas
a tin	una lata	*oo*·na *la*·ta
some ...	unos ... m pl	*oo*·nos ...
	unas ... f pl	*oo*·nas ...
that one	ése/ésa m/f	*e*·se/*e*·sa
this one	éste/ésta m/f	*es*·te/*es*·ta

Enough.	Ya.
	ya

A bit more.	Un poco más.
	oon *po*·ko mas

Less.	Menos.
	me·nos

🔍 LOOK FOR

Carnicería	kar·nee·se·*ree*·a	Butcher
Fiambrería	fyam·bre·*ree*·a	Delicatessen
Frutería	froo·te·*ree*·a	Fruit Shop
Heladería	e·la·de·*ree*·a	Ice-Cream Parlour
Lechería	le·che·*ree*·a	Dairy Shop
Mercado	mer·*ka*·do	Market
Panadería	pa·na·de·*ree*·a	Baker
Pastelería	pas·te·le·*ree*·a	Cake Shop
Pescadería	pes·ka·de·*ree*·a	Fish Shop
Pollería	po·ye·*ree*·a	Poultry Shop
Supermercado	soo·per·mer·*ka*·do	Supermarket
Tabaquero	ta·ba·*ke*·ro	Tobacconist
Verdulería	ver·doo·le·*ree*·a	Greengrocer

Can I have a bag, please?	¿Me da una bolsa, por favor? me da *oo*·na *bol*·sa por fa·*vor*
Where can I find the ... section?	¿Dónde está la sección de ...? *don*·de es·*ta* la sek·*syon* de ...

dairy	productos lácteos	pro·*dook*·tos *lak*·te·os
frozen goods	productos congelados	pro·*dook*·tos kon·khe·*la*·dos
fruit and vegetable	frutas y verduras	*froo*·tas ee ver·*doo*·ras
meat	carne	*kar*·ne
poultry	aves	*a*·ves

Cooking

cooked	cocido/a m/f ko·*see*·do/a
dried	seco/a m/f *se*·ko/a
fresh	fresco/a m/f *fres*·ko/a
frozen	congelado/a m/f kon·khe·*la*·do/a
powdered	en polvo en *pol*·vo
raw	crudo/a m/f *kroo*·do/a
vacuum-packed	envasado/a m/f al vacío en·va·*sa*·do/a al va·*see*·o

 **LOOK FOR**

apropriado/a m/f para cocinar en microondas	a·pro·*prya*·do/a pa·ra ko·see·*nar* en mee·kro·*on*·das microwaveable
consúmase antes del ...	kon·*soo*·ma·se *an*·tes del ... use by ...
consúmase dentro de (cuatro) días de abierto	kon·*soo*·ma·se *den*·tro de (*kwa*·tro) *dee*·as de a·*byer*·to consume within (four) days of opening
manténgase en el refrigerador	man·*ten*·ga·se en el re·free·khe·ra·*dor* keep refrigerated

Could I please borrow (a bottle opener)?	¿Me puede prestar (un abrebotellas)? me *pwe*·de pres·*tar* (oon a·bre·bo·*te*·yas)
Where's (a can opener)?	¿Dónde hay (un abrelatas)? *don*·de ai (oon a·bre·*la*·tas)

For more cooking implements, see the **dictionary**.

> ### *¿Cuánto vale ...?*
> *kwan*·to va·le ...
> *How much is ...?*

Vegetarian & Special Meals

KEY PHRASES

Do you have vegetarian food?	¿Tienen comida vegetariana?	*tye*·nen ko·*mee*·da ve·khe·ta·*rya*·na
Could you prepare a meal without ...?	¿Me puede preparar una comida sin ...?	me *pwe*·de pre·pa·*rar oo*·na ko·*mee*·da seen ...
I'm allergic to ...	Soy alérgico/a a ... **m/f**	soy a·*ler*·khee·ko/a a ...

Special Diets & Allergies

Is there a halal restaurant near here?	¿Hay un restaurante halal por aquí? ai oon res·tow·*ran*·te a·*lal* por a·*kee*
Is there a kosher restaurant near here?	¿Hay un restaurante kosher por aquí? ai oon res·tow·*ran*·te ko·sher por a·*kee*
Is there a vegetarian restaurant near here?	¿Hay un restaurante vegetariano por aquí? ai oon res·tow·*ran*·te ve·khe·ta·*rya*·no por a·*kee*
I'm vegan.	Soy vegetariano/a estricto/a. **m/f** soy ve·khe·ta·*rya*·no/a es·*treek*·to/a
I'm on a special diet.	Estoy a dieta especial. es·*toy* a *dye*·ta es·pe·*syal*

I'm allergic to ...	Soy alérgico/a ... **m/f**
	soy a·*ler*·khee·ko/a ...

dairy produce	a los productos lácteos	a los pro·*dook*·tos *lak*·te·os
eggs	a los huevos	a los *we*·vos
fish	al pescado	al pes·*ka*·do
gelatin	a la gelatina	a la khe·la·*tee*·na
honey	a la miel	a la myel
nuts	a las nueces	a las *nwe*·ses
peanuts	al maní	al ma·*nee*
seafood	al marisco	al ma·*rees*·ko

Ordering Food

Do you have (vegetarian) food?	¿Tienen comida (vegetariana)?
	tye·nen ko·*mee*·da (ve·khe·ta·*rya*·na)
I don't eat (red meat).	No como (carne roja).
	no *ko*·mo (*kar*·ne *ro*·kha)
Is it cooked in/with ...?	¿Está cocinado en/con ...?
	es·*ta* ko·see·*na*·do en/kon ...
Could you prepare a meal without ...?	¿Me puede preparar una comida sin ...?
	me *pwe*·de pre·pa·*rar oo*·na ko·*mee*·da seen ...

butter	mantequilla	man·te·*kee*·ya
meat/fish stock	caldo de carne/ pescado	*kal*·do de *kar*·ne/ pes·*ka*·do
pork	cerdo	*ser*·do
poultry	aves	*a*·ves

FOOD | **VEGETARIAN & SPECIAL MEALS**

🔊 LISTEN FOR

Le preguntaré al cocinero.	le pre·goon·ta·re al ko·see·ne·ro	I'll check with the cook.
¿Puede comer ...?	pwe·de ko·mer ...	Can you eat ...?
Todo lleva (carne).	to·do ye·va (kar·ne)	It all has (meat) in it.

Is this ...?	**¿Esto es ...?**	es·to es ...

cholesterol-free	sin colesterol	seen ko·les·te·rol
decaffeinated	sin cafeína	seen ka·fe·ee·na
free of animal produce	sin productos de animales	seen pro·dook·tos de a·nee·ma·les
free-range	de corral	de ko·ral
genetically modified	transgénico/a m/f	trans·khe·nee·ko/a
gluten-free	sin gluten	seen gloo·ten
low-fat	bajo/a m/f en grasas	ba·kho/a en gra·sas
low in sugar	bajo/a m/f en azúcar	ba·kho/a en a·soo·kar
organic	orgánico/a m/f	or·ga·nee·ko/a
salt-free	sin sal	seen sal

A

Menu
~ DECODER ~

léxico culinario

This miniguide to Latin American cuisine lists dishes and
ingredients in Spanish alphabetical order (see **alphabet**, p13).
Spanish nouns have their gender indicated by ⓜ or ⓕ. If it's a plural
noun, you'll also see pl.

~ A ~

a la plancha a la *plan*·cha grilled

a punto a *poon*·to medium (steak)

aceite ⓜ a·*say*·te oil

aceitunas ⓕ pl a·say·*too*·nas olives

— alinadas (Cub) a·lee·*na*·das olives
marinated in cummin, hot pepper,
lemon, garlic & vinegar

— rellenas re·*ye*·nas stuffed olives

achicoria ⓕ a·chee·*ko*·rya chicory •
endive

achuras ⓕ pl a·*choo*·ras offal

adobo ⓜ a·*do*·bo paste of garlic,
oregano, paprika, peppercorn, salt,
olive, lime juice & vinegar for
seasoning meat

agua ⓕ a·*gwa* water

— de canilla de ka·*nee*·ya tap water

— de jamaica (CAm) de kha·*mai*·ka
sweet, red, iced tea made from
hibiscus flowers

— de la llave de la *ya*·ve tap water

— de panel (Col) de pa·*nel* unrefined
sugar melted in hot water

— de vertiente de ver·*tyen*·te spring
water

— del tubo del *too*·bo tap water

— mineral mee·ne·*ral* mineral water

aguacate ⓜ a·gwa·*ka*·te avocado

— salsa (Cub) *sal*·sa avocado sauce
containing tomato, capsicum, olive,
tomato & white rum

aguardiente ⓜ (Col) a·gwar·*dyen*·te
spirit flavoured with anise

ahumado/a ⓜ/ⓕ a·oo·*ma*·do/a
smoked

ají ⓜ a·*khee* chilli sauce • red chilli

ajiaco ⓜ a·*khya*·ko spicy potato
stew • in Colombia, soup with
chicken & three varieties of potato,
served with corn & capers

ajili-mójili ⓜ (Pue) a·khee·lee
mo·khee·lee tangy garlic sauce

ajillo, al a·*khee*·yo, al in garlic

ajo ⓜ a·*kho* garlic

ajoporro ⓜ a·kho·*po*·ro leek

al ajillo al a·*khee*·yo in garlic

al horno al *or*·no baked

al vapor al va·*por* steamed

albahaca ⓕ al·*ba*·ka basil

albóndigas ⓕ pl al·*bon*·dee·gas
meatballs

alcachofa ⓕ al·ka·*cho*·fa artichoke

alcaparra ⓕ al·ka·*pa*·ra caper

alcaucil ⓜ (SAm) al·*kow*·seel
artichoke

alcohol ⓜ al·*kol* alcohol

B

aliado ⓜ (Chi) *a·lya·*do sandwich with cold ham & cheese
alita ⓕ *a·lee·*ta wing (bird or poultry)
allioli ⓜ *al·yo·*lee garlic sauce
almejas ⓕ pl *al·me·*khas clams
almendra ⓕ *al·men·*dra almond
almuerzo ⓜ *al·mwer·*so lunch
alubias ⓕ pl *a·loo·*byas kidney beans
amarillos ⓜ pl (Pue) *a·ma·ree·*yos fried ripe plantains coated with cinnamon, sugar & wine sauce
ananá(s) ⓜ *a·na·na(s)* pineapple
anca ⓕ *an·*ka haunch
anchoas ⓕ pl *an·cho·*as anchovies
anguila ⓜ *an·gee·*la eel
anís ⓜ *a·nees* anise • aniseed
anticucho ⓜ (Bol, Chi, Per) *an·tee·koo·*cho kebab
apio ⓜ *a·*pyo celery
arenque ⓜ *a·ren·*ke herring
arepa ⓕ (Col, Ven) *a·re·*pa small toasted or fried maize pancake
areperas ⓕ (Ven) *a·re·pe·*ras snack bars selling **arepas**
arreglados ⓜ pl (Cos) *a·re·gla·*dos savoury filled puff pastries
arrollado ⓜ *a·ro·ya·*do rolled pork
arroz ⓜ *a·ros* rice
— con habichuelas (Pue) kon *a·bee·chwe·*las dish of rice & beans
— con leche kon *le·*che rice pudding
— con pollo kon *po·*yo dish of rice & chicken
arveja ⓕ (Ecu) *ar·ve·*kha pea stew
— seca *se·*ka split pea
arvejas ⓕ pl *ar·ve·*khas peas
asado ⓜ (SAm) *a·sa·*do mixed grill
— al espiedo al *es·pye·*do spit roast
asado/a ⓜ/ⓕ *a·sa·*do/a roasted
— al horno al *or·*no oven-roasted
asopao ⓜ **de pollo** (Pue) *a·so·pa·*o de *po·*yo chicken stew with **adobo** seasoning
atún ⓜ *a·toon* tuna
— con ron (Cub) kon ron tuna with a rum sauce

auyama ⓕ (Col, Ven) *ow·ya·*ma pumpkin
ave ⓜ *a·*ve fowl • poultry
avellana ⓕ *a·ve·ya·*na hazelnut
azafrán ⓜ *a·sa·fran* saffron
azúcar ⓜ *a·soo·*kar sugar

~ B ~

bacalao ⓜ *ba·ka·la·*o (salted) cod
baho ⓜ (Nic) *ba·*o stew of beef, various types of plantains & **yuca**
baleadas ⓕ pl (Hon) *ba·le·a·*das white-flour tortillas filled with refried beans, cream & crumbled cheese
banana ⓕ (Arg, Per) *ba·na·*na banana
banano ⓜ (CAm,Col) *ba·na·*no banana
bandeja ⓕ (Col) *ban·de·*kha main course
— paisa (Col) *pai·*sa traditional dish consisting of ground beef, sausage, red beans, rice, green banana, egg, salt, pork & avocado
baracoa ⓜ **special** (Cub) *ba·ra·ko·*a spe·*syal* cocktail of rum , coconut cream, grapefruit juice & limejuice
Barros Jarpa ⓜ (Chi) *ba·ros khar·*pa sandwich with cold ham & melted cheese, named after a Chilean painter
Barros Luco ⓜ (Chi) *ba·ros loo·*ko steak sandwich with melted cheese, named after a Chilean president
batata ⓕ *ba·ta·*ta sweet potato
bebida ⓕ *be·bee·*da drink (beverage)
beicon ⓜ **con queso** *bay·*kon kon *ke·*so cold bacon with cheese
berberechos ⓜ pl *ber·be·re·*chos cockles
berenjena ⓕ *be·ren·khe·*na aubergine • eggplant
berro ⓜ *be·*ro watercress
besugo ⓜ *be·soo·*go bream
betarraga ⓕ (Bol, Chi) *ba·ta·ra·*ga beetroot

bien asado/a ⓜ/ⓕ byen a·*sa*·do/a well-done

bien hecho/a ⓜ/ⓕ byen e·*cho*/a well-done

bife ⓜ (Arg, Par, Uru) *bee*·fe steak

— a caballo a ka·*ba*·yo steak served with two eggs & chips

— asado a·*sa*·do roast beef

— de chorizo de cho·*ree*·so rump steak

— de costilla de kos·*tee*·ya T-bone steak (also called **chuleta**)

— de lomo ⓜ de *lo*·mo tenderloin

bistec ⓜ bees·*tek* steak

— con patatas kon pa·*ta*·tas steak & chips

blanco ⓜ *blan*·ko white (wine)

bocadillo ⓜ (Cub) bo·ka·*dee*·yo sandwich filled with ham or cheese

bocaditos ⓜ pl (Cub) bo·ka·*dee*·tos substantial snack dishes

bocas ⓕ pl (Cos, Pan) *bo*·kas savoury side dishes served at bars

bollos ⓜ pl *bo*·yos bread rolls

boniatillo ⓜ (Cub) bo·nya·*tee*·yo dessert made from sweet potato, sugar, cinnamon, lime, egg yolks & sherry

boniato ⓜ (Arg) bo·*nya*·to sweet potato

bori-bori ⓜ (Par) bo·ree *bo*·ree chicken soup with corn meal balls

botella ⓕ bo·*te*·ya bottle

breva ⓕ *bre*·va fig

brócoli ⓜ *bro*·ko·lee broccoli

budín ⓜ boo·*deen* pudding

buey ⓜ bway ox

~ C ~

caballa ⓕ ka·*ba*·ya mackerel

cabeza ⓜ ka·*be*·sa head

cabra ⓕ *ka*·bra goat

cacao ⓜ ka·*ka*·o cocoa

cachapa ⓕ (Ven) ka·*cha*·pa large round corn pancake often served with cheese, ham or both

cachito ⓜ (Ven) ka·*chee*·to a type of hot croissant filled with chopped ham

café ⓜ ka·fe coffee

— chico (Arg) *chee*·ko small cup of coffee

— doble *do*·ble long black coffee

— marrón (Ven) ma·*ron* coffee consisting of half coffee & half milk

— negro *ne*·gro black coffee

— tinto (Col) *teen*·to black coffee

— solo *so*·lo black coffee

cafecito ⓜ ka·fe·*see*·to small cup of coffee

cajeta ⓕ (Cos) ka·*khe*·ta similar to **dulce de leche**

calabacín ⓜ ka·la·ba·*seen* courgette • zucchini

calabaza ⓕ ka·la·*ba*·sa gourd • marrow • pumpkin

calamares ⓜ pl ka·la·*ma*·res calamari • squid

caldereta ⓕ kal·de·*re*·ta stew

caldillo ⓜ **cubano** (Cub) kal·*dee*·yo koo·*ba*·no hotpot made with steak, onions, tomatoes, potatoes, hot pepper, garlic, brown sugar & cumin

caldo ⓜ *kal*·do broth • stock

— de gallina de ga·*yee*·na chicken soup

— de patas (Ecu) de *pa*·tas soup made of boiled cattle hooves

caliente ka·*lyen*·te hot

callampas ⓕ (Chi) ka·*yam*·pas mushrooms

camarón ⓜ ka·ma·*ron* shrimp • small prawn

cambur ⓜ (Ven) kam·*boor* banana

camomila ⓕ ka·mo·*mee*·la camomile tea

camote ⓜ ka·*mo*·te sweet potato

caña ⓕ *ka*·nya **aguardiente** • cane alcohol

— de azúcar de a·*soo*·kar sugar cane

canela ⓕ ka·*ne*·la cinnamon

canelones ⓜ pl ka·ne·*lo*·nes cannelloni

cangrejo ⓜ kan·*gre*·kho crab

— de río de *ree*·o crayfish

cañita ① (Pue) ka·*nyee*·ta homemade, illegal rum

capitán ① (Chi) ka·pee·*tan* vermouth

capón ⓜ (SAm) ka·*pon* mutton

carabinero ⓜ ka·ra·bee·*ne*·ro large prawn

caracol ⓜ ka·ra·*kol* snail

carbonada ① (Arg) kar·bo·*na*·da beef stew of rice, potatoes, maize, squash, apples & peaches

carimañola ① (Pan) ka·ree·ma·*nyo*·la deep-fried roll filled with meat, made from ground & boiled **yuca**

carne ① *kar*·ne meat

— de caballo de ka·*ba*·yo horsemeat

— de vaca de *va*·ka beef

— fría *free*·a cold meat

— mechada (Pue) me·*cha*·da roast beef

— molida mo·*lee*·da minced meat

carnicería ① kar·nee·se·*ree*·a butcher's shop

carpa ① *kar*·pa carp

casado ⓜ (Cos) ka·*sa*·do platter of rice, black beans, plantain, meat or fish, cabbage, an egg or avocado

— vegetariano (Cos) ve·khe·ta·*rya*·no vegetarian version of **casado**

casamiento ⓜ (Sal) ka·sa·*myen*·to rice & beans mixed together

castaña ① kas·*ta*·nya chestnut

— de Pará de pa·*ra* brazil nut

cave ⓜ (Hon) *ka*·ve a type of coffee liqueur

caza ① *ka*·sa game (meat)

— de temporada de tem·po·*ra*·da game in season

cazuela ① ka·*swe*·la casserole • fish stew (Arg)

— de mariscos (Chi) de ma·*rees*·kos shellfish soup

cebada ① se·*ba*·da barley

cebolla ① se·*bo*·ya onion

cerdo ⓜ *ser*·do pig • pork

cereales ⓜ pl se·re·*a*·les cereal

cereza ① se·*re*·sa cherry

cerveza ① ser·*ve*·sa beer

— de barril de ba·*reel* beer on tap • draught beer

— de malta de *mal*·ta dark beer

— lager *la*·ger lager beer

— negra *ne*·gra stout

ceviche ⓜ se·vee·che raw fish marinated in lemon juice, chilli or onions or both

chacarero ⓜ (Chi) cha·ka·*re*·ro beefsteak with tomato & vegetables

chairo ⓜ (Bol) *chai*·ro mutton or beef soup served with **chuños**, fresh potato & dried maize

chajchu ⓜ (Bol) *chakh*·choo beef with freeze-dried potatoes, hard-boiled egg, cheese & hot red-pepper sauce

chalote ⓜ cha·*lo*·te shallot • spring onion

champán ⓜ cham·*pan* champagne

champiñones ⓜ pl cham·pee·*nyo*·nes mushrooms

— al ajillo al a·*khee*·yo garlic mushrooms

chapalele ⓜ (Chi) cha·pa·*le*·le boiled potato & flour bread

chaque ⓜ (Bol) *cha*·ke similar to **chupe** but much thicker & with more grain

charque ⓜ (Bol) *char*·ke dried beef, llama or other red meat

— kan kan **charque** served with mashed hominy

chauchas ① pl *chow*·chas string beans

chicha ① (Bol, Per) *chee*·cha maize beer associated with ceremonial & ritual occasions in Peru

chicharrón ⓜ chee·cha·*ron* fried pork fat

chifa ① (Bol, CAm, Per) *chee*·fa Chinese restaurant

chilcano ⓜ (Chi, Per) cheel·*ka*·no ginger ale (may be served with **pisco**)

C

chile ⓜ *chee*·le pimento (small red pepper)

chimichurri ⓜ (Arg, Uru) chee·mee·*choo*·ree strong olive oil, parsley & garlic barbecue sauce

chinchulines ⓜ pl cheen·choo·*lee*·nes small intestines – a common **asado** dish

chipa ⓕ **de almidón** (Par) *chee*·pa de al·mee·*don* like **chipa guazú** but made with manioc flour rather than corn meal

chipa ⓕ **guazú** (Par) *chee*·pa gwa·*soo* dish resembling a cheese souffle containing corn meal

chipirón ⓜ chee·pee·*ron* small squid

chirimoya ⓕ chee·ree·*mo*·ya custard apple

chispa tren ⓕ (Cub) *chees*·pa tren 'train sparks' – Cuban firewater

chivito ⓜ (Uru) chee·*vee*·to tasty & filling steak sandwich with a variety of additions including cheese, lettuce, tomato & bacon

— al plato al *pla*·to steak served with a fried egg, potato salad, green salad & French fries

chivo ⓜ *chee*·vo baby goat • kid

choclo ⓜ *cho*·klo corn on the cob • maize

choco ⓜ *cho*·ko cuttlefish

chocolate ⓜ cho·ko·*la*·te chocolate

— caliente ka·*lyen*·te hot chocolate drink

— santafereño (Col) san·ta·fe·re·*nyo* cup of hot chocolate accompanied by a piece of cheese & bread

chola ⓕ (Bol) *cho*·la bread roll filled with meat, onion, tomato & **escabeche**

chop ⓜ chop draught beer

choripán ⓜ (Arg) cho·ree·*pan* spicy sausage sandwich

chorizo ⓜ cho·*ree*·so spicy pork sausage

— al horno al *or*·no spicy baked sausage

chorlito ⓜ chor·*lee*·to plover (small game bird)

chuleta ⓕ choo·le·ta chop • cutlet • T-bone steak (Arg)

— de puerco de *pwer*·ko pork chop

chuños ⓜ pl (Bol) *choo*·nyos freeze-dried potatoes made by leaving potatoes out in the winter cold

chupe ⓜ *choo*·pe soup • stew • in Bolivia, a vegetable, meat & grain soup with a clear broth flavoured with **ají**, tomato, cumin or onion

— de camarones (Per) de ka·ma·ro·nes prawn soup

— de cóngrio (Chi) de *kon*·gryo conger-eel stew

— de locos (Chi) de *lo*·kos abalone stew

churrasco ⓜ choo·*ras*·ko rib steak • in Ecuador, a hearty dish of rice, fried beef, fried eggs, vegetables, fried potatoes, a slice of avocado, tomato & rice

ciruela ⓕ see·*rwe*·la plum

— seca *se*·ka prune

ckocko ⓜ (Bol) *ko*·ko spicy chicken cooked in wine or **chicha** & served with maize, olives, raisins & aromatic condiments

clericó ⓜ (Uru) kle·ree·*ko* usually a mixture of white wine, fruit juice, a liqueur, fruit salad, ice & a carbonated soft drink or cider

cocina ⓕ ko·*see*·na cuisine • kitchen

cocinado/a ⓜ/ⓕ ko·see·*na*·do/a cooked

cocinar ko·see·*nar* to cook

cocinero/a ⓜ/ⓕ ko·see·*ne*·ro/a chef

coco ⓜ *ko*·ko coconut

codorniz ⓕ ko·dor·*nees* quail

coles ⓜ pl **de Bruselas** *ko*·les de broo·se·las Brussels sprouts

coliflor ⓕ ko·lee·*flor* cauliflower

combinado ⓜ kom·bee·*na*·do cocktail

D

completo ⓜ (Chi) kom·*ple*·to a hot dog with the lot

con gas kon gas fizzy

con leche kon *le*·che with milk

coñac ⓜ ko·*nyak* brandy

conejo ⓜ ko·*ne*·kho rabbit

confitería ⓕ kon·fee·te·*ree*·a a candy store • sweet shop

confites ⓜ pl (Bol) kon·*fee*·tes festive candies consisting of coloured sugar syrup, nuts, aniseed, fruits, biscuit or coconut

copa ⓕ *ko*·pa glass

corazón ⓜ ko·ra·*son* heart

cordero ⓜ kor·*de*·ro lamb

cortado ⓜ (Arg) kor·*ta*·do coffee with a little milk

costilla ⓕ kos·*tee*·ya loin • spare rib

— de cerdo de *ser*·do pork chop

costillar ⓜ **de cordero** kos·tee·*yar* de kor·*de*·ro rack of lamb

crema ⓕ *kre*·ma cream

— batida ba·*tee*·da whipped cream

croquetas ⓕ pl (Cub) kro·*ke*·tas fried ham or chicken croquettes

crudo/a ⓜ/ⓕ *kroo*·do/a raw

crustáceos ⓜ pl kroos·*ta*·se·os shellfish

cuadril ⓜ kwa·*dreel* rump steak

cubo ⓜ **de hielo** *koo*·bo de *ye*·lo ice cube

curanto ⓜ (Chi) koo·*ran*·to hearty stew of fish, shellfish, chicken, pork, lamb, beef & potato

curtido ⓜ (Sal) koor·*tee*·do mixture of pickled beets, cabbage & carrots served with **pupusas**

cuy ⓜ kooy grilled or roasted guinea pig

~ D ~

damasco ⓜ da·*mas*·ko apricot

dátil ⓜ *da*·teel date

descafeinado/a ⓜ/ⓕ des·ka·fay·*na*·do/a decaffeinated

desnatado/a ⓜ/ⓕ des·na·*ta*·do/a low-fat

digestivo ⓜ dee·khes·*tee*·vo digestif

dorado/a ⓜ/ⓕ do·*ra*·do/a browned

dulce ⓜ **de leche** (Arg) *dool*·se de *le*·che caramelised condensed milk • filling in sweet pastries

dulce *dool*·se sweet

dulces ⓜ pl *dool*·ses sweets

~ E ~

(de) elaboración propia (de) e·la·bo·ra·*syon pro*·pya made on the premises

elote ⓜ (CAm) e·*lo*·te corn • corn on the cob

empanada ⓕ em·pa·*na*·da stuffed meat & vegetable turnover

empanadilla ⓕ (Pue) em·pa·na·*dee*·ya pocket of plantain or **yuca** dough stuffed with meat

empanadillas ⓕ pl **de jueyes** (Pue) em·pa·na·*dee*·yas de *khwe*·yes highly seasoned land crab meat baked into an **empanadilla** of cassava paste

empana ⓕ (Cub) em·*pa*·na meat or vegetable pattie

en escabeche (Pue) en es·ka·*be*·che way of preparing seafood by frying, then chilling & pickling it

en rodajas en ro·*da*·khas sliced

enchilladas ⓕ pl (Hon, Mex) en·chee·ya·das crisp fried tortilla topped with spicy meat, salad & crumbled cheese

endulzado/a ⓜ/ⓕ en·dool·*sa*·do/a sweetened

eneldo ⓜ e·*nel*·do dill

ensalada ⓕ en·sa·*la*·da salad • in El Salvador, a mixed fruit juice served with fruit salad floating on top

— mixta *meeks*·ta mixed salad

— rusa *roo*·sa vegetable salad with mayonnaise

— verde *ver*·de green salad

entremeses ⓜ pl en·tre·me·ses hors-d'oeuvres

erizos ⓜ pl (Chi) e·ree·sos sea urchins

escabeche ⓜ (Bol) es·ka·be·che vegetables, onion & peppers preserved in vinegar

espagueti ⓜ pl es·pa·ge·tee spaghetti

espárrago ⓜ es·pa·ra·go asparagus

especialidad ⓕ es·pe·sya·lee·da speciality

— de la casa de la ka·sa speciality of the house

— del día del dee·a speciality of the day

espinacas ⓕ pl es·pee·na·kas spinach

espumoso/a ⓜ/ⓕ es·poo·mo·so/a sparkling

estofado ⓜ es·to·fa·do stew

estofado/a ⓜ/ⓕ es·to·fa·do/a braised

estragón ⓜ es·tra·gon tarragon

~ F ~

faba ⓜ fa·ba type of dried bean

facturas ⓕ pl (Arg) fak·too·ras buns • cakes

faisán ⓜ fai·san pheasant

falso conejo ⓜ (Bol) fal·so ko·ne·kho 'false rabbit' – greasy, glutinous meat-based dish

fideos ⓜ pl fee·de·os noodles

filete ⓜ fee·le·te fillet of meat or fish

— de bife de bee·fe beef fillet

flan ⓜ flan creme caramel • egg custard

frambuesa ⓕ fram·bwe·sa raspberry

fresa ⓕ fre·sa strawberry

fresco/a ⓜ/ⓕ fres·ko/a fresh

frescos ⓜ pl (Hon) fres·kos fruit drinks blended with water & sugar

fricasés ⓜ (Bol) free·ka·ses pork or chicken stew with maize grits

frijol ⓜ free·khol bean

— blanco blan·ko large butter bean

frijoles ⓜ pl free·kho·les beans

— con arroz (Gua) kon a·ros beans & rice

frío/a ⓜ/ⓕ free·o/a cold

fritada ⓕ free·ta·da scraps of fried or roast pork

fritanga ⓕ free·tan·ga hotpot or stew • in Bolivia, spicy hot pork with mint & beans

frito/a ⓜ/ⓕ free·to/a fried

— a la sartén a la sar·ten pan-fried

fruta ⓕ froo·ta fruit

frutilla ⓕ froo·tee·ya strawberry

fuerte fwer·te strong

~ G ~

galleta ⓕ ga·ye·ta biscuit • cookie

gallina ⓕ ga·yee·na chicken

gallito ⓜ ga·yee·to cockerel

gallo ⓜ ga·yo rooster

gallo pinto (Cos, Nic, Pan) ga·yo peen·to lightly spiced mixture of rice & black beans traditionally served for breakfast, sometimes with **natilla** or fried eggs

gallos ⓜ pl (Cos) ga·yos tortilla sandwiches containing meat, beans or cheese

gambas ⓕ pl **rebozadas** gam·bas re·bo·sa·das batter-fried scampi (large prawns)

ganso ⓜ gan·so goose

garbanzo ⓜ gar·ban·so chickpea

gaseoso/a ⓜ/ⓕ ga·se·o·so/a fizzy

gazpacho ⓜ ga·spa·cho cold tomato & vegetable soup

ginebra ⓕ bols (Arg) khee·ne·bra bols alcoholic drink similar to gin

girasol ⓕ khee·ra·sol sunflower

glaseado/a ⓜ/ⓕ gla·se·a·do/a glazed • iced

gol ⓜ (Chi) gol translucent alcoholic mixture of butter, sugar & milk

granada ① gra·na·da pomegranate

grande gran·de big • large

grasa ① gra·sa fat • grease

gratinado/a ⓜ/① gra·tee·na·do/a au gratin

grosella ① gro·se·ya redcurrant

— espinosa es·pee·no·sa gooseberry

— negra ne·gra blackcurrant

güifiti ⓜ (Hon) gi·fee·tee mix of **aguardiente** with aromatic & marine plants – a Garífuna specialty

guinda (Per) geen·da sweet cherry brandy

guindado ⓜ (Chi) geen·da·do fermented alcoholic drink made from a cherry-like fruit, brandy, cinnamon & cloves

guindilla ① geen·dee·ya hot chilli

guisantes ⓜ pl gee·san·tes peas

guiso ⓜ (Cos) gee·so stew

güisqui ⓜ gwees·kee whisky

~ H ~

haba ① a·ba broad bean • Lima bean

hallaca ① (Ven) a·ya·ka chopped pork, beef and/or chicken with vegetables & olives, all folded in a maize dough, wrapped in banana leaves & steamed

hamburguesa ① am·boor·ge·sa hamburger

harina ① a·ree·na flour

hecho/a ⓜ/① e·cho/a made • prepared

heladería ① e·la·de·ree·a ice-cream parlour

helado/a ⓜ/① e·la·do/a chilled • iced

helado ⓜ e·la·do ice cream

hervido/a ⓜ/① er·vee·do/a boiled

— a fuego lento a fwe·go len·to simmered

hervir er·veer boil

hierba ① yer·ba herb

hierbabuena ① yer·ba·bwe·na mint

hígado ⓜ ee·ga·do liver

higo ⓜ ee·go fig

hocico ⓜ o·see·ko snout

hongo ⓜ on·go button mushroom

horchata ① (Cos) or·cha·ta rice-based drink flavoured with cinnamon

— de cebada (Sal) de se·ba·da sweet barley-based beverage spiced with cinnamon

hormiga culona (Col) or·mee·ga koo·lo·na large fried ants – unique to Santander

horneado/a ⓜ/① or·ne·a·do/a baked

hornear or·ne·ar bake

horno ⓜ or·no oven

horno, al or·no, al oven-baked

hortalizas ① pl or·ta·lee·sas vegetables

hueso ⓜ we·so bone

huevos ⓜ pl we·vos eggs

— cocidos ko·see·dos boiled eggs

— de paslama de pas·la·ma turtle eggs – a popular dish in Nicaragua though ecologically suspect

— duros doo·ros hard-boiled eggs

— estrellados es·tre·ya·dos fried eggs

— fritos free·tos fried eggs

— pericos pe·ree·kos scrambled eggs with fried onions

— revueltos re·vwel·tos scrambled eggs

humitas ① pl (Bol) oo·mee·tas corn **tamales** filled with spiced beef, vegetables & potatoes

— en chala (Chi) en cha·la popular & tasty snack of steamed **tamales** wrapped in corn husks

húngaros ⓜ pl (Uru) oon·ga·ros spicy sausages on a hot-dog roll

~ I ~

infusión ① een·foo·syon herbal tea

~ J ~

jabalí ⓜ kha·ba·lee wild boar
jamón ⓜ kha·mon ham
— dulce dool·se boiled ham
— serrano se·ra·no cured ham
jengibre ⓜ khen·khee·bre ginger
jochi ⓜ kho·chee agouti (a rodent prized for its meat)
jolque ⓜ (Bol) khol·ke kidney soup
jueyes ⓜ pl (Pue) khwe·yes land crabs – an island staple
jugo ⓜ khoo·go juice
— exprimido ⓜ ek·spree·mee·do freshly squeezed juice
jugoso/a ⓜ/ⓕ khoo·go·so/a succulent

~ K ~

kala purkha ⓕ (Bol) ka·la poor·ka soup made from maize cooked in a ceramic dish by adding a steaming chunk of heavy pumice
kosher ko·sher kosher
kuchen ⓜ (Chi) koo·chen pastries filled with local fruit, baked by Chileans of German descent

~ L ~

lager la·ger lager • light-coloured or pale beer
langosta ⓕ lan·gos·ta spiny lobster
langostino ⓜ lan·gos·tee·no lobster • prawn
lawa ⓕ (Bol) la·wa soup made from a broth thickened with corn starch or wheat flour
leche ⓕ le·che milk
— desnatada des·na·ta·da skimmed milk
lechón ⓜ le·chon suckling pig – a speciality of Cochabamba in Bolivia
lechona ⓕ (Col) le·cho·na pig carcass stuffed with its own meat, rice & dried peas & baked in an oven

lechuga ⓕ le·choo·ga lettuce
legumbre ⓕ le·goom·bre pulse
lengua ⓕ len·gwa tongue
lenguado ⓜ len·gwa·do dab • lemon sole
lenteja ⓕ len·te·kha lentil • in Ecuador, a lentil stew
lentejas ⓕ pl len·te·khas lentils
licuados ⓜ pl lee·kwa·dos milk-blended fruit drinks
lima ⓕ lee·ma lime
limón ⓜ lee·mon lemon
limonadas ⓕ pl lee·mo·na·das lemonade made with lime or lemon juice, water & sugar
lista ⓕ **de vinos** lees·ta de vee·nos wine list
llajhua ⓕ (Bol) ya·khwa hot **salsa** made from tomatoes & hot-pepper pods
llano/a ⓜ/ⓕ ya·no/a plain
llapingachos ⓜ pl (Ecu) ya·peen·ga·chos fried pancakes made from mashed potato & cheese, often served with **fritada**
llaucha ⓕ pl **paceña** (Bol) yow·cha pa·se·nya doughy cheese bread
locotos ⓜ pl (Bol) lo·ko·tos small hot-pepper pods
locro ⓜ lo·kro in Argentina & Paraguay, a maize stew • in Ecuador, potato soup with corn & avocado or cheese topping
lomo ⓜ lo·mo loin
— a lo pobre (Chi) a lo po·bre huge slab of beef topped with two fried eggs & served with French fries
— con pimientos kon pee·myen·tos pork sausage with peppers
— de cerdo de ser·do pork loin • sausage
— saltado (Per) sal·ta·do chopped steak fried with onions, tomatoes, potatoes & served with rice
longaniza ⓕ lon·ga·nee·sa dark pork sausage

M

~ M ~

macarrones ⓜ pl ma·ka·ro·nes macaroni

maíz ⓜ ma·ees corn • maize • sweet corn

mallorca ① (Pue) ma·yor·ka sweet pastry covered with powdered sugar

malta ① (Pue) mal·ta nonalcoholic, vitamin-fortified malt beverage

mandarina ① man·da·ree·na tangerine

mango ⓜ man·go mango

maní ⓜ ma·nee peanut

mantequilla ① man·te·kee·ya butter

manzana ① man·sa·na apple

maracuyá ① ma·ra·koo·ya passionfruit

marinado/a ⓜ/① ma·ree·na·do/a marinated

mariscos ⓜ pl ma·rees·kos seafood • shellfish

masaco ⓜ (Bol) ma·sa·ko llama **charque** served with mashed plantain or **yuca**

matambre relleno (Arg) ma·tam·bre re·ye·no stuffed & rolled flank steak, baked or eaten cold as an appetiser

mate ⓜ ma·te tea prepared from **yerba mate** – the most popular hot beverage in Argentina, Paraguay & Uruguay

— de coca (Bol, Per) de ko·ka coca-leaf tea

mavi ⓜ (Pue) ma·vee a root beer–like drink made from the bark of the ironwood tree

mayonesa ① ma·yo·ne·sa mayonnaise

mazamorro ⓜ ma·sa·mo·ro in Costa Rica, a pudding made from corn starch • in Paraguay, corn mush

mazapan ⓜ ma·sa·pan almond paste • marzipan

mazorca ① ma·sor·ka corn on the cob

mbaipy heé ① (Par) mba·ee·pee e·e dessert of corn, milk & molasses

mbaipy soó ⓜ (Par) mba·ee·pee so·o hot maize pudding with meat chunks

mbeyú ⓜ (Par) mbe·yoo grilled manioc pancake

medialunas ① pl me·dya·loo·nas 'half moons' – small croissants (a popular breakfast food in Argentine cafes)

mediana ① me·dya·na bottle (third of a litre)

medianoche ⓜ (Pue) me·dya·no·che ham, pork & cheese sandwich

medio y medio ⓜ (Uru) me·dyo ee me·dyo mixture of sparkling wine & white wine

mejilla ① me·khee·ya cheek

mejillones ⓜ pl me·khee·yo·nes mussels

— al vapor al va·por steamed mussels

melocotón ⓜ me·lo·ko·ton peach

melón ⓜ me·lon melon

membrillo ⓜ mem·bree·yo quince

menta ⓜ men·ta mint

menú ⓜ me·noo menu

menudencias ① pl (SAm) me·noo·den·syas giblets

menudo de pollo me·noo·do de po·yo gizzard • poultry entrails

mercado ⓜ mer·ka·do market

merengadas ① pl (Ven) me·ren·ga·das milkshake with juice

merluza ① mer·loo·sa hake – in Argentina, it's served batter-fried with mashed potatoes

— a la plancha ① a la plan·cha grilled hake

mermelada ① mer·me·la·da jam

miel ① myel honey

migas ① pl mee·gas fried breadcrumb dish

mil hojas ① pl (Pue) meel o·khas 'a thousand leaves' – layers of thin pastry filled with almond & honey paste

milanesa ① mee·la·ne·sa schnitzel

milcao ⓜ (Chi) meel·kow potato bread

mojama ① mo·kha·ma cured tuna

mojo ⓜ **isleño** (Pue) mo·kho ees·le·nyo piquant sauce of vinegar, tomato sauce, olive oil, onions, capers, pimentos, olives, bay leaves & garlic – often served with fried fish

molleja ① mo·ye·kha sweetbread

mondongo ⓜ (Ven) mon·don·go seasoned tripe cooked in bouillon with maize, potatoes & other vegetables

montado ⓜ mon·ta·do tiny sandwich served as an appetiser

mora ① mo·ra blackberry

morcilla ① mor·see·ya blood sausage – a common **asado** dish

moros y cristianos ⓜ pl (Cub) mo·ros ee krees·tya·nos 'Moors & Christians' – dish of black beans & rice

mostaza ① mos·ta·sa mustard

mosto ⓜ (Par) mos·to sugar-cane juice

mote ⓜ **con huesillo** (Chi) mo·te kon we·see·yo peach nectar with barley kernels

muchacho ⓜ (Ven) moo·cha·cho roast loin of beef served in sauce

muslo ⓜ moos·lo thigh

muy hecho/a ⓜ/① mooy e·cho/a well-done

~ N ~

nabo ⓜ na·bo turnip

nacatamales ⓜ pl (Nic) na·ka·ta·ma·les cornmeal, meat, vegetables & herbs wrapped in banana leaves

naranja ① na·ran·kha orange

naranjadas ① pl na·ran·kha·das lemonades made with orange juice

nata ① na·ta cream

natilla ① (Cos) na·tee·ya sour cream

natillas ① pl na·tee·yas creamy milk dessert • custard

nuez ⓜ nwes nut • walnut

~ O ~

ocas ① pl (Bol) o·kas tough, purple, potato-like tubers

ojo ⓜ **de bife** o·kho de bee·fe eye of round steak

olímpicos ⓜ pl (Uru) o·leem·pee·kos club sandwiches

oporto ⓜ o·por·to port

orejón ⓜ o·re·khon dried apricot

orgánico/a ⓜ/① or·ga·nee·ko/a organic

ostión ⓜ os·tyon scallop

ostiones ⓜ pl (Cub) os·tyo·nes drink or appetiser containing mussels or oysters, rum, lime juice, salt & pepper

ostras ① pl os·tras oysters

oveja ① o·ve·kha ewe

~ P ~

pabellón ⓜ (Ven) pa·be·yon main course consisting of shredded beef, rice, beans & fried plantain – Venezuela's national dish

pacumutas ① pl (Bol) pa·koo·moo·tas enormous chunks of grilled meat accompanied by **yuca**, onions & other trimmings

paila ① **marina** (Chi) pai·la ma·ree·na fish & shellfish chowder

pajarito ⓜ pa·kha·ree·to small bird

paleta ① pa·le·ta shoulder

palmitos ⓜ pl (Cos) pal·mee·tos hearts of palm – usually served in a vinegar dressing

paloma ① pa·lo·ma pigeon

palta ① (SAm) pal·ta avocado

— a la jardinera (Per) a la khar·dee·ne·ra avocado stuffed with cold vegetables & mayonnaise

— a la reina (Per) a la ray·na avocado stuffed with chicken salad

pan ⓜ pan bread
— de coco (Hon) de ko·ko coconut bread
panapen ⓜ (Pue) pa·na·pen breadfruit
panchos ⓜ pl (Arg, Uru) pan·chos mild sausages on a hot-dog roll
panes ⓜ pl (Sal) pa·nes French breads sliced open & stuffed with chicken or turkey
papas ① pl pa·pas potatoes
— fritas free·tas chips • French fries
— rellenas (Bol) re·ye·nas stuffed potatoes – a speciality from the central highlands
papitas ① pl pa·pee·tas crisps • potato chips
parrilla ① pa·ree·ya grill
parrillada ① pa·ree·ya·da mixed grill – huge slabs of grilled meat prepared over hot coals, served with spicy sauces & vegetables • steak house – an institution in Argentina
pasa ⓜ pa·sa raisin
pasankalla ① (Bol) pa·san·ka·ya puffed maize with caramel – very sticky & chewy concoction
pasta ① pas·ta pasta
pastel ⓜ pas·tel cake • pastry • in Puerto Rico, a sweeter version of an **empanadilla** with a stuffing of raisins, beans, fish or pork
— de choclo (Chi) de cho·klo maize casserole filled with vegetables, chicken & beef
pastelillos ⓜ pl (Pue) pas·te·lee·yos smaller version of a **pastel** stuffed with meat & cheese
patacones ⓜ pl (Cos, Pan) pa·ta·ko·nes fried green plantains cut into thin pieces, salted, then pressed & fried
patita ① **de cerdo** pa·tee·ta de ser·do pig's trotter
pato ⓜ pa·to duck
pavo ⓜ pa·vo turkey

pebre ⓜ (Chi) pe·bre tasty condiment made from chopped tomatoes, onion, garlic, chilli peppers, coriander & parsley
pechuga ① pe·choo·ga breast meat
pedido ⓜ pe·dee·do order
pejibaye ⓜ (Cos) pe·khee·ba·ye starchy palm fruit also eaten as a salad
pepinillo ⓜ pe·pee·nee·yo gherkin
pepino ⓜ pe·pee·no cucumber
pera ① pe·ra pear
perca ① per·ka perch
perdiz ① per·dees partridge
perejil ⓜ pe·re·kheel parsley
perico ⓜ (Col) pe·ree·ko small milk coffee
pescadilla ① pes·ka·dee·ya whiting
pescado ⓜ pes·ka·do fish
— de agua dulce de a·gwa dool·se freshwater fish
— de mar ⓜ de mar saltwater fish
pescaíto ⓜ pes·ka·ee·to tiny fried fish
pez ⓜ **espada** pes es·pa·da swordfish
picada ① (Arg) pee·ka·da snack
picadillo ⓜ pee·ka·dee·yo minced meat • in Cuba, ground beef hash with capsicum, raisins, ham, spices, olives & rice
picante pee·kan·te spicy
pierna ① pyer·na leg
pil pil ⓜ peel peel often spicy garlic sauce
pimentón ⓜ pee·men·ton paprika
pimienta ① pee·myen·ta pepper
pimiento ⓜ pee·myen·to bell pepper • capsicum
piña ① pee·nya pineapple
pinchita ① (Pue) peen·chee·ta homemade, illegal rum
pincho ⓜ peen·cho kebab
piñón ⓜ pee·nyon pine nut
pintado ⓜ (Col) peen·ta·do small milk coffee

piononos ⑩ pl (Pue) pyo·no·nos deep-fried cones made from plantains stuffed with cheese (or meat) & coated with egg batter

pipas ① pl (Cos) pee·pas green coconuts with a straw to drink the milk

pique ⑩ **a lo macho** (Bol) pee·ke a lo ma·cho chunked grilled beef & sausage served with French fries, lettuce, tomatoes, onions, capsicum & **locotos**

pisco ⑩ (Chi, Per) pees·ko grape brandy – often served as a **pisco sauer** with egg white, lemon juice & powdered sugar

pistacho ⑩ pees·ta·cho pistachio

plancha ① plan·cha grill

plátano ⑩ pla·ta·no banana • plantain

— maduro (Pan) ma·doo·ro slices of ripe plantains baked or broiled with butter, brown sugar & cinnamon

platija ① pla·tee·kha flounder

plato ⑩ pla·to dish • plate

poché po·che poached

poco hecho/a ⑩/① po·ko e·cho/a rare

pollo ⑩ po·yo chicken

— a la canasta (Bol) a la ka·nas·ta 'chicken in a basket' – chicken served with mustard, fries or **yuca** & **ají**

polvo ⑩ pol·vo powder

pomelo ⑩ po·me·lo grapefruit

porotos ⑩ pl po·ro·tos beans

porrón ⑩ **de cerveza** po·ron de ser·ve·sa bottled beer

postre ⑩ pos·tre dessert

potaje ⑩ po·ta·khe stew

primer ⑩ **plato** pree·mer pla·to entree • first course

puchero ⑩ (Arg) poo·che·ro casserole with beef, chicken, bacon, sausage, blood sausage, maize, peppers, tomatoes, onions, cabbage, sweet potatoes & squash

puerros ⑩ pl pwe·ros leek

pukacapa ① (Bol) poo·ka·ka·pa circular **empanada** filled with cheese, olives, onions & hot-pepper sauce

pulpo ⑩ pool·po octopus

— a la gallega a la ga·ye·ga octopus in sauce

punto, a poon·to, a medium (steak)

pupusas ① pl (Sal) poo·poo·sas cornmeal pastry stuffed with farmer's cheese, refried beans, **chicharrón,** or all three (called **revuelta**)

~ **Q** ~

queque ⑩ ke·ke cake

— seco se·ko pound cake

quesillos ⑩ pl (Nic) ke·see·yos soft cheese & onions folded in a **tortilla**

quesito ⑩ (Pue) ke·see·to sweet baked shell stuffed with cheese & topped with honey

queso ⑩ ke·so cheese

— fruta bomba (Cub) froo·ta bom·ba appetiser of warm papaya & cheese

quinoa ⑩ (Bol) kee·no·a nutritious indigenous grain high in protein & used to thicken stews

quinto ⑩ keen·to very small bottle

~ **R** ~

rábano ⑩ ra·ba·no radish

rabo ⑩ ra·bo tail

ración ① ra·syon small tapas plate or dish

rancio/a ⑩/① ran·syo/a stale

ranga ① (Bol) ran·ga potato soup with chopped liver

rape ⑩ ra·pe monkfish

raspados ⑩ pl (Pan) ras·pa·dos cones made of shaved ice topped with fruit syrup & sweetened condensed milk

refresco ⑩ (Bol) re·fres·ko fruit-based juice with a dried peach in it

refrescos ⑩ pl re·fres·kos soft drinks

relleno ⓜ re·ye·no stuffing • in Bolivia, a stuffed corn fritter similar to **humitas**

relleno/a ⓜ/ⓕ re·ye·no/a stuffed

remolacha ⓕ re·mo·la·cha beetroot

repollo ⓜ re·po·yo cabbage

revoltijo ⓜ re·vol·tee·kho scrambled egg

revuelta ⓕ (Sal) re·vwel·ta cornmeal pastry stuffed with farmer's cheese, refried beans and fried pork fat

riñón ⓜ ree·nyon kidney

rodaja ⓕ ro·da·kha slice

romero ⓜ ro·me·ro rosemary

ron ⓜ ron rum

rondón ⓜ (Cos) ron·don thick seafood-based soup blended with coconut milk

ropa vieja (Pan) ro·pa vye·kha 'old clothes' – spicy shredded-beef combination served over rice

rosado ⓜ ro·sa·do rosé

rostro asado (Bol) ros·tro a·sa·do roasted sheep's head

ruibarbo ⓜ rooy·bar·bo rhubarb

~ S ~

sal ⓕ sal salt

salado/a ⓜ/ⓕ sa·la·do salted • salty

salchichas ⓕ pl sal·chee·chas sausages similar to hot dogs

salmón ⓜ sal·mon salmon

salpicón ⓜ (Cub) sal·pee·kon salad made from cold meat, potatoes, olives, capers, onion, lettuce, pineapple, capsicum & vinegar

salsa ⓕ sal·sa sauce

— de carne de kar·ne gravy

salteado/a ⓜ/ⓕ sal·te·a·do/a sauteed

salteñas ⓕ pl (Bol) sal·te·nyas delicious rugby ball–shaped meat & vegetable pasties that originated in Salta, Argentina

salvaje sal·va·khe wild

sancocho ⓜ san·ko·cho in Panama, a spicy chicken & vegetable stew • in Puerto Rico, vegetable soup containing plantains, tomatoes, green pepper, chilli pepper, cilantro leaves, onion & corn kernels • in Venezuela, vegetable stew with meat, fish or chicken

sandía ⓕ san·dee·a watermelon

sangre ⓕ san·gre blood

sangría ⓕ san·gree·a red-wine punch

sardina ⓕ sar·dee·na sardine

seco ⓜ (Ecu) se·ko 'dry' – meat stew served with rice

seco/a ⓜ/ⓕ se·ko/a dried • dry

segundo plato se·goon·do pla·to main course

sémola ⓕ se·mo·la semolina

sepia ⓕ se·pya cuttlefish

sésamo ⓜ se·sa·mo sesame

sesos ⓜ pl se·sos brains

sidra ⓕ see·dra cider

silpancho ⓜ (Bol) seel·pan·cho a thin greasy schnitzel

sin cubierto seen koo·byer·to no cover charge

sin gas seen gas still

sin grasa seen gra·sa lean

sobrasada ⓕ so·bra·sa·da soft pork sausage

sofrito ⓜ (Pue) so·free·to seasoning consisting of garlic, onions & pepper browned in olive oil, then flavoured with annatto seeds

soja ⓕ so·kha soya

solomillo ⓜ so·lo·mee·yo sirloin

sooyo sopy ⓜ (Par) soo·yo so·pee thick soup of ground meat, accompanied by rice or noodles

sopa ⓕ so·pa soup

— a la criolla (Per) a la kree·o·ya lightly spiced noodle soup with beef, egg, milk & vegetables

— de caracol (Hon) de ka·ra·kol conch soup made with coconut

— de mariscos (Chi) de ma·*rees*·kos shellfish soup
— de mondongo (Hon) de mon·*don*·go tripe soup – reputed to be a good hangover remedy
— de pescado de pes·*ka*·do fish soup
— paraguaya ① (Par) pa·ra·*gwa*·ya corn bread with cheese & onion
sopaipa ① (Chi) so·*pai*·pa dark-brown unbaked wheat & flour bread
sopaipillas ① (Bol) so·pai·*pee*·yas sweet fried breads
sopón ⑩ **de pescado** (Pue) so·*pon* de pes·*ka*·do fish soup flavoured with garlic, onions & sherry
submarino ⑩ (Arg) soob·ma·*ree*·no breakfast beverage consisting of a semisweet chocolate bar dissolved in steamed milk
suflé ⑩ soo·*fle* souffle

~ T ~

tajadas ① pl (Nic, Pan, Ven) ta·*kha*·das sliced plantains served as a base for grilled meat & cabbage salad
tajaditas ① pl (Hon) ta·kha·*dee*·tas crispy, fried banana chips
tallarines ⑩ pl ta·ya·*ree*·nes noodles mixed with pork, chicken, beef or vegetables sold at **chifas**
tamales ⑩ pl ta·*ma*·les cornmeal dough filled with spiced beef, vegetables & potatoes, wrapped in a maize husk & fried, grilled or baked • in Colombia, chopped pork with rice & vegetables folded in a maize dough, wrapped in banana leaves & steamed
— asados (Cos) a·*sa*·dos sweet cornmeal cakes
tarta ① *tar*·ta cake
tasajo ⑩ (Pan) ta·*sa*·kho dried meat cooked with vegetables
tatú ⑩ ta·*too* armadillo

tawa-tawas ⑩ (Bol) ta·wa·*ta*·was type of doughnut
té ⑩ te tea
— con leche kon *le*·che tea with milk
— con limón kon lee·*mon* tea with lemon
— de menta de *men*·ta mint tea
— sin leche seen *le*·che black tea
tembleque ⑩ (Pue) tem·*ble*·ke pudding-like concoction of coconut milk & cinnamon
tereré (Par) te·re·*re* ice-cold **mate**
ternera ① ter·*ne*·ra veal
thimpu ⑩ (Bol) *teem*·poo spicy lamb & vegetable stew
tibio/a ⑩/① *tee*·byo/a warm
timochenko ⑩ (Hon) tee·mo·*chen*·ko **aguardiente** mixed with aromatic plants of the region
tinto ⑩ *teen*·to red (wine) • in Colombia, a small cup of black coffee
tira ① **de asado** *tee*·ra de a·*sa*·do a narrow strip of rib roast
tocino ⑩ to·*see*·no bacon
— ahumado a·oo·*ma*·do smoked bacon
— con queso kon *ke*·so cold bacon with cheese
tojorí ⑩ (Bol) to·kho·*ree* oatmeal-like concoction of mashed corn, cinnamon & sugar
tomatada ① **de cordero** (Bol) to·ma·*ta*·da de kor·*de*·ro lamb stew with tomato sauce
tomate ⑩ to·*ma*·te tomato
torta ① *tor*·ta cake • flan • tart
tortilla ① tor·*tee*·ya omelette
— de maíz (Ecu, Pan) de ma·*ees* thick, fried cornmeal tortilla
tortillas ① pl **con quesillo** (Hon) tor·*tee*·yas kon ke·*see*·lyo two crisp fried tortillas with melted white cheese between them
tortuga ① tor·*too*·ga turtle
tostada ① tos·*ta*·da toast
tostones ⑩ pl (Pue) tos·*to*·nes fried green plantains

U

trigo ⓜ *tree*·go wheat
tripa ⓕ *tree*·pa tripe
— **gorda** *gor*·da large intestine (a common **asado** dish)
tripas ⓕ pl *tree*·pas offal
trozo ⓜ *tro*·so piece • slice
trucha ⓕ *troo*·cha trout
trufa ⓕ *troo*·fa truffle
tubo ⓜ *too*·bo tall glass
tucumana ⓕ (Bol) too·koo·*ma*·na heavily spiced puff-pastry shell packed with egg, potatoes, chicken & onions
tuétano ⓜ *twe*·ta·no bone marrow
turrón ⓜ too·*ron* almond nougat

~ U ~

ubre ⓕ *oo*·bre udder
uva ⓕ *oo*·va grape

~ V ~

vaca ⓕ *va*·ka beef
vacío ⓜ va·*see*·o flank steak – textured & chewy, but tasty
vainilla ⓕ vai·*nee*·ya vanilla
vapor ⓜ va·*por* steam
vapor, al va·*por*, al steamed
vaso ⓜ *va*·so glass
vegetal ⓜ ve·khe·*tal* vegetable
vegetariano/a ⓜ/ⓕ ve·khe·ta·*rya*·no/a vegetarian
venado ⓜ ve·*na*·do venison
venera ⓕ ve·*ne*·ra scallop
verduras ⓕ pl ver·*doo*·ras green vegetables

vigorón ⓜ (Nic) vee·go·*ron* cassava steamed & topped with fried pork rind & cabbage salad, usually served on a banana leaf
vinagre ⓜ vee·*na*·gre vinegar
vino ⓜ *vee*·no wine
— **de la casa** de la *ka*·sa house wine
— **espumoso** es·poo·*mo*·so sparkling wine
— **(muy) seco** (mooy) *se*·ko (very) dry wine

~ W ~

wafle ⓜ *wa*·fle waffle
witu ⓜ (Bol) gwee·too beef stew with pureed tomatoes

~ Y ~

yaguarlocro ⓜ (Ecu) ya·gwar·*lo*·kro potato soup with chunks of barely congealed blood sausage floating in it
yerba ⓕ **mate** yer·ba *ma*·te dried chopped leaf of Ilex Paraguayensis which is made into a tea in Argentina, Uruguay & Paraguay
yogur ⓜ yo·*goor* yogurt
yuca ⓕ *yoo*·ka cassava – a common staple in Latin American cuisine

~ Z ~

zanahoria ⓕ sa·na·o·rya carrot
zapallo ⓜ (SAm) sa·*pa*·yo pumpkin
zarzuela ⓕ **de marisco** sar·*swe*·la de ma·*rees*·ko seafood stew

Dictionary
ENGLISH *to* SPANISH
inglés – español

Nouns in the dictionary have their gender indicated by ⓜ or ⓕ. If it's a plural noun, you'll also see pl. When a word that could be either a noun or a verb has no gender indicated, it's a verb.

A

(be) able poder po·*der*
aboard a bordo a *bor*·do
abortion aborto ⓜ a·*bor*·to
about sobre *so*·bre
above arriba a·*ree*·ba
abroad en el extranjero en el ek·stran·*khe*·ro
accept aceptar a·sep·*tar*
accident accidente ⓜ ak·see·*den*·te
accommodation alojamiento ⓜ a·lo·kha·*myen*·to
across a través a tra·*ves*
activist activista ⓜ&ⓕ ak·tee·*vees*·ta
acupuncture acupuntura ⓕ a·koo·poon·*too*·ra
adaptor adaptador ⓜ a·dap·ta·*dor*
addicted adicto/a ⓜ/ⓕ a·*deek*·to/a
address dirección ⓕ dee·rek·*syon*
administration administración ⓕ ad·mee·nees·tra·*syon*
admission price precio ⓜ de entrada *pre*·syo de en·*tra*·da
admit (accept) admitir ad·mee·*teer*
admit (acknowledge) reconocer re·ko·no·*ser*
admit (allow to enter) dejar entrar de·*khar* en·*trar*

adult adulto/a ⓜ/ⓕ a·*dool*·to/a
advertisement anuncio ⓜ a·*noon*·syo
advice consejo ⓜ kon·*se*·kho
advise aconsejar a·kon·se·*khar*
after después de des·*pwes* de
aftershave loción ⓕ para después del afeitado lo·*syon* pa·ra des·*pwes* del a·fay·*ta*·do
again otra vez *o*·tra ves
age edad ⓕ e·*da*
aggressive agresivo/a ⓜ/ⓕ a·gre·*see*·vo/a
agree estar de acuerdo es·*tar* de a·*kwer*·do
agriculture agricultura ⓕ a·gree·kool·*too*·ra
AIDS SIDA ⓜ *see*·da
air aire ⓜ *ai*·re
(by) airmail por vía aérea por *vee*·a a·*e*·re·a
air-conditioned con aire acondicionado kon *ai*·re a·kon·dee·syo·*na*·do
airline aerolínea ⓕ a·e·ro·*lee*·ne·a
airport aeropuerto ⓜ a·e·ro·*pwer*·to
airport tax tasa ⓕ del aeropuerto *ta*·sa del a·e·ro·*pwer*·to

aisle (plane, train) pasillo ⓜ
pa·see·yo
alarm clock despertador ⓜ
des·per·ta·dor
all (singular) todo/a ⓜ/ⓕ sg
to·do/a
all (plural) todos/as ⓜ/ⓕ pl
to·dos/as
allergy alergia ⓕ a·ler·khya
allow permitir per·mee·teer
almond almendra ⓕ al·men·dra
almost casi ka·see
alone solo/a ⓜ/ⓕ so·lo/a
already ya ya
also también tam·byen
altitude altura ⓕ al·too·ra
altitude sickness soroche ⓜ
so·ro·che
always siempre syem·pre
ambassador embajador(a)ⓜ/ⓕ
em·ba·kha·dor/em·ba·kha·do·ra
ambulance ambulancia ⓕ
am·boo·lan·sya
among entre en·tre
amount cantidad ⓕ kan·tee·da
anarchist anarquista ⓜ&ⓕ
a·nar·kees·ta
ancient antiguo/a ⓜ/ⓕ
an·tee·gwo/a
and y ee
angry enojado/a ⓜ/ⓕ
e·no·kha·do/a
animal animal ⓜ a·nee·mal
animal rights derechos ⓜ pl de
animales de·re·chos de
a·nee·ma·les
ankle tobillo ⓜ to·bee·yo
annoyed fastidiado/a ⓜ/ⓕ
fas·tee·dya·do/a
answer respuesta ⓕ res·pwes·ta
answering machine contestador ⓜ
automático kon·tes·ta·dor
ow·to·ma·tee·ko
ant hormiga ⓕ or·mee·ga
antibiotics antibióticos ⓜ pl
an·tee·byo·tee·kos

antihistamines antihistaminicos ⓜ pl
an·tee·ees·ta·mee·nee·kos
antimalarial tablets pastillas ⓕ pl
antipalúdicas pas·tee·yas
an·tee·pa·loo·dee·kas
antique antigüedad ⓕ an·tee·gwe·da
antiseptic antiséptico ⓜ
an·tee·sep·tee·ko
any (singular) alguno/a ⓜ/ⓕ sg
al·goo·no/a
any (plural) algunos/as ⓜ/ⓕ pl
al·goo·nos/as
appendix apéndice ⓜ a·pen·dee·se
apple manzana ⓕ man·sa·na
appointment cita ⓕ see·ta
apricot damasco da·mas·ko
archaeological arqueológico/a ⓜ/ⓕ
ar·ke·o·lo·khee·ko/a
architect arquitecto/a ⓜ/ⓕ
ar·kee·tek·to/a
architecture arquitectura ⓕ
ar·kee·tek·too·ra
Argentina Argentina ⓕ
ar·khen·tee·na
argue discutir dees·koo·teer
arm brazo ⓜ bra·so
armadillo armadillo ⓜ ar·ma·dee·yo
army ejercito ⓜ e·kher·see·to
arrest detener de·te·ner
arrivals llegadas ⓕ pl ye·ga·das
arrive llegar ye·gar
art arte ⓜ ar·te
art gallery museo ⓜ de arte
moo·se·o de ar·te
artist artista ⓜ&ⓕ ar·tees·ta
ashtray cenicero ⓜ se·nee·se·ro
ask (a question) preguntar
pre·goon·tar
ask (for something) pedir pe·deer
aspirin aspirina ⓕ as·pee·ree·na
asthma asma ⓜ as·ma
athletics atletismo ⓜ at·le·tees·mo
atmosphere atmósfera ⓕ
at·mos·fe·ra
aubergine berenjena ⓕ
be·ren·khe·na

aunt tía ① *tee*·a
automatic automático/a ⓜ/① ow·to·*ma*·tee·ko/a
ATM cajero ⓜ automático ka·*khe*·ro ow·to·*ma*·tee·ko
autumn otoño ⓜ o·*to*·nyo
avenue avenida ① a·ve·*nee*·da
avocado palta ① *pal*·ta

B&W (film) blanco y negro *blan*·ko ee *ne*·gro
baby bebé ⓜ&① be·*be*
baby food comida ① de bebé ko·*mee*·da de be·*be*
baby powder talco ⓜ *tal*·ko
back (body) espalda ① es·*pal*·da
backpack mochila ① mo·*chee*·la
bacon tocino ⓜ to·*see*·no
bad malo/a ⓜ/① *ma*·lo/a
bag (general) bolso ⓜ *bol*·so
bag (shopping) bolsa ① (de compras) *bol*·sa (de *kom*·pras)
baggage equipaje ⓜ e·kee·*pa*·khe
baggage allowance límite ⓜ de equipaje *lee*·mee·te de e·kee·*pa*·khe
baggage claim recogida ① de equipajes re·ko·*khee*·da de e·kee·*pa*·khes
bakery panadería ① pa·na·de·*ree*·a
balance (account) saldo ⓜ *sal*·do
balcony balcón ⓜ bal·*kon*
ball pelota ① pe·*lo*·ta
ballpoint pen bolígrafo ⓜ bo·*lee*·gra·fo
banana (CAm) plátano ⓜ *pla*·ta·no
banana (SAm) banana ① ba·*na*·na
banana (Ven) cambur ⓜ kam·*boor*
band (music) grupo ⓜ *groo*·po
bandage vendaje ⓜ ven·*da*·khe
Band-Aids curitas ① pl koo·*ree*·tas
bank (money) banco ⓜ *ban*·ko
bank account cuenta ① bancaria *kwen*·ta ban·*ka*·rya
banknotes billetes ⓜ pl de banco bee·*ye*·tes de *ban*·ko

baptism bautizo ⓜ bow·*tee*·so
barber barbero ⓜ bar·*be*·ro
basket canasta ① ka·*nas*·ta
bath baño ⓜ *ba*·nyo
bath tub bañera ① ba·*nye*·ra
bathing suit malla ① de baño • traje ⓜ de baño *ma*·ya de *ba*·nyo • *tra*·khe de *ba*·nyo
bathroom baño ⓜ *ba*·nyo
battery (car) batería ① ba·te·*ree*·a
battery (general) pila ① *pee*·la
be estar • ser es·*tar* • ser
beach playa ① *pla*·ya
beans frijoles ⓜ pl free·*kho*·les
beautician esteticista ⓜ&① es·te·tee·*sees*·ta
beautiful bello/a ⓜ/① *be*·yo/a
beauty salon salón ⓜ de belleza sa·*lon* de be·*ye*·sa
because porque *por*·ke
bed cama ① *ka*·ma
bedding ropa ① de cama *ro*·pa de *ka*·ma
bedroom habitación ① a·bee·ta·*syon*
bee abeja ① a·*be*·kha
beef carne ① de vaca *kar*·ne de *va*·ka
beer cerveza ① ser·*ve*·sa
beetroot remolacha ① re·mo·*la*·cha
before antes *an*·tes
beggar mendigo/a ⓜ/① men·*dee*·go/a
begin comenzar ko·men·*sar*
behind detrás de de·*tras* de
bell pepper pimiento ⓜ pee·*myen*·to
below abajo a·*ba*·kho
Belize Belice ① be·*lee*·se
best mejor me·*khor*
bet apuesta ① a·*pwes*·ta
better mejor me·*khor*
between entre *en*·tre
bible biblia ① *bee*·blya
bicycle bicicleta ① bee·see·*kle*·ta
big grande *gran*·de
bike bici ① *bee*·see
bike chain cadena ① de bici ka·*de*·na de *bee*·see

B

bike path camino ⓜ de bici
ka·*mee*·no de *bee*·see

bill (account) cuenta ⓕ *kwen*·ta

biography biografía ⓕ byo·gra·*fee*·a

bird pájaro ⓜ *pa*·kha·ro

birth certificate partida ⓕ
de nacimiento par·*tee*·da de
na·see·*myen*·to

birthday cumpleaños ⓜ
koom·ple·a·nyos

biscuit galleta ⓕ ga·*ye*·ta

bite (dog) mordedura ⓕ
mor·de·*doo*·ra

bite (insect) picadura ⓕ
pee·ka·*doo*·ra

black negro/a ⓜ/ⓕ *ne*·gro/a

blanket frazada ⓕ fra·*sa*·da

blind ciego/a ⓜ/ⓕ *sye*·go/a

blister ampolla ⓕ am·*po*·ya

blocked atascado/a ⓜ/ⓕ
a·tas·*ka*·do/a

blood sangre ⓕ *san*·gre

blood group grupo ⓜ sanguíneo
groo·po san·*gee*·ne·o

blood pressure presión ⓕ arterial
pre·*syon* ar·te·*ryal*

blood test análisis ⓜ de sangre
a·*na*·lee·sees de *san*·gre

blue azul a·*sool*

board (plane, ship) embarcarse
em·bar·*kar*·se

boarding house pensión ⓕ pen·*syon*

boarding pass tarjeta ⓕ de
embarque tar·*khe*·ta de em·*bar*·ke

boat barco ⓜ *bar*·ko

body cuerpo ⓜ *kwer*·po

Bolivia Bolivia ⓕ bo·*lee*·vya

bomb bomba ⓕ *bom*·ba

bone hueso ⓜ *we*·so

book libro ⓜ *lee*·bro

book (reserve) reservar re·ser·*var*

booked out lleno/a ⓜ/ⓕ *ye*·no/a

bookshop librería ⓕ lee·bre·*ree*·a

boots botas ⓕ pl *bo*·tas

border (frontier) frontera ⓕ
fron·*te*·ra

borders (photography) marcos ⓜ pl
mar·kos

(be) bored (estar) aburrido/a ⓜ/ⓕ
(es·*tar*) a·boo·*ree*·do/a

boring aburrido/a ⓜ/ⓕ
a·boo·*ree*·do/a

borrow pedir pe·*deer*

botanic garden jardín ⓜ botánico
khar·*deen* bo·*ta*·nee·ko

both ambos/as ⓜ/ⓕ pl *am*·bos/as

bottle botella ⓕ bo·*te*·ya

bottle opener abrebotellas ⓜ
a·bre·bo·*te*·yas

(at the) bottom (al) fondo (de)
(al) *fon*·do (de)

bowl bol ⓜ bol

box caja ⓕ *ka*·kha

boxing boxeo ⓜ bok·*se*·o

boy chico ⓜ *chee*·ko

boyfriend novio ⓜ *no*·vyo

bra corpiño ⓜ kor·*pee*·nyo

brake freno ⓜ pl *fre*·no

brandy coñac ⓜ ko·*nyak*

brave valiente va·*lyen*·te

Brazil Brasil ⓜ bra·*seel*

bread pan ⓜ pan

bread rolls bollos ⓜ pl *bo*·yos

break romper rom·*per*

break down descomponerse
des·kom·po·*ner*·se

breakfast desayuno ⓜ de·sa·*yoo*·no

breast (poultry) pechuga ⓕ
pe·*choo*·ga

breasts senos ⓜ pl *se*·nos

breathe respirar res·pee·*rar*

bribe (CAm) mordida ⓕ mor·*dee*·da

bribe (SAm) coima ⓕ *koy*·ma

bribe coimear koy·me·*ar*

bridge puente ⓜ *pwen*·te

briefcase maletín ⓜ ma·le·*teen*

brilliant brillante bree·*lyan*·te

bring traer tra·*er*

broken roto/a ⓜ/ⓕ *ro*·to/a

broken down (machine)
averiado/a ⓜ/ⓕ a·ve·*rya*·do/a

brother hermano ⓜ er·*ma*·no

brown marrón ma·*ron*
bruise moretón ⓜ mo·re·*ton*
bucket balde ⓜ *bal*·de
budget presupuesto ⓜ
pre·soo·*pwes*·to
Buddhist budista ⓜ&ⓕ boo·*dees*·ta
bug bicho ⓜ *bee*·cho
build construir kons·troo·*eer*
building edificio ⓜ e·dee·*fee*·syo
bulb bombillo ⓜ bom·*bee*·yo
bulb (Ecu, Per) foco ⓜ *fo*·ko
bull toro ⓜ *to*·ro
bullfight corrida ⓕ ko·*ree*·da
bullring plaza ⓕ de toros *pla*·sa
de *to*·ros
bum (body) culo ⓜ *koo*·lo
burn quemadura ⓕ ke·ma·*doo*·ra
burn quemar ke·*mar*
bus (city) autobús ⓜ ow·to·*boos*
bus (intercity) ómnibus ⓜ
om·nee·boos
bus station (city) estación ⓕ de
autobuses es·ta·*syon* de ow·to·*boo*·ses
bus station (intercity) estación ⓕ
de ómnibuses es·ta·*syon* de
om·nee·boo·ses
bus stop (city) parada ⓕ de
autobús pa·*ra*·da de ow·to·*boos*
bus stop (intercity) parada ⓕ de
ómnibus pa·*ra*·da de *om*·nee·boos
business negocio ⓜ ne·*go*·syo
business class clase ⓕ preferente
kla·se pre·fe·*ren*·te
business person comerciante ⓜ&ⓕ
ko·mer·*syan*·te
busker artista callejero/a ⓜ/ⓕ
ar·*tees*·ta ka·ye·*khe*·ro/a
busy ocupado/a ⓜ/ⓕ o·koo·*pa*·do/a
but pero *pe*·ro
butcher's shop carnicería ⓕ
kar·nee·se·*ree*·a
butter mantequilla ⓕ man·te·*kee*·ya
butterfly mariposa ⓕ ma·ree·*po*·sa
button botón ⓜ bo·*ton*
buy comprar kom·*prar*
buzzard gallinazo ⓜ ga·yee·*na*·so

C

cabbage repollo ⓜ re·*po*·yo
cable cable ⓜ *ka*·ble
cable car teleférico ⓜ te·le·*fe*·ree·ko
cafe cafetería ⓕ ka·fe·te·*ree*·a
cake torta ⓕ *tor*·ta
cake shop pastelería ⓕ
pas·te·le·*ree*·a
calculator calculadora ⓕ
kal·koo·la·*do*·ra
calendar calendario ⓜ ka·len·*da*·ryo
call llamar ya·*mar*
camera cámara ⓕ (fotográfica)
ka·ma·ra (fo·to·*gra*·fee·ka)
camera shop tienda ⓕ de fotografía
tyen·da de fo·to·gra·*fee*·a
camp acampar a·kam·*par*
campsite cámping ⓜ *kam*·peen
camping store tienda ⓕ de
provisiones de cámping *tyen*·da de
pro·vee·*syo*·nes de *kam*·peen
can (tin) lata ⓕ *la*·ta
can (be able) poder po·*der*
can opener abrelatas ⓜ a·bre·*la*·tas
cancel cancelar kan·se·*lar*
candle vela ⓕ *ve*·la
candy dulces ⓜ pl *dool*·ses
cantaloupe cantalupo ⓜ kan·ta·*loo*·po
capsicum pimiento ⓜ pee·*myen*·to
car carro ⓜ *ka*·ro
car hire alquiler ⓜ de carro al·kee·*ler*
de *ka*·ro
car owner's title papeles ⓜ pl del
auto pa·*pe*·les del *ow*·to
car park parking ⓜ *par*·keen
car registration matrícula ⓕ
ma·*tree*·koo·la
caravan caravana ⓕ ka·ra·*va*·na
cards cartas ⓕ pl *kar*·tas
care (about something)
preocuparse por pre·o·koo·*par*·se por
care (for someone) cuidar de
kwee·*dar* de
caring bondadoso/a ⓜ/ⓕ
bon·da·*do*·so/a

C

carriage (train) vagón ⓜ va·*gon*

carpenter carpintero ⓜ
kar·peen·*te*·ro

carrot zanahoria ⓕ sa·na·o·*rya*

carry llevar ye·*var*

cash dinero ⓜ en efectivo dee·*ne*·ro
en e·fek·*tee*·vo

cash (a cheque) cobrar (un cheque)
ko·*brar* (oon *che*·ke)

cash register caja ⓕ registradora
ka·kha re·khees·tra·*do*·ra

cashew castaña ⓕ de cajú
kas·*ta*·nya de ka·*khoo*

cashier cajero/a ⓜ/ⓕ ka·*khe*·ro/a

castle castillo ⓜ kas·*tee*·yo

casual work trabajo ⓜ eventual
tra·*ba*·kho e·ven·*twal*

cat gato/a ⓜ/ⓕ *ga*·to/a

cathedral catedral ⓕ ka·te·*dral*

Catholic católico/a ⓜ/ⓕ
ka·*to*·lee·ko/a

cauliflower coliflor ko·lee·*flor*

cave cueva ⓕ *kwe*·va

cavity (tooth) caries ⓕ *ka*·ryes

CD cómpact ⓜ *kom*·pak

celebration celebración ⓕ
se·le·bra·*syon*

cell phone teléfono ⓜ móvil
te·*le*·fo·no *mo*·veel

cemetery cementerio ⓜ
se·men·*te*·ryo

cent centavo ⓜ sen·*ta*·vo

centimetre centímetro ⓜ
sen·*tee*·me·tro

Central America Centroamérica ⓕ
sen·tro·a·*me*·ree·ka

Central American
centroaméricano/a ⓜ/ⓕ
sen·tro·a·me·ree·*ka*·no/a

central heating calefacción ⓕ
central ka·le·fak·*syon* sen·*tral*

centre centro ⓜ *sen*·tro

ceramic cerámica ⓕ se·*ra*·mee·ka

cereal cereales ⓜ pl se·re·*a*·les

certificate certificado ⓜ
ser·tee·fee·*ka*·do

chain cadena ⓕ ka·*de*·na

chair silla ⓕ *see*·ya

chance oportunidad ⓕ
o·por·too·nee·*da*

change (money) cambio ⓜ *kam*·byo

change cambiar kam·*byar*

changing room vestuario ⓜ
ves·*twa*·ryo

charming encantador(a) ⓜ/ⓕ
en·kan·ta·*dor*/en·kan·ta·*do*·ra

chat up tratar de ligar tra·*tar* de
lee·*gar*

cheap barato/a ⓜ/ⓕ ba·*ra*·to/a

cheat tramposo/a ⓜ/ⓕ
tram·*po*·so/a

check (bill) cuenta ⓕ *kwen*·ta

check revisar re·vee·*sar*

check-in (airport) facturación ⓕ
fak·too·ra·*syon*

check-in (baggage) facturación ⓕ
de equipaje fak·too·ra·*syon* de
e·kee·*pa*·khe

check-in (hotel) registrar
re·khees·*trar*

checkpoint control ⓜ kon·*trol*

cheese queso ⓜ *ke*·so

chef cocinero/a ⓜ/ⓕ ko·see·*ne*·ro/a

chemist (shop) farmacia ⓕ
far·*ma*·sya

chemist (person)
farmacéutico/a ⓜ/ⓕ
far·ma·see·oo·tee·ko/a

cheque cheque ⓜ *che*·ke

chess ajedrez ⓜ a·khe·*dres*

chest pecho ⓜ *pe*·cho

chewing gum chicle ⓜ *chee*·kle

chicken pollo ⓜ *po*·yo

chickpeas garbanzos ⓜ pl
gar·*ban*·sos

child niño/a ⓜ/ⓕ *nee*·nyo/a

child's car seat asiento ⓜ de
seguridad para bebés a·*syen*·to de
se·goo·ree·*da* pa·ra be·*bes*

childminding service guardería ⓕ
gwar·de·*ree*·a

Chile Chile ⓕ *chee*·le

chilli ají ⓜ *a·khee*

chilli sauce salsa ⓕ de ají *sal·sa de a·khee*

chocolate chocolate ⓜ *cho·ko·la·te*

choose escoger *es·ko·kher*

chopping board tabla ⓕ de cortar *ta·bla de kor·tar*

Christian cristiano/a ⓜ/ⓕ *krees·tya·no/a*

Christmas Navidad ⓕ *na·vee·da*

church iglesia ⓕ *ee·gle·sya*

cider sidra ⓕ *see·dra*

cigar cigarro ⓜ *see·ga·ro*

cigarette cigarillo ⓜ *see·ga·ree·yo*

cigarette lighter mechero ⓜ *me·che·ro*

cigarette paper papel ⓜ de fumar *pa·pel de foo·mar*

cinema cine ⓜ *see·ne*

circus circo ⓜ *seer·ko*

citizenship ciudadanía ⓕ *syoo·da·da·nee·a*

city ciudad ⓕ *syoo·da*

city centre centro ⓜ de la ciudad *sen·tro de la syoo·da*

civil rights derechos ⓜ pl civiles *de·re·chos see·vee·les*

classical clásico/a ⓜ/ⓕ *kla·see·ko/a*

clean limpio/a ⓜ/ⓕ *leem·pyo/a*

cleaning limpieza ⓕ *leem·pye·sa*

client cliente/a ⓜ/ⓕ *klyen·te/a*

cliff acantilado ⓜ *a·kan·tee·la·do*

climb subir *soo·beer*

cloak capote ⓜ *ka·po·te*

cloakroom guardarropa ⓜ *gwar·da·ro·pa*

clock reloj ⓜ *re·lokh*

close (nearby) cerca *ser·ka*

close (shut) cerrar *se·rar*

closed cerrado/a ⓜ/ⓕ *se·ra·do/a*

clothes line cuerda ⓕ para tender la ropa *kwer·da pa·ra ten·der la ro·pa*

clothing ropa ⓕ *ro·pa*

clothing store tienda ⓕ de ropa *tyen·da de ro·pa*

cloud nube ⓕ *noo·be*

cloudy nublado/a ⓜ/ⓕ *noo·bla·do/a*

clutch embrague ⓜ *em·bra·ge*

coach (sport) entrenador(a) ⓜ/ⓕ *en·tre·na·dor/en·tre·na·do·ra*

coast costa ⓕ *kos·ta*

coat saco ⓜ *sa·ko*

coke (drug) coca ⓕ *ko·ka*

cocaine cocaína ⓕ *ko·ka·ee·na*

coca plant coca ⓕ *ko·ka*

cockroach cucaracha ⓕ *koo·ka·ra·cha*

cocoa cacao ⓜ *ka·kow*

coconut coco ⓜ *ko·ko*

coconut palm palma ⓕ de coco *pal·ma de ko·ko*

codeine codeína ⓕ *ko·de·ee·na*

coffee café ⓜ *ka·fe*

coins monedas ⓕ pl *mo·ne·das*

coke (drug) coca ⓕ *ko·ka*

cold frío/a ⓜ/ⓕ *free·o/a*

(have a) cold (tener) resfrío (te·*ner*) *res·free·o*

colleague colega ⓜ&ⓕ *ko·le·ga*

collect call llamada ⓕ a cobro revertido *ya·ma·da a ko·bro re·ver·tee·do*

college (hall of residence) residencia ⓕ de estudiantes *re·see·den·sya de es·too·dyan·tes*

college (school) colegio ⓜ *ko·le·khyo*

college (university) universidad ⓕ *oo·nee·ver·see·da*

Colombia Colombia ⓕ *ko·lom·bya*

colour color ⓜ *ko·lor*

comb peine ⓜ *pay·ne*

come venir *ve·neer*

comedy comedia ⓕ *ko·me·dya*

comfortable cómodo/a ⓜ/ⓕ *ko·mo·do/a*

communion comunión ⓕ *ko·moo·nyon*

communist comunista ⓜ&ⓕ *ko·moo·nees·ta*

companion compañero/a ⓜ/ⓕ *kom·pa·nye·ro/a*

C

ENGLISH *to* **LATIN AMERICAN SPANISH**

company compañía ①
kom·pa·nyee·a

compass brújula ① broo·khoo·la

complain quejarse ke·khar·se

computer computadora ①
kom·poo·ta·do·ra

computer game juego ⓜ
de computadora khwe·go de
kom·poo·ta·do·ra

concert concierto ⓜ kon·syer·to

conditioner acondicionador ⓜ
a·kon·dee·syo·na·dor

condom condón ⓜ kon·don

confession confesión ① kon·fe·syon

confirm confirmar kon·feer·mar

connection conexión ①
ko·nek·syon

conservative conservador(a) ⓜ/①
kon·ser·va·dor/kon·ser·va·do·ra

constipation estreñimiento ⓜ
es·tre·nyee·myen·to

consulate consulado ⓜ
kon·soo·la·do

contact lenses lentes ① pl de
contacto len·tes de kon·tak·to

contemporary
contemporáneo/a ⓜ/①
kon·tem·po·ra·ne·o/a

contraceptive anticonceptivo ⓜ
an·tee·kon·sep·tee·vo

contract contrato ⓜ kon·tra·to

convenience store tienda ①
de artículos básicos tyen·da de
ar·tee·koo·los ba·see·kos

convent convento ⓜ kon·ven·to

cook cocinero/a ⓜ/① ko·see·ne·ro/a

cook cocinar ko·see·nar

cookie galleta ① ga·ye·ta

corkscrew sacacorchos ⓜ
sa·ka·kor·chos

corn maíz ⓜ ma·ees

cornflakes copos ⓜ pl de maíz
ko·pos de ma·ees

corner esquina ① es·kee·na

corrupt corrupto/a ⓜ/①
ko·roop·to/a

cost ⓜ coste ⓜ kos·te

cost costar kos·tar

Costa Rica Costa Rica ① kos·ta
ree·ka

cottage cheese requesón ⓜ
re·ke·son

cotton algodón ⓜ al·go·don

cotton balls bolas ① pl de algodón
bo·las de al·go·don

cough tos ① tos

cough medicine jarabe ⓜ kha·ra·be

count contar kon·tar

counter (shop) mostrador ⓜ
mos·tra·dor

country (nation) país ⓜ pa·ees

countryside campo ⓜ kam·po

courgette calabacín ⓜ ka·la·ba·seen

court (legal) tribunal ⓜ tree·boo·nal

court (tennis) cancha ① kan·cha

cousin primo/a ⓜ/① pree·mo/a

cover charge (restaurant) precio ⓜ
del cubierto pre·syo del koo·byer·to

cover charge (venue) precio ⓜ de
entrada pre·syo de en·tra·da

cow vaca ① va·ka

craft market mercado ⓜ de
artesanía mer·ka·do de ar·te·sa·nee·a

craft artesanía ① ar·te·sa·nee·a

crash (accident) choque ⓜ cho·ke

crazy loco/a ⓜ/① lo·ko/a

cream crema ① kre·ma

cream cheese queso ⓜ cremoso
ke·so kre·mo·so

creche guardería ① gwar·de·ree·a

credit card tarjeta ① de crédito
tar·khe·ta de kre·dee·to

crocodile cocodrilo ⓜ ko·ko·dree·lo

crop cosecha ① ko·se·cha

crowded abarrotado/a ⓜ/①
a·ba·ro·ta·do/a

Cuba Cuba ① koo·ba

cucumber pepino ⓜ pe·pee·no

cup taza ① ta·sa

cupboard armario ⓜ ar·ma·ryo

currency exchange cambio ⓜ (de
dinero) kam·byo (de dee·ne·ro)

current corriente ① ko·*ryen*·te
current affairs informativo ⓜ
een·for·ma·*tee*·vo
curry powder curry ⓜ en polvo
koo·ree en *pol*·vo
customs aduana ① a·*dwa*·na
cut cortar kor·*tar*
cutlery cubiertos ⓜ pl koo·*byer*·tos
CV historial ⓜ profesional ees·to·*ryal*
pro·fe·syo·*nal*
cycle andar en bicicleta an·*dar* en
bee·see·*kle*·ta
cycling ciclismo ⓜ see·*klees*·mo
cyclist ciclista ⓜ&① see·*klees*·ta

D

dad papá ⓜ pa·*pa*
daily diariamente dya·rya·*men*·te
dance baile ① *bai*·le
dance bailar bai·*lar*
dangerous peligroso/a ⓜ/①
pe·lee·*gro*·so/a
dark oscuro/a ⓜ/① os·*koo*·ro/a
date (appointment) cita ① *see*·ta
date (day) fecha ① *fe*·cha
date (a person) salir con sa·*leer* kon
date of birth fecha ① de nacimiento
fe·cha de na·see·*myen*·to
daughter hija ① *ee*·kha
dawn alba ① *al*·ba
day día ⓜ *dee*·a
day after tomorrow pasado mañana
pa·*sa*·do ma·*nya*·na
day before yesterday anteayer
an·te·a·*yer*
dead muerto/a ⓜ/① *mwer*·to/a
deaf sordo/a ⓜ/① *sor*·do/a
decide decidir de·see·*deer*
deep profundo/a ⓜ/①
pro·*foon*·do/a
deforestation deforestación ①
de·fo·res·ta·*syon*
delay demora ① de·*mo*·ra
deliver entregar en·tre·*gar*
democracy democracia ①
de·mo·*kra*·see·a

demonstration (protest)
manifestación ① ma·nee·fes·ta·*syon*
dengue fever fiebre ① del dengue
fye·bre del *den*·ge
dental floss hilo ⓜ dental *ee*·lo
den·*tal*
dentist dentista ⓜ&① den·*tees*·ta
deodorant desodorante ⓜ
de·so·do·*ran*·te
depart (person) partir par·*teer*
depart (plane etc) salir sa·*leer*
department store grande
almacén ⓜ *gran*·de al·ma·*sen*
departure (person) partida ①
par·*tee*·da
departure (plane etc) salida ①
sa·*lee*·da
deposit (bank) depósito ⓜ
de·po·*see*·to
descendant descendiente ⓜ
de·sen·*dyen*·te
desert desierto ⓜ de·*syer*·to
design diseño ⓜ dee·se·*nyo*
destination destino ⓜ des·*tee*·no
detail detalle ⓜ de·*ta*·ye
detective novel novela ① negra
no·*ve*·la *ne*·gra
diabetes diabetes ⓜ dya·be·tes
dial tone tono ⓜ *to*·no
diaper pañal ⓜ pa·*nyal*
diaphragm diafragma ⓜ
dya·*frag*·ma
diarrhoea diarrea ① dya·*re*·a
diary agenda ① a·*khen*·da
dictionary diccionario ⓜ
deek·syo·*na*·ryo
die morir mo·*reer*
diet (customary food) dieta ① *dye*·ta
diet (slimming) régimen ⓜ
re·khee·men
different diferente dee·fe·*ren*·te
difficult difícil dee·*fee*·seel
dining car vagón ⓜ restaurante
va·*gon* res·tow·*ran*·te
digital camera cámara ① digital
ka·ma·ra dee·khee·*tal*

E

dinner cena ① *se*·na

direct directo/a ⓜ/① dee·*rek*·to/a

direct-dial servicio ⓜ telefónico automático ser·*vee*·syo te·le·*fo*·nee·ko ow·to·ma·tee·ko

director director(a) ⓜ/① dee·*rek*·tor/dee·rek·to·ra

dirty sucio/a ⓜ/① *soo*·syo/a

disabled minusválido/a ⓜ/① mee·noos·*va*·lee·do/a

disco discoteca ① dees·ko·*te*·ka

discount descuento ⓜ des·*kwen*·to

discover descubrir des·koo·*breer*

discrimination discriminación ① dees·kree·mee·na·*syon*

disease enfermedad ① en·fer·mee·*da*

disk disco ⓜ *dees*·ko

disposable camera cámara ① descartable *ka*·ma·ra des·kar·*ta*·ble

diving submarinismo ⓜ soob·ma·ree·*nees*·mo

diving equipment equipo ⓜ de inmersión e·*kee*·po de een·mer·*syon*

dizzy mareado/a ⓜ/① ma·re·a·do/a

do hacer a·*ser*

doctor médico/a ⓜ/① *me*·dee·ko/a

dog perro/a ⓜ/① *pe*·ro/a

dole subsidio ⓜ de desempleo soob·*see*·dyo de des·em·*ple*·o

doll muñeca ① moo·*nye*·ka

domestic (country) nacional na·syo·*nal*

domestic flight vuelo ⓜ doméstico *vwe*·lo do·*mes*·tee·ko

Dominican Republic República ① Dominicana re·*poo*·blee·ka do·mee·nee·*ka*·na

donkey burro ⓜ *boo*·ro

door puerta ① *pwer*·ta

dope droga ① *dro*·ga

double doble *do*·ble

double bed cama ① de matrimonio *ka*·ma de ma·*tree*·mo·nyo

double copies (photos) dos copias ① pl dos *ko*·pyas

double room habitación ① doble a·bee·ta·*syon do*·ble

down hacia abajo a·*see*·a a·*ba*·kho

downhill cuesta abajo *kwes*·ta a·*ba*·kho

dozen docena ① do·*se*·na

draw dibujar dee·boo·*khar*

dream soñar so·*nyar*

dress vestido ⓜ ves·*tee*·do

drink copa ① *ko*·pa

drink tomar to·*mar*

drinkable potable po·*ta*·ble

drive conducir kon·doo·*seer*

drivers licence carnet ⓜ kar·*net*

drug (medicinal) medicina ① me·dee·*see*·na

drug addiction drogadicción ① dro·ga·deek·*syon*

drug dealer traficante ⓜ de drogas tra·fee·*kan*·te de *dro*·gas

drugs (illegal) drogas ① pl *dro*·gas

drums batería ① ba·te·*ree*·a

drunk borracho/a ⓜ/① bo·*ra*·cho/a

dry seco/a ⓜ/① *se*·ko/a

dry secar se·*kar*

duck pato ⓜ *pa*·to

dummy (pacifier) chupete ⓜ choo·*pe*·te

during durante doo·*ran*·te

DVD DVD ⓜ de oo·ve *de*

dysentry disentería ① dee·sen·te·*ree*·a

E

each cada *ka*·da

ear oreja ① o·*re*·kha

early temprano tem·*pra*·no

earn ganar ga·*nar*

earplugs tapones ⓜ pl para los oídos ta·*po*·nes *pa*·ra los o·*ee*·dos

earrings aretes ⓜ pl a·*re*·tes

Earth Tierra ① *tye*·ra

earthquake terremoto ⓜ te·re·*mo*·to

east este ⓜ *es*·te

Easter Pascua ① *pas*·kwa

easy fácil *fa*·seel

eat comer ko·*mer*
economy class clase ① turística
kla·se too·*rees*·tee·ka
Ecuador Ecuador ⓜ e·kwa·*dor*
education educación ①
e·doo·ka·*syon*
egg huevo ⓜ *we*·vo
eggplant berenjena ① be·ren·*khe*·na
elections elecciones ① pl
e·lek·*syo*·nes
electrician electricista ⓜ&①
e·lek·tree·*sees*·ta
electricity electricidad ①
e·lek·tree·see·*da*
elevator ascensor ⓜ a·sen·*sor*
El Salvador El Salvador ⓜ el
sal·va·*dor*
embarrassed avergonzado/a ⓜ/①
a·ver·gon·*sa*·do/a
embassy embajada ① em·ba·*kha*·da
emergency emergencia ①
e·mer·*khen*·sya
emotional emocional e·mo·syo·*nal*
employee empleado/a ⓜ/①
em·ple·*a*·do/a
employer patrón/patrona ⓜ/①
pa·*tron*/pa·*tro*·na
empty vacío/a ⓜ/① va·*see*·o/a
end fin ⓜ feen
end acabar a·ka·*bar*
endangered species especies ① pl
en peligro de extinción es·*pe*·syes en
pe·*lee*·gro de ek·steen·*syon*
engagement (marriage)
compromiso ⓜ kom·pro·*mee*·so
engine motor ⓜ mo·*tor*
engineer ingeniero/a ⓜ/①
een·khe·*nye*·ro/a
engineering ingeniería ①
een·khe·nye·*ree*·a
England ① Inglaterra een·gla·*te*·ra
English (language) inglés ⓜ een·*gles*
English inglés/inglesa ⓜ/①
een·*gles*/een·*gle*·sa
enjoy (oneself) divertirse
dee·ver·*teer*·se

enough suficiente soo·fee·*syen*·te
enter entrar en·*trar*
entertainment guide guía ①
de los espectáculos *gee*·a de los
es·pek·*ta*·koo·los
envelope sobre ⓜ *so*·bre
environment medio ⓜ ambiente
me·dyo am·*byen*·te
epilepsy epilepsia ① e·pee·*lep*·sya
equality igualdad ① ee·gwal·*da*
equipment equipo ⓜ e·*kee*·po
escalator escalera ① mecánica
es·ka·*le*·ra me·*ka*·nee·ka
euthanasia eutanasia ①
e·oo·ta·*na*·sya
evening noche ① *no*·che
everything todo *to*·do
example ejemplo ⓜ e·*khem*·plo
excellent excelente ek·se·*len*·te
excess baggage exceso ⓜ de
equipage ek·*se*·so de e·kee·*pa*·khe
exchange cambio ⓜ de dinero
kam·byo de dee·*ne*·ro
exchange cambiar kam·*byar*
exchange rate tipo ⓜ de cambio
tee·po de *kam*·byo
excluded no incluido/a ⓜ/① no
een·kloo·ee·do/a
exhaust (car) escape ⓜ es·*ka*·pe
exhibition exposición ①
ek·spo·see·*syon*
exit salida ① sa·*lee*·da
expensive caro/a ⓜ/① *ka*·ro/a
experience experiencia ①
ek·spe·*ryen*·sya
exploitation explotación ①
ek·splo·ta·*syon*
express expreso/a ⓜ/①
ek·*spre*·so/a
express mail correo ⓜ urgente
ko·*re*·o oor·*khen*·te
extension (visa) prolongación ①
pro·lon·ga·*syon*
eye ojo ⓜ o·*kho*
eye drops gotas ① pl para los ojos
go·tas *pa*·ra los o·*khos*

F

F

fabric tela ① *te*·la

face cara ① *ka*·ra

factory fábrica ① *fa*·bree·ka

factory worker obrero/a ⓜ/① o·*bre*·ro/a

fall (tumble) caída ① ka·*ee*·da

fall (season) otoño ⓜ o·*to*·nyo

family familia ① fa·*mee*·lya

family name apellido ⓜ a·pe·*yee*·do

famous conocido/a ⓜ/① ko·no·*see*·do/a

fan (person) hincha ⓜ&① *een*·cha

fan (machine) ventilador ⓜ ven·tee·la·*dor*

fan belt correa ① del ventilador ko·*re*·a del ven·tee·la·*dor*

fantasy fantasía ① fan·ta·*see*·a

far lejos *le*·khos

farm granja ① *gran*·kha

farmer agricultor(a) ⓜ/① a·gree·kool·*tor*/a·gree·kool·*to*·ra

fast rápido/a ⓜ/① *ra*·pee·do/a

fat gordo/a ⓜ/① *gor*·do/a

father padre ⓜ *pa*·dre

father-in-law suegro ⓜ *swe*·gro

faucet grifo ⓜ *gree*·fo

fault (someone's) culpa ① *kool*·pa

faulty defectuoso/a ⓜ/① de·fek·*two*·so/a

feel sentir sen·*teer*

feelings sentimientos ⓜ pl sen·tee·*myen*·tos

fence cerca ① *ser*·ka

fencing (sport) esgrima ① es·*gree*·ma

fever fiebre ① *fye*·bre

few pocos/as ⓜ/① pl *po*·kos/as

fiance(e) prometido/a ⓜ/① pro·me·*tee*·do/a

fiction (literature) (literatura de) ficción ①(lee·te·ra·*too*·ra de) feek·*syon*

fig higo ⓜ *ee*·go

fight pelea ① pe·*le*·a

film (roll for camera) película ① pe·*lee*·koo·la

film speed sensibilidad ① sen·see·bee·lee·*da*

filtered con filtro kon *feel*·tro

find encontrar en·kon·*trar*

fine multa ① *mool*·ta

finger dedo ⓜ *de*·do

finish terminar ter·mee·*nar*

fire fuego ⓜ *fwe*·go

firewood leña ① *le*·nya

first primero/a ⓜ/① pree·*me*·ro/a

first class primera clase ① pree·*me*·ra *kla*·se

first-aid kit maletín ⓜ de primeros auxilios ma·le·*teen* de pree·*me*·ros ow·*ksee*·lyos

fish pez ⓜ pes

fish (as food) pescado ⓜ pes·*ka*·do

fish shop pescadería ① pes·ka·de·*ree*·a

fishing pesca ① *pes*·ka

flag bandera ① ban·*de*·ra

flamingo flamenco ⓜ fla·*men*·ko

flashlight (torch) linterna ① leen·*ter*·na

flannel (wash cloth) toallita ① to·a·*yee*·ta

flat llano/a ⓜ/① *ya*·no/a

flea pulga ① *pool*·ga

flood inundación ① ee·noon·da·*syon*

floor (ground) suelo ⓜ *swe*·lo

floor (storey) piso ⓜ *pee*·so

florist florista ⓜ&① flo·*rees*·ta

flour harina ① a·*ree*·na

flower flor ① flor

flu gripe ① *gree*·pe

fly mosca ① *mos*·ka

fly volar vo·*lar*

foggy brumoso/a ⓜ/① broo·*mo*·so/a

follow seguir se·*geer*

food comida ① ko·*mee*·da

food poisoning intoxicación ① alimenticia een·tok·see·ka·*syon* a·lee·men·*tee*·sya

food supplies víveres ⓜ pl
vee·ve·res
foot pie ⓜ pye
football (soccer) fútbol ⓜ foot·bol
footpath acera ① a·se·ra
footpath (CAm) andén ⓜ an·den
footpath (SAm) vereda ① ve·re·da
foreign extranjero/a ⓜ/①
ek·stran·khe·ro/a
foreigner extranjero/a ⓜ/①
ek·stran·khe·ro/a
forest bosque ⓜ bos·ke
forever para siempre pa·ra syem·pre
forget olvidar ol·vee·dar
forgive perdonar per·do·nar
fork tenedor ⓜ te·ne·dor
fortnight quincena ① keen·se·na
foyer vestíbulo ⓜ ves·tee·boo·lo
fragile frágil fra·kheel
France Francia ① fran·sya
free (gratis) gratis gra·tees
free (not bound) libre lee·bre
freeze congelar kon·khe·lar
fridge refrigeradora ①
re·free·khe·ra·do·ra
friend amigo/a ⓜ/① a·mee·go/a
frog rana ① ra·na
frost escarcha ① es·kar·cha
frostbite congelación ①
kon·khe·la·syon
frozen foods productos ⓜ pl
congelados pro·dook·tos
kon·khe·la·dos
fruit fruta ① froo·ta
fruit picking recolección ① de fruta
re·ko·lek·syon de froo·ta
fry freir fre·eer
frying pan sartén ① sar·ten
full lleno/a ⓜ/① ye·no/a
full-time a tiempo completo a
tyem·po kom·ple·to
fun diversión ① dee·ver·syon
funeral funeral ⓜ foo·ne·ral
funny gracioso/a ⓜ/① gra·syo·so/a
furniture muebles ⓜ pl mwe·bles
future futuro ⓜ foo·too·ro

G

game (play) juego ⓜ khwe·go
game (sport) partido ⓜ par·tee·do
garage (car repair) taller ⓜ ta·yer
garage (car shelter) garage ⓜ
ga·ra·khe
garden jardín ⓜ khar·deen
gardening jardinería ①
khar·dee·ne·ree·a
garlic ajo ⓜ a·kho
gas (petrol) gasolina ① ga·so·lee·na
gas cartridge cartucho ⓜ de gas
kar·too·cho de gas
gate verja ① ver·kha
gears marchas ① pl mar·chas
general general khe·ne·ral
Germany ① Alemania a·le·ma·nya
gift regalo ⓜ re·ga·lo
gig actuación ① ak·twa·syon
ginger jengibre ⓜ khen·khee·bre
girl chica ① chee·ka
girlfriend novia ① no·vya
give dar dar
glandular fever fiebre ① glandular
fye·bre glan·doo·lar
glass (drinking) vaso ⓜ va·so
glass (material) vidrio ⓜ vee·dryo
glasses anteojos ⓜ pl an·te·o·khos
glossy brillante bree·yan·te
gloves guantes ⓜ pl gwan·tes
go ir eer
go out with salir con sa·leer kon
goat cabra ① ka·bra
god dios dyos
goggles anteojos ⓜ pl an·te·o·khos
gold oro ⓜ o·ro
golf ball pelota ① de golf pe·lo·ta
de golf
golf course cancha ① de golf
kan·cha de golf
good bueno/a ⓜ/① bwe·no/a
government gobierno ⓜ go·byer·no
grams gramos ⓜ pl gra·mos
grandchild nieto/a ⓜ/① nye·to/a
grandfather abuelo ⓜ a·bwe·lo

grandmother abuela ⓕ a·*bwe*·la

grapefruit pomelo ⓜ po·*me*·lo

grapes uvas ⓕ pl *oo*·vas

grass hierba ⓕ *yer*·ba

grave tumba ⓕ *toom*·ba

great fantástico/a ⓜ/ⓕ
fan·*tas*·tee·ko/a

green verde *ver*·de

greengrocer verdulero/a ⓜ/ⓕ
ver·doo·*le*·ro/a

grey gris grees

grocery almacén ⓜ al·ma·*sen*

groundnut maní ⓜ ma·*nee*

group grupo ⓜ *groo*·po

grow crecer kre·*ser*

Guatemala Guatemala ⓕ
gwa·te·*ma*·la

guess adivinar a·dee·vee·*nar*

guide (audio) guía ⓕ audio *gee*·a
ow·dyo

guide (person) guía ⓜ&ⓕ *gee*·a

guide dog perro ⓜ guía *pe*·ro *gee*·a

guidebook guía ⓕ *gee*·a

guided tour recorrido ⓜ guiado
re·ko·*ree*·do gee·a·do

guilty culpable kool·*pa*·ble

guinea pig cuy ⓜ kooy

guitar guitarra ⓕ gee·*ta*·ra

gum (chewing) chicle ⓜ *chee*·kle

gum (mouth) encía ⓕ en·*see*·a

gymnastics gimnasia ⓕ
kheem·*na*·sya

gynaecologist ginecólogo/a ⓜ/ⓕ
khee·ne·*ko*·lo·go/a

H

hail granizo ⓜ gra·*nee*·so

hair pelo ⓜ *pe*·lo

haircut corte ⓜ de pelo *kor*·te de
pe·lo

hairdresser peluquero/a ⓜ/ⓕ
pe·loo·*ke*·ro/a

half medio/a ⓜ/ⓕ *me*·dyo/a

hallucinate alucinar a·loo·see·*nar*

ham jamón ⓜ kha·*mon*

hammer martillo ⓜ mar·*tee*·yo

hammock hamaca ⓕ a·*ma*·ka

hand mano ⓕ *ma*·no

handbag bolso ⓜ *bol*·so

handicraft artesanía ⓕ
ar·te·sa·*nee*·a

handkerchief pañuelo ⓜ pa·*nywe*·lo

handlebar manillar ⓜ ma·nee·*yar*

handmade hecho/a ⓜ/ⓕ a mano
e·cho/a a *ma*·no

handsome buen mozo/a ⓜ/ⓕ bwen
mo·so/a

happy feliz fe·*lees*

harassment acoso ⓜ a·*ko*·so

harbour puerto ⓜ *pwer*·to

hard (not easy) difícil dee·*fee*·seel

hard (not soft) duro/a ⓜ/ⓕ
doo·ro/a

hardware store ferretería ⓕ
fe·re·te·*ree*·a

hash hachís ⓜ a·*chees*

hat sombrero ⓜ som·*bre*·ro

have tener te·*ner*

hay fever alergia ⓕ de polén
a·*ler*·khya de po·*len*

he él el

head cabeza ⓕ ka·*be*·sa

headache dolor ⓜ de cabeza do·*lor*
de ka·*be*·sa

headlights faros ⓜ pl *fa*·ros

health salud ⓕ sa·*loo*

hear oír o·*eer*

hearing aid audífono ⓜ
ow·*dee*·fo·no

heart corazón ⓜ ko·ra·*son*

heart condition condición ⓕ
cardíaca kon·dee·*syon* kar·*dee*·a·ka

heat calor ⓜ ka·*lor*

heater estufa ⓕ es·*too*·fa

heating calefacción ⓕ ka·le·fak·*syon*

heavy pesado/a ⓜ/ⓕ pe·*sa*·do/a

helmet casco ⓜ *kas*·ko

help ayudar a·yoo·*dar*

her su soo

herbalist herborista ⓜ&ⓕ
er·bo·*rees*·ta

herbs hierbas ⓕ pl *yer*·bas

here aquí a·*kee*
heroin heroína ① e·ro·*ee*·na
herring arenque ⑩ a·*ren*·ke
high alto/a ⑩/① *al*·to/a
high school instituto ⑩
een·stee·*too*·to
hike ir de excursión eer de
ek·skoor·*syon*
hiking excursionismo ⑩
ek·skoor·syo·*nees*·mo
hiking boots botas ① pl de
montaña *bo*·tas de mon·*ta*·nya
hiking route camino ⑩ rural
ka·*mee*·no roo·*ral*
hill colina ① ko·*lee*·na
Hindu hindú ⑩&① een·*doo*
hire alquilar al·kee·*lar*
his su soo
historical histórico/a ⑩/①
ees·to·*ree*·ko/a
hitchhike hacer dedo a·*ser de*·do
HIV positive seropositivo/a ⑩/①
se·ro·po·see·*tee*·vo/a
holiday día ⑩ festivo *dee*·a fes·*tee*·vo
holidays vacaciones ① pl
va·ka·*syo*·nes
home casa ① *ka*·sa
homeless sin techo seen *te*·cho
homemaker ama ① de casa a·ma
de *ka*·sa
Honduras Honduras ① on·*doo*·ras
honey miel ① myel
honeymoon luna ① de miel *loo*·na
de myel
horoscope horóscopo ⑩ o·*ros*·ko·po
horse caballo ⑩ ka·*ba*·yo
horse riding equitación ①
e·kee·ta·*syon*
horseradish rábano ⑩ picante
ra·ba·no pee·*kan*·te
hospital hospital ⑩ os·pee·*tal*
hospitality hospitalidad ①
os·pee·ta·lee·*da*
hot caliente ka·*lyen*·te
hot water agua ① caliente *a*·gwa
ka·*lyen*·te

hotel hotel ⑩ o·*tel*
house casa ① *ka*·sa
how como *ko*·mo
how much cuanto *kwan*·to
hug abrazo ⑩ a·*bra*·so
huge enorme e·*nor*·me
human rights derechos ⑩ pl
humanos de·*re*·chos oo·*ma*·nos
hummingbird colibrí ⑩ ko·lee·*bree*
(be) hungry tener hambre te·*ner*
am·bre
hunting caza ① *ka*·sa
(be in a) hurry tener prisa te·*ner*
pree·sa
hurt dañar da·*nyar*
husband esposo ⑩ es·*po*·so
hut cabaña ① ka·*ba*·nya

I yo yo
ice hielo ⑩ *ye*·lo
ice axe piolet ⑩ pyo·*let*
ice cream helado ⑩ e·*la*·do
ice-cream parlour heladería ①
e·la·de·*ree*·a
ice hockey hockey ⑩ sobre hielo
kho·kee *so*·bre *ye*·lo
identification identificación ①
ee·den·tee·fee·ka·*syon*
identification card (ID)
cédula ⑩ de identidad *se*·doo·la de
ee·den·tee·*da*
idiot idiota ⑩&① ee·*dyo*·ta
if si see
ill enfermo/a ⑩/① en·*fer*·mo/a
illegal ilegal ee·le·*gal*
immigration inmigración ①
een·mee·gra·*syon*
important importante
eem·por·*tan*·te
impossible imposible
eem·po·*see*·ble
included incluido/a ⑩/①
een·kloo·ee·do/a
income tax impuesto ⑩ sobre la
renta eem·*pwes*·to *so*·bre la *ren*·ta

J

indicators (car) direccionales ⓜ pl
dee·rek·syo·na·les
indigestion indigestión ⓕ
een·dee·khes·tyon
industry industria ⓕ een·doos·trya
infection infección ⓕ een·fek·syon
inflammation inflamación ⓕ
een·fla·ma·syon
information información ⓕ
een·for·ma·syon
influenza gripe ⓕ gree·pe
ingredient ingrediente ⓜ
een·gre·dyen·te
inhaler inhalador ⓜ ee·na·la·dor
inject inyectarse een·yek·tar·se
injection inyección ⓕ een·yek·syon
injury herida ⓕ e·ree·da
innocent inocente ee·no·sen·te
inside adentro a·den·tro
instructor instructor(a) ⓜ/ⓕ
een·strook·tor/een·strook·to·ra
instructor (skiing) monitor(a) ⓜ/ⓕ
mo·nee·tor/mo·nee·to·ra
insurance seguro ⓜ se·goo·ro
interesting interesante
een·te·re·san·te
intermission descanso ⓜ
des·kan·so
international internacional
een·ter·na·syo·nal
internet cafe cibercafé ⓜ
see·ber·ka·fe
interpreter intérprete ⓜ&ⓕ
een·ter·pre·te
interview entrevista ⓕ
en·tre·vees·ta
invite invitar een·vee·tar
iron (clothes) plancha ⓕ plan·cha
island isla ⓕ ees·la
IT informática ⓕ een·for·ma·tee·ka
itch picazón ⓕ pee·ka·son
itemised detallado/a ⓜ/ⓕ
de·ta·ya·do/a
itinerary itinerario ⓜ ee·tee·ne·ra·ryo
IUD (contraceptive device) DIU ⓜ
de ee oo

J

jacket chaqueta ⓕ cha·ke·ta
jaguar jaguar ⓜ kha·gwar
jail cárcel ⓕ kar·sel
jam mermelada ⓕ mer·me·la·da
Japan Japón ⓜ kha·pon
jar jarra ⓕ kha·ra
jaw mandíbula ⓕ man·dee·boo·la
jealous celoso/a ⓜ/ⓕ se·lo·so/a
jeep yip ⓜ yeep
jewellery joyería ⓕ kho·ye·ree·a
Jewish judío/a ⓜ/ⓕ khoo·dee·o/a
job trabajo ⓜ tra·ba·kho
jogging footing ⓜ foo·teen
joke broma ⓕ bro·ma
journalist periodista ⓜ&ⓕ
pe·ryo·dees·ta
judge juez ⓜ&ⓕ khwes
juice jugo ⓜ khoo·go
jump saltar sal·tar
jumper (sweater) chompa ⓜ
chom·pa
jumper leads cables ⓜ pl de
arranque ka·bles de a·ran·ke

K

ketchup salsa ⓕ de tomate sal·sa
de to·ma·te
key llave ⓕ ya·ve
keyboard teclado ⓜ te·kla·do
kick patada ⓕ pa·ta·da
kick dar una patada dar oo·na
pa·ta·da
kill matar ma·tar
kilogram kilo ⓜ kee·lo
kilometre kilómetro ⓜ kee·lo·me·tro
kind amable a·ma·ble
kindergarten jardín ⓜ de infancia •
kinder ⓜ khar·deen de een·fan·sya •
keen·der
king rey ⓜ ray
kiss beso ⓜ be·so
kiss besar be·sar
kitchen cocina ⓕ ko·see·na
kitten gatito/a ⓜ/ⓕ ga·tee·to/a

knapsack mochila ① mo-*chee*-la
knee rodilla ① ro-*dee*-ya
knife cuchillo ⓜ koo-*chee*-yo
know (someone) conocer ko-no-*ser*
know (something) saber sa-*ber*

L

labourer obrero/a ⓜ/① o-*bre*-ro/a
lace encaje ⓜ en-*ka*-khe
lager cerveza ① rubia ser-*ve*-sa *roo*-bya
lake lago ⓜ *la*-go
lamb cordero ⓜ kor-*de*-ro
land tierra ① *tye*-ra
landlady propietaria ① pro-pye-*ta*-rya
landlord propietario ⓜ pro-pye-*ta*-ryo
language idioma ⓜ ee-*dyo*-ma
laptop computadora ① portátil kom-poo-ta-*do*-ra por-*ta*-teel
lard manteca ① de cerdo man-*te*-ka de ser-do
large grande *gran*-de
laser pointer puntero ⓜ láser poon-*te*-ro *la*-ser
late tarde *tar*-de
Latin America Latinoamérica ① la-tee-no-a-*me*-ree-ka
Latin American latinoamericano/a ⓜ/① la-tee-no-a-me-ree-*ka*-no/a
laugh reírse re-*eer*-se
laundrette lavandería ① la-van-de-*ree*-a
laundry lavandería ① la-van-de-*ree*-a
law ley ① lay
lawyer abogado/a ⓜ/① a-bo-*ga*-do/a
laxatives laxantes ⓜ pl lak-*san*-tes
lazy perezoso/a ⓜ/① pe-re-*so*-so/a
leader jefe/a ⓜ/① *khe*-fe/a
leaf hoja ① *o*-kha
learn aprender a-pren-*der*
leather cuero ⓜ *kwe*-ro
leave partir par-*teer*

lecturer profesor(a) ⓜ/① pro-fe-*sor*/pro-fe-*so*-ra
leek puerro ⓜ *pwe*-ro
left (direction) izquierda ① ees-*kyer*-da
left-luggage office consigna ① kon-*seeg*-na
left-wing izquierdista ees-kyer-*dees*-ta
leg (body) pierna ① *pyer*-na
legal legal le-*gal*
legislation legislación ① le-khees-la-*syon*
lemon limón ⓜ lee-*mon*
lemonade limonada ① lee-mo-*na*-da
lens objetivo ⓜ ob-khe-*tee*-vo
lentils lentejas ① pl len-*te*-khas
lesbian lesbiana ① les-*bya*-na
less de menos de *me*-nos
letter carta ① *kar*-ta
lettuce lechuga ① le-*choo*-ga
liar mentiroso/a ⓜ/① men-tee-*ro*-so/a
library biblioteca ① bee-blyo-*te*-ka
lice piojos ⓜ pl *pyo*-khos
license plate number matrícula ① ma-*tree*-koo-la
lie (not stand) tumbarse toom-*bar*-se
life vida ① *vee*-da
lifejacket chaleco ⓜ salvavidas cha-*le*-ko sal-va-*vee*-das
lift (elevator) ascensor ⓜ a-sen-*sor*
lift levantar le-van-*tar*
light luz ① loos
light (colour) claro/a ⓜ/① *kla*-ro/a
light (not heavy) ligero/a ⓜ/① lee-*khe*-ro/a
light bulb bombilla ① bom-*bee*-ya
light meter fotómetro ⓜ fo-*to*-me-tro
lighter encendedor ⓜ en-sen-de-*dor*
lights (on car) faros ⓜ pl *fa*-ros
like (affection) gustar(le) goos-*tar*(-le)
lime lima ① *lee*-ma

line línea ① *lee*·ne·a
lip balm bálsamo ⓜ de labios
bal·sa·mo de *la*·byos
lips labios ⓜ pl *la*·byos
lipstick lápiz ⓜ de labios *la*·pees
de *la*·byos
liquor store bodega ① bo·*de*·ga
listen escuchar es·koo·*char*
live vivir vee·*veer*
liver hígado ⓜ *ee*·ga·do
lizard lagartija ① la·gar·*tee*·kha
local local lo·*kal*
lock (door) cerradura ① se·ra·*doo*·ra
lock cerrar se·*rar*
locked cerrado/a ⓜ/① con llave
se·*ra*·do/a kon *ya*·ve
lollies caramelos ⓜ pl ka·ra·*me*·los
long largo/a ⓜ/① *lar*·go/a
long-distance larga distancia *lar*·ga
dees·*tan*·sya
look mirar mee·*rar*
look after cuidar de kwee·*dar* de
look for buscar boos·*kar*
lookout mirador ⓜ mee·ra·*dor*
loose change monedas ① pl sueltas
mo·*ne*·das *swel*·tas
lose perder per·*der*
lost perdido/a ⓜ/① per·*dee*·do/a
lost-property office oficina ① de
objetos perdidos o·fee·*see*·na de
ob·*khe*·tos per·*dee*·dos
loud ruidoso/a ⓜ/① rwee·*do*·so/a
love querer ke·*rer*
lover amante ⓜ&① a·*man*·te
low bajo/a ⓜ/① *ba*·kho/a
lubricant lubricante ⓜ
loo·bree·*kan*·te
luck suerte ① *swer*·te
lucky afortunado/a ⓜ/①
a·for·too·na·do/a
luggage equipaje ⓜ e·kee·*pa*·khe
luggage lockers consigna ①
automática kon·*seeg*·na
ow·to·*ma*·tee·ka
luggage tag etiqueta ① de equipaje
e·tee·*ke*·ta de e·kee·*pa*·khe

lump bulto ⓜ *bool*·to
lunch almuerzo ⓜ al·*mwer*·so
lungs pulmones ⓜ pl pool·*mo*·nes
luxurious de lujo de *loo*·kho

M

macaw papagayo ⓜ pa·pa·*ga*·yo
machine máquina ① *ma*·kee·na
made of (cotton) hecho/a ⓜ/① de
(algodón) e·*cho*/a de (al·go·*don*)
magazine revista ① re·*vees*·ta
magician mago/a ⓜ/① *ma*·go/a
mail correo ⓜ ko·*re*·o
mailbox buzón ⓜ boo·*son*
main principal preen·see·*pal*
make hacer a·*ser*
make-up maquillaje ⓜ
ma·kee·*ya*·khe
malaria malaria ① ma·*la*·rya
mallet mazo ⓜ *ma*·so
mammogram mamograma ⓜ
ma·mo·*gra*·ma
man hombre ⓜ *om*·bre
manager director(a) ⓜ/①
dee·rek·*tor*/dee·rek·*to*·ra
mandarin mandarina ①
man·da·*ree*·na
manual manual ma·*nwal*
many muchos/as ⓜ/① pl
moo·chos/as
map mapa ⓜ *ma*·pa
margarine margarina ①
mar·ga·*ree*·na
marital status estado ⓜ civil
es·*ta*·do see·*veel*
market mercado ⓜ mer·*ka*·do
marmalade mermelada ①
mer·me·*la*·da
marriage matrimonio ⓜ
ma·tree·*mo*·nyo
married casado/a ⓜ/① ka·*sa*·do/a
marry casarse ka·*sar*·se
martial arts artes ⓜ pl marciales
ar·tes mar·*sya*·les
mass (Catholic) misa ① *mee*·sa
massage masaje ⓜ ma·*sa*·khe

masseur/masseuse masajista ⓜ&ⓕ
ma·sa·*khees*·ta

mat esterilla ⓕ es·te·*ree*·ya

match (sport) partido ⓜ par·*tee*·do

matches fósforos ⓜ pl *fos*·fo·ros

mattress colchón ⓜ kol·*chon*

maybe quizás kee·*sas*

mayonnaise mayonesa ⓕ
ma·yo·*ne*·sa

mayor alcalde ⓜ&ⓕ al·*kal*·de

measles sarampión ⓜ sa·ram·*pyon*

meat carne ⓕ *kar*·ne

mechanic mecánico/a ⓜ/ⓕ
me·*ka*·nee·ko/a

media medios ⓜ pl de
comunicación *me*·dyos de
ko·moo·nee·ka·*syon*

medicine medicina ⓕ
me·dee·*see*·na

meditation meditación ⓕ
me·dee·ta·*syon*

meet encontrar en·kon·*trar*

melon melón ⓜ me·*lon*

member miembro ⓜ&ⓕ *myem*·bro

menstruation menstruación ⓕ
mens·trwa·*syon*

menu menú ⓜ me·*noo*

message mensaje ⓜ men·*sa*·khe

metre (distance) metro ⓜ *me*·tro

metro subterráneo ⓜ soob·te·ra·ne·o

metro station estación ⓕ de
subterráneo es·ta·*syon* de
soob·te·*ra*·ne·o

Mexico México ⓜ *me*·khee·ko

microwave oven microondas ⓜ
mee·kro·on·das

midnight medianoche ⓕ
me·dya·no·che

migraine migraña ⓕ mee·*gra*·nya

military militares ⓜ pl
mee·lee·ta·res

military service servicio ⓜ militar
ser·*vee*·syo mee·lee·*tar*

milk leche ⓕ *le*·che

millimetre milímetro ⓜ
mee·*lee*·me·tro

million millón ⓜ mee·*yon*

mince (meat) carne ⓕ molida
kar·ne mo·*lee*·da

mind (look after) cuidar kwee·*dar*

mineral water agua ⓜ mineral
a·gwa mee·ne·*ral*

mints pastillas ⓕ pl de menta
pas·*tee*·yas de *men*·ta

minute minuto ⓜ mee·*noo*·to

mirror espejo ⓜ es·*pe*·kho

miscarriage aborto ⓜ natural
a·bor·to na·too·*ral*

miss (feel absence of) extrañar
ek·stra·*nyar*

mistake error ⓜ e·*ror*

mix mezclar mes·*klar*

mobile phone teléfono ⓜ móvil/
celular te·*le*·fo·no mo·*veel*/se·loo·*lar*

moisturiser crema ⓕ hidratante
kre·ma ee·dra·*tan*·te

monastery monasterio ⓜ
mo·nas·*te*·ryo

money dinero ⓜ dee·*ne*·ro

month mes ⓜ mes

monument monumento ⓜ
mo·noo·*men*·to

moon luna ⓕ *loo*·na

more más mas

morning mañana ⓕ ma·*nya*·na

morning sickness náuseas ⓕ pl del
embarazo *now*·se·as del em·ba·*ra*·so

mosque mezquita ⓕ mes·*kee*·ta

mosquito mosquito ⓜ mos·*kee*·to

mosquito coil espiral ⓜ repelente
contra mosquitos es·pee·*ral*
re·pe·*len*·te kon·tra mos·*kee*·tos

mosquito net mosquitera ⓕ
mos·kee·*te*·ra

mother madre ⓕ *ma*·dre

mother-in-law suegra ⓕ *swe*·gra

motorboat motora ⓕ mo·*to*·ra

motorcycle motocicleta ⓕ
mo·to·see·*kle*·ta

motorway autopista ⓕ
ow·to·*pees*·ta

mountain montaña ⓕ mon·*ta*·nya

mountain bike bicicleta ⓕ de montaña bee·see·*kle*·ta de mon·*ta*·nya

mountain path sendero ⓜ sen·*de*·ro

mountain range cordillera ⓕ kor·dee·*ye*·ra

mountaineering alpinismo ⓜ al·pee·*nees*·mo

mouse ratón ⓜ ra·*ton*

mouth boca ⓕ *bo*·ka

movie película ⓕ pe·*lee*·koo·la

mp3 player reproductor ⓜ de mp3 re·pro·dook·*tor* de e·me pe tres

mud lodo ⓜ *lo*·do

mum mamá ⓕ ma·*ma*

muscle músculo ⓜ *moos*·koo·lo

museum museo ⓜ moo·*se*·o

mushroom champiñón ⓜ cham·pee·*nyon*

music música ⓕ *moo*·see·ka

musician músico/a ⓜ/ⓕ *moo*·see·ko/a

Muslim musulmán/musulmana ⓜ/ⓕ moo·sool·*man*/moo·sool·*ma*·na

mussels mejillones ⓜ pl me·khee·*yo*·nes

mustard mostaza ⓕ mos·*ta*·sa

mute mudo/a ⓜ/ⓕ *moo*·do/a

my mi mee

N

nail clippers cortauñas ⓜ kor·ta·oo·nyas

name nombre ⓜ *nom*·bre

napkin servilleta ⓕ ser·vee·*ye*·ta

nappy pañal ⓜ pa·*nyal*

nappy rash irritación ⓕ de pañal ee·ree·ta·*syon* de pa·*nyal*

national nacional na·syo·*nal*

national park parque ⓜ nacional *par*·ke na·syo·*nal*

nationality nacionalidad ⓕ na·syo·na·lee·*da*

nature naturaleza ⓕ na·too·ra·*le*·sa

naturopathy naturopatía ⓕ na·too·ro·pa·*tya*

nausea náusea ⓕ *now*·se·a

near (to) cerca (de) *ser*·ka (de)

nearby cerca *ser*·ka

nearest más cercano/a ⓜ/ⓕ mas ser·*ka*·no/a

necessary necesario/a ⓜ/ⓕ ne·se·*sa*·ryo/a

neck cuello ⓜ *kwe*·yo

need necesitar ne·se·see·*tar*

needle (sewing) aguja ⓕ a·*goo*·kha

needle (syringe) jeringuilla ⓕ khe·reen·*gee*·ya

neither tampoco tam·*po*·ko

net red ⓕ re

Netherlands Holanda ⓕ o·*lan*·da

never nunca *noon*·ka

new nuevo/a ⓜ/ⓕ *nwe*·vo/a

New Year Año ⓜ Nuevo *a*·nyo *nwe*·vo

New Zealand Nueva Zelanda ⓕ *nwe*·va se·*lan*·da

news noticias ⓕ pl no·*tee*·syas

newsagency quiosco ⓜ kee·*os*·ko

newspaper periódico ⓜ pe·*ryo*·dee·ko

next próximo/a ⓜ/ⓕ *prok*·see·mo/a

next to al lado de al *la*·do de

Nicaragua Nicaragua ⓕ nee·ka·*ra*·gwa

nice (object) bueno/a ⓜ/ⓕ *bwe*·no/a

nice (person) simpático/a ⓜ/ⓕ seem·*pa*·tee·ko/a

nickname apodo ⓜ a·*po*·do

night noche ⓕ *no*·che

night life vida ⓕ nocturna *vee*·da nok·*toor*·na

noisy ruidoso/a ⓜ/ⓕ rwee·*do*·so/a

non-direct indirecto/a een·dee·*rek*·to/a

none nada *na*·da

nonfiction literatura ⓕ no novelesca lee·te·ra·*too*·ra no no·ve·*les*·ka

nonsmoking no fumadores no foo·ma·*do*·res

noodles fideos ⓜ pl fee·*de*·os

noon mediodía ⓜ me·dyo·*dee*·a

north norte ⓜ *nor*·te

nose nariz ⓕ na·*rees*

notebook cuaderno ⓜ kwa·*der*·no

nothing nada *na*·da

novel novela ⓕ no·*ve*·la

now ahora a·o·ra

nuclear energy energía ⓕ nuclear e·ner·*khee*·a noo·kle·*ar*

nuclear testing pruebas ⓕ pl nucleares *prwe*·bas noo·kle·a·res

nuclear waste desperdicios ⓜ pl nucleares des·per·*dee*·syos noo·kle·a·res

number número ⓜ *noo*·me·ro

nun monja ⓕ *mon*·kha

nurse enfermero/a ⓜ/ⓕ en·fer·*me*·ro/a

nut nuez ⓕ nwes

O

oats avena ⓕ a·*ve*·na

ocean océano ⓜ o·*se*·a·no

off (spoiled) pasado/a ⓜ/ⓕ pa·*sa*·do/a

office oficina ⓕ o·fee·*see*·na

office worker oficinista ⓜ&ⓕ o·fee·see·*nees*·ta

often a menudo a me·*noo*·do

oil aceite ⓜ a·*say*·te

old viejo/a ⓜ/ⓕ *vye*·kho/a

olive aceituna ⓕ a·say·*too*·na

olive oil aceite ⓜ de oliva a·*say*·te de o·*lee*·va

on en en

once una vez *oo*·na ves

one-way ticket boleto ⓜ sencillo bo·*le*·to sen·*see*·yo

onion cebolla ⓕ se·*bo*·ya

only sólo *so*·lo

open abierto/a ⓜ/ⓕ a·*byer*·to/a

open abrir a·*breer*

opening hours horas ⓕ pl de apertura o·ras de a·per·*too*·ra

opera house teatro ⓜ de la ópera te·*a*·tro de la o·*pe*·ra

operation (medical) operación ⓕ o·pe·ra·*syon*

operator operador(a) ⓜ/ⓕ o·pe·ra·*dor*/o·pe·ra·*do*·ra

opinion opinión ⓕ o·pee·*nyon*

opposite frente a *fren*·te a

or o o

orange (fruit) naranja ⓕ na·*ran*·kha

orange (colour) naranjo/a ⓜ/ⓕ na·*ran*·kho/a

orange juice jugo ⓜ de naranja *khoo*·go de na·*ran*·kha

orchestra orquesta ⓕ or·*kes*·ta

orchid orquídea ⓕ or·*kee*·de·a

order (command) orden ⓕ *or*·den

order (placement) orden ⓜ *or*·den

order ordenar or·de·*nar*

ordinary corriente ko·*ryen*·te

orgasm orgasmo ⓜ or·*gas*·mo

original original o·ree·khee·*nal*

other otro/a ⓜ/ⓕ o·*tro*/a

our nuestro/a ⓜ/ⓕ *nwes*·tro/a

outside afuera a·*fwe*·ra

ovarian cyst quiste ⓜ ovárico *kees*·te o·*va*·ree·ko

oven horno ⓜ *or*·no

over (above) sobre *so*·bre

overcoat abrigo ⓜ a·*bree*·go

overdose sobredosis ⓕ so·bre·*do*·sees

owner dueño/a ⓜ/ⓕ *dwe*·nyo/a

oxygen oxígeno ⓜ ok·*see*·khe·no

oyster ostra ⓕ *os*·tra

ozone layer capa ⓕ de ozono *ka*·pa de o·*so*·no

P

pacemaker marcapasos ⓜ mar·ka·*pa*·sos

pacifier chupete ⓜ choo·*pe*·te

package paquete ⓜ pa·*ke*·te

packet paquete ⓜ pa·*ke*·te

padlock candado ⓜ kan·*da*·do

page página ⓕ *pa*·khee·na

pain dolor ⓜ do·*lor*

painful doloroso/a ⓜ/ⓕ do·lo·ro·so/a

painkillers analgésicos ⓜ pl a·nal·khe·see·kos

paint pintar peen·tar

painter pintor(a) ⓜ/ⓕ peen·tor/peen·to·ra

painting (art) pintura ⓕ peen·too·ra

painting (canvas) cuadro ⓜ kwa·dro

pair (couple) pareja ⓕ pa·re·kha

palace palacio ⓜ pa·la·syo

pan olla ⓕ o·ya

panoramic panorámico/a ⓜ/ⓕ pa·no·ra·mee·ko/a

Panama Panamá ⓕ pa·na·ma

panther pantera ⓕ pan·te·ra

pants pantalones ⓜ pl pan·ta·lo·nes

panty liners salvaeslips ⓜ pl sal·va·e·sleeps

pantyhose medias ⓕ pl me·dyas

pap smear citología ⓕ see·to·lo·khee·a

paper papel ⓜ pa·pel

paperwork trabajo ⓜ administrativo tra·ba·kho ad·mee·nees·tra·tee·vo

Paraguay Paraguay ⓜ pa·ra·gway

parcel paquete ⓜ pa·ke·te

parents padres ⓜ pl pa·dres

park parque ⓜ par·ke

park (car) estacionar es·ta·syo·nar

parliament parlamento ⓜ par·la·men·to

parrot loro ⓜ lo·ro

part parte ⓕ par·te

partner (relationship) pareja ⓜ&ⓕ pa·re·kha

part-time a tiempo parcial a tyem·po par·syal

party (celebration) fiesta ⓕ fyes·ta

party (politics) partido ⓜ par·tee·do

pass (mountain) paso ⓜ pa·so

pass (permit) pase ⓜ pa·se

passenger pasajero/a ⓜ/ⓕ pa·sa·khe·ro/a

passport pasaporte ⓜ pa·sa·por·te

passport number número ⓜ de pasaporte noo·me·ro de pa·sa·por·te

past pasado ⓜ pa·sa·do

path sendero ⓜ sen·de·ro

pay pagar pa·gar

payment pago ⓜ pa·go

pea guisante ⓕ gee·san·te

peace paz ⓕ pas

peach durazno ⓜ doo·ras·no

peak cumbre ⓕ koom·bre

peanut maní ⓜ ma·nee

pear pera ⓕ pe·ra

pedestrian peatón ⓜ&ⓕ pe·a·ton

pegs (tent) estacas ⓕ pl es·ta·kas

pen (ballpoint) bolígrafo ⓜ bo·lee·gra·fo

pencil lápiz ⓜ la·pees

penis pene ⓜ pe·ne

penicillin penicilina ⓕ pe·nee·see·lee·na

penknife navaja ⓕ na·va·kha

pensioner pensionado/a ⓜ/ⓕ pen·syo·na·do/a

people gente ⓕ khen·te

pepper (spice) pimienta ⓕ pee·myen·ta

per (day) por (día) por (dee·a)

percent por ciento por syen·to

performance actuación ⓕ ak·twa·syon

perfume perfume ⓜ per·foo·me

period pain dolor ⓜ menstrual do·lor mens·trwal

permission permiso ⓜ per·mee·so

permit permiso ⓜ per·mee·so

permit permitir per·mee·teer

person persona ⓕ per·so·na

perspire sudar soo·dar

Peru Perú ⓜ pe·roo

petition petición ⓕ pe·tee·syon

petrol gasolina ⓕ ga·so·lee·na

pharmacy farmacia ⓕ far·ma·sya

pharmacist farmacéutico/a ⓜ/ⓕ far·ma·see·oo·tee·ko/a

phone book guía ⓕ telefónica gee·a te·le·fo·nee·ka

phone box cabina ⓕ telefónica
ka-*bee*-na te-le-*fo*-nee-ka

phone card tarjeta ⓕ de teléfono
tar-*khe*-ta de te-*le*-fo-no

photo fotografía ⓕ fo-to-gra-*fee*-a

photocopier fotocopiadora ⓕ
fo-to-ko-pya-*do*-ra

photographer fotógrafo/a ⓜ/ⓕ
fo-*to*-gra-fo/a

photography fotografía ⓕ
fo-to-gra-*fee*-a

phrasebook libro ⓜ de frases
lee-bro de *fra*-ses

pick (up) levantar le-van-*tar*

pickaxe piqueta ⓕ pee-*ke*-ta

pickles pepinillos ⓜ pl
pe-pee-*nee*-yos

pie empanada ⓕ em-pa-*na*-da

piece pedazo ⓜ pe-*da*-so

pig cerdo ⓜ *ser*-do

pill pastilla ⓕ pas-*tee*-ya

the Pill la píldora ⓕ la *peel*-do-ra

pillow almohada ⓕ al-mo-a-da

pillowcase funda ⓕ de almohada
foon-da de al-mo-a-da

pineapple ananá(s) ⓜ a-na-*na*(s)

pink rosa *ro*-sa

pistachio pistacho ⓜ pees-*ta*-cho

place lugar ⓜ loo-*gar*

place of birth lugar ⓜ de nacimiento
loo-*gar* de na-see-*myen*-to

plane avión ⓜ a-*vyon*

planet planeta ⓜ pla-*ne*-ta

plant planta ⓕ *plan*-ta

plant sembrar sem-*brar*

plastic plástico ⓜ *plas*-tee-ko

plate plato ⓜ *pla*-to

plateau meseta ⓕ me-*se*-ta

platform plataforma ⓕ pla-ta-*for*-ma

play obra ⓕ o-bra

play (a game) jugar khoo-*gar*

play (the guitar) tocar (la guitarra)
to-*kar* (la gee-*ta*-ra)

play (tennis) jugar (al tenis)
khoo-*gar* (al *te*-nees)

plug (bath) tapón ⓜ ta-*pon*

plug (electricity) enchufe ⓜ
en-*choo*-fe

plum ciruela ⓕ see-*rwe*-la

pocket bolsillo ⓜ bol-*see*-yo

poetry poesía ⓕ po-e-*see*-a

point punto ⓜ *poon*-to

point apuntar a-poon-*tar*

poisonous venenoso/a ⓜ/ⓕ
ve-ne-*no*-so/a

police policía ⓕ po-lee-*see*-a

police station comisaría ⓕ
ko-mee-sa-*ree*-a

policy política ⓕ po-*lee*-tee-ka

policy (insurance) póliza ⓕ
po-lee-sa

politician político/a ⓜ/ⓕ
po-*lee*-tee-ko/a

politics política ⓕ po-*lee*-tee-ka

polls sondeos ⓜ pl son-*de*-os

pollution contaminación ⓕ
kon-ta-mee-na-*syon*

pony potro ⓜ *po*-tro

pool (game) billar ⓜ bee-*yar*

pool (swimming) piscina ⓕ
pee-*see*-na

poor pobre *po*-bre

popular popular po-poo-*lar*

pork cerdo ⓜ *ser*-do

port puerto ⓜ *pwer*-to

port (wine) oporto ⓜ o-*por*-to

portable CD player reproductor ⓜ
de compacts portátil re-pro-dook-*tor*
de *kom*-paks por-ta-*teel*

possible posible po-*see*-ble

post code código ⓜ postal
ko-dee-go pos-*tal*

post office correos ⓜ pl ko-*re*-os

postage franqueo ⓜ fran-*ke*-o

postcard postal ⓕ pos-*tal*

pot (ceramic) cacharro ⓜ ka-*cha*-ro

pot (kitchen) olla ⓕ o-ya

pot (dope) chocolate ⓜ cho-ko-*la*-te

potato papa ⓕ *pa*-pa

pottery alfarería ⓕ al-fa-re-*ree*-a

pound (money) libra ⓕ *lee*-bra

poverty pobreza ⓕ po-*bre*-sa

Q

power poder ⓜ po·*der*

prawn langostino ⓜ lan·gos·*tee*·no

prayer oración ⓕ o·ra·*syon*

prefer preferir pre·fe·*reer*

pregnancy test kit prueba ⓕ del embarazo *prwe*·ba del em·ba·*ra*·so

pregnant embarazada ⓕ em·ba·ra·*sa*·da

premenstrual tension tensión ⓕ premenstrual ten·*syon* pre·mens·*trwal*

prepare preparar pre·pa·*rar*

present (gift) regalo ⓜ re·*ga*·lo

presentation presentación ⓕ pre·sen·ta·*syon*

president presidente/a ⓜ/ⓕ pre·see·*den*·te/a

pressure presión ⓕ pre·*syon*

pretty bonito/a ⓜ/ⓕ bo·*nee*·to/a

prevent prevenir pre·ve·*neer*

price precio ⓜ *pre*·syo

priest sacerdote ⓜ sa·ser·*do*·te

prime minister (man) primer ministro ⓜ pree·*mer* mee·*nees*·tro

prime minister (woman) primera ministra ⓕ pree·*me*·ra mee·*nees*·tra

prison cárcel ⓕ *kar*·sel

prisoner prisionero/a ⓜ/ⓕ pree·syo·ne·ro/a

private privado/a ⓜ/ⓕ pree·*va*·do/a

produce producir pro·doo·*seer*

profit beneficio ⓜ be·ne·*fee*·syo

programme programa ⓜ pro·*gra*·ma

projector proyector ⓜ pro·yek·*tor*

promise promesa ⓕ pro·*me*·sa

proposal propuesta ⓕ pro·*pwes*·ta

protect proteger pro·te·*kher*

protected protegido/a ⓜ/ⓕ pro·te·*khee*·do/a

protest protesta ⓕ pro·*tes*·ta

protest protestar pro·tes·*tar*

provisions provisiones ⓕ pl pro·vee·*syo*·nes

prune ciruela ⓕ pasa see·*rwe*·la *pa*·sa

public telephone teléfono ⓜ público te·*le*·fo·no poo·blee·ko

public toilet baños ⓜ pl *ba*·nyos

Puerto Rico Puerto ⓜ Rico *pwer*·to *ree*·ko

pull jalar kha·*lar*

pump bomba ⓕ *bom*·ba

pumpkin calabaza ⓕ ka·la·*ba*·sa

puncture pinchar peen·*char*

punish castigar kas·tee·*gar*

puppy cachorro ⓜ ka·*cho*·ro

pure puro/a ⓜ/ⓕ *poo*·ro/a

purple morado/a ⓜ/ⓕ mo·*ra*·do/a

push empujar em·poo·*khar*

put poner po·*ner*

Q

qualifications cualificaciones ⓕ pl kwa·lee·fee·ka·*syo*·nes

quality calidad ⓕ ka·lee·*da*

quarantine cuarentena ⓕ kwa·ren·*te*·na

quarrel pelea ⓕ pe·*le*·a

quarter cuarto ⓜ *kwar*·to

queen reina ⓕ *ray*·na

question pregunta ⓕ pre·*goon*·ta

queue cola ⓕ *ko*·la

quick rápido/a ⓜ/ⓕ *ra*·pee·do/a

quiet tranquilo/a ⓜ/ⓕ tran·*kee*·lo/a

R

rabbit conejo ⓜ ko·*ne*·kho

race (people) raza ⓕ *ra*·sa

race (sport) carrera ⓕ ka·*re*·ra

racetrack (sport) pista ⓕ *pees*·ta

racing bike bicicleta ⓕ de carreras bee·see·*kle*·ta de ka·*re*·ras

racquet raqueta ⓕ ra·*ke*·ta

radiator radiador ⓜ ra·dya·*dor*

radish rábano ⓜ *ra*·ba·no

railway ferrocarril ⓜ fe·ro·ka·*reel*

railway station estación ⓕ de tren es·ta·*syon* de tren

rain lluvia ⓕ *yoo*·vya

raincoat impermeable ⓜ eem·per·me·*a*·ble

raisin pasa ⓕ de uva *pa*·sa de oo·va

R

rape violar vyo·*lar*

rare raro/a ⓜ/ⓕ ra·ro/a

rash irritación ⓕ ee·rree·ta·*syon*

raspberry frambuesa ⓕ fram·*bwe*·sa

rat rata ⓕ *ra*·ta

raw crudo/a ⓜ/ⓕ *kroo*·do/a

razor afeitadora ⓕ a·fay·ta·*do*·ra

razor blade hoja ⓕ de afeitar o·kha de a·fay·*tar*

read leer le·*er*

ready listo/a ⓜ/ⓕ *lees*·to/a

real estate agent agente ⓜ inmobiliario a·*khen*·te een·mo·bee·*lya*·ryo

realistic realista re·a·*lees*·ta

reason razón ⓕ ra·*son*

receipt recibo ⓜ re·*see*·bo

receive recibir re·see·*beer*

recently recientemente re·syen·te·*men*·te

recognise reconocer re·ko·no·*ser*

recommend recomendar re·ko·men·*dar*

recording grabación ⓕ gra·ba·*syon*

recyclable reciclable re·see·*kla*·ble

recycle reciclar re·see·*klar*

red rojo/a ⓜ/ⓕ *ro*·kho/a

referee árbitro ⓜ *ar*·bee·tro

references (work) referencias ⓕ pl re·fe·*ren*·syas

refrigerator refrigeradora ⓕ re·free·khe·ra·*do*·ra

refugee refugiado/a ⓜ/ⓕ re·foo·*khya*·do/a

refund reembolso ⓜ re·em·*bol*·so

refuse negar(se) ne·*gar*(·se)

registered mail correo ⓜ certificado ko·*re*·o ser·tee·fee·*ka*·do

relationship relación ⓕ re·la·*syon*

relax relajarse re·la·*khar*·se

relic reliquia ⓕ re·*lee*·kya

religion religión ⓕ re·lee·*khyon*

religious religioso/a ⓜ/ⓕ re·lee·*khyo*·so/a

remote remoto/a ⓜ/ⓕ re·*mo*·to/a

remote control mando ⓜ a distancia *man*·do a dees·*tan*·sya

rent alquiler ⓜ al·kee·*ler*

rent alquilar al·kee·*lar*

repair reparar re·pa·*rar*

republic república ⓕ re·*poo*·blee·ka

reservation reserva ⓕ re·*ser*·va

reserve hacer una reserva a·*ser* oo·na re·*ser*·va

rest descansar des·kan·*sar*

restaurant restaurante ⓜ res·tow·*ran*·te

resume currículum ⓜ koo·*ree*·koo·loom

retired jubilado/a ⓜ/ⓕ khoo·bee·*la*·do/a

return volver vol·*ver*

return ticket boleto ⓜ de ida y vuelta (bo·*le*·to) de *ee*·da ee *vwel*·ta

reverse charge call llamada ⓕ a cobro revertido ya·*ma*·da a *ko*·bro re·ver·*tee*·do

review crítica ⓕ *kree*·tee·ka

rhythm ritmo ⓜ *reet*·mo

rice arroz ⓜ a·*ros*

rich rico/a ⓜ/ⓕ *ree*·ko/a

ride paseo ⓜ pa·*se*·o

ride montar mon·*tar*

right (correct) correcto/a ⓜ/ⓕ ko·*rek*·to/a

right (direction) derecha de·*re*·cha

right-wing derechista de·re·*chees*·ta

ring (on finger) anillo ⓜ a·*nee*·yo

ring (by phone) llamar por teléfono ya·*mar* por te·*le*·fo·no

rip-off estafa ⓕ es·*ta*·fa

risk riesgo ⓜ *ryes*·go

river río ⓜ *ree*·o

road calle ⓕ *ka*·ye

rob robar ro·*bar*

rock (stone) roca ⓕ *ro*·ka

rock climbing escalada ⓕ es·ka·*la*·da

rock group grupo ⓜ de rock *groo*·po de rok

roll (bread) bollo ⓜ *bo*·yo

S

romance novel novela ⓕ rosa no·ve·la *ro*·sa
romantic romántico/a ⓜ/ⓕ ro·*man*·tee·ko/a
roof techo ⓜ *te*·cho
room habitación ⓕ a·bee·ta·*syon*
room number número ⓜ de habitación *noo*·me·ro de a·bee·ta·*syon*
rope cuerda ⓕ *kwer*·da
round redondo/a ⓜ/ⓕ re·*don*·do/a
roundabout glorieta ⓕ glo·*rye*·ta
route ruta ⓕ *roo*·ta
rowing remo ⓜ *re*·mo
rubbish basura ⓕ ba·*soo*·ra
rug alfombra ⓕ al·*fom*·bra
ruins ruinas ⓕ pl *rwee*·nas
rules reglas ⓕ pl *re*·glas
rum ron ⓜ ron
running (sport) footing ⓜ *foo*·teen

S

sad triste *trees*·te
saddle sillín ⓜ see·*yeen*
safe caja ⓕ fuerte *ka*·kha *fwer*·te
safe seguro/a ⓜ/ⓕ se·*goo*·ro/a
safe sex sexo ⓜ seguro *sek*·so se·*goo*·ro
sail vela ⓕ *ve*·la
sailing boat barco ⓜ de vela *bar*·ko de *ve*·la
saint santo/a ⓜ/ⓕ *san*·to/a
salad ensalada ⓕ en·sa·*la*·da
salary salario ⓜ sa·*la*·ryo
sales tax IVA ⓜ *ee*·va
salt sal ⓕ sal
same igual ee·*gwal*
sand arena ⓕ a·*re*·na
sandals sandalias ⓕ pl san·*da*·lyas
sanitary napkins compresas ⓕ pl kom·*pre*·sas
saucepan olla ⓕ *o*·ya
sauna sauna ⓕ *sow*·na
sausage salchicha ⓕ sal·*chee*·cha
say decir de·*seer*
scale (climb) trepar tre·*par*

scarf bufanda ⓕ boo·*fan*·da
school escuela ⓕ es·*kwe*·la
science ciencia ⓕ *syen*·sya
science fiction ciencia ⓕ ficción *syen*·sya feek·*syon*
scientist científico/a ⓜ/ⓕ syen·*tee*·fee·ko/a
scissors tijeras ⓕ pl tee·*khe*·ras
score marcar mar·*kar*
scoreboard marcador ⓜ mar·ka·*dor*
screen pantalla ⓕ pan·*ta*·ya
sea mar ⓜ mar
seasickness mareo ⓜ ma·*re*·o
seaside orilla ⓕ del mar o·*ree*·ya del mar
season estación ⓕ es·ta·*syon*
seat asiento ⓜ a·*syen*·to
seatbelt cinturón ⓜ de seguridad seen·too·*ron* de se·goo·ree·*da*
second segundo ⓜ se·*goon*·do
second segundo/a ⓜ/ⓕ se·*goon*·do/a
second-hand de segunda mano de se·*goon*·da *ma*·no
secretary secretario/a ⓜ/ⓕ se·kre·*ta*·ryo/a
see ver ver
selfish egoísta ⓜ&ⓕ e·go·*ees*·ta
self-service autoservicio ⓜ ow·to·ser·*vee*·syo
sell vender ven·*der*
send enviar en·*vyar*
sensible juicioso/a ⓜ/ⓕ khwee·*syo*·so/a
sensual sensual sen·*swal*
separate separado/a ⓜ/ⓕ se·pa·*ra*·do/a
separate separar se·pa·*rar*
series serie ⓕ *se*·rye
serious serio/a ⓜ/ⓕ *se*·ryo/a
service charge servicio ⓜ ser·*vee*·syo
service station gasolinera ⓕ ga·so·lee·*ne*·ra
several varios/as ⓜ/ⓕ *va*·ryos/as
sew coser ko·*ser*

sex sexo ⓜ *sek·*so

sexism sexismo ⓜ sek·*sees·*mo

shade sombra ⓕ *som·*bra

shadow sombra ⓕ *som·*bra

shampoo champú ⓜ cham·*poo*

shape forma ⓕ *for·*ma

share (with) compartir kom·par·*teer*

shave afeitarse a·fay·*tar·*se

shaving cream espuma ⓕ de afeitar es·*poo·*ma de a·fay·*tar*

she ella e·ya

sheep oveja ⓕ o·*ve·*kha

sheet (bed) sábana ⓕ *sa·*ba·na

ship barco ⓜ *bar·*ko

shirt camisa ⓕ ka·*mee·*sa

shoe shop zapatería ⓕ sa·pa·te·*ree·*a

shoes zapatos ⓜ pl sa·*pa·*tos

shoot disparar dees·pa·*rar*

shop tienda ⓕ *tyen·*da

shoplifting hurto en tiendas oor·to en *tyen·*das

(go) shopping ir de compras eer de *kom·*pras

shopping centre centro ⓜ comercial *sen·*tro ko·mer·*syal*

short (height) bajo/a ⓜ/ⓕ *ba·*kho/a

short (length) corto/a ⓜ/ⓕ *kor·*to/a

shortage escasez ⓕ es·ka·*ses*

shorts pantalones ⓜ pl cortos pan·ta·*lo·*nes *kor·*tos

short stories cuentos ⓜ pl *kwen·*tos

shoulders hombros ⓜ pl *om·*bros

shout gritar gree·*tar*

show espectáculo ⓜ es·pek·*ta·*koo·lo

show mostrar mos·*trar*

shower ducha ⓕ *doo·*cha

shrine capilla ⓕ ka·*pee·*ya

shut cerrado/a ⓜ/ⓕ se·*ra·*do/a

shy tímido/a ⓜ/ⓕ *tee·*mee·do/a

sick enfermo/a ⓜ/ⓕ en·*fer·*mo/a

side lado ⓜ *la·*do

sign señal ⓕ se·*nyal*

signature firma ⓕ *feer·*ma

silk seda ⓕ *se·*da

silver plata ⓕ *pla·*ta

SIM card tarjeta ⓕ SIM tar·*khe·*ta seem

simple sencillo/a ⓜ/ⓕ sen·*see·*yo/a

since (time) desde *des·*de

sing cantar kan·*tar*

singer cantante ⓜ&ⓕ kan·*tan·*te

single (unmarried) soltero/a ⓜ/ⓕ sol·*te·*ro/a

single room habitación ⓕ individual a·bee·ta·*syon* een·dee·vee·*dwal*

singlet camiseta ⓕ ka·mee·*se·*ta

sister hermana ⓕ er·*ma·*na

sit sentarse sen·*tar·*se

size (clothes) talla ⓕ *ta·*ya

size (general) tamaño ⓜ ta·*ma·*nyo

skateboarding monopatinaje ⓜ mo·no·pa·tee·*na·*khe

ski esquiar es·*kyar*

skiing esquí ⓜ es·*kee*

ski lift telesquí ⓜ te·le·*skee*

skis esquís ⓜ pl es·*kees*

skimmed milk leche ⓕ desnatada *le·*che des·na·*ta·*da

skin piel ⓕ pyel

skirt falda ⓕ *fal·*da

sky cielo ⓜ *sye·*lo

sleep dormir dor·*meer*

sleeping bag saco ⓜ de dormir *sa·*ko de dor·*meer*

sleeping car coche ⓜ cama ko·che *ka·*ma

sleeping pills pastillas ⓕ pl para dormir pas·*tee·*yas *pa·*ra dor·*meer*

(be) sleepy tener sueño te·*ner swe·*nyo

slide (film) diapositiva ⓕ dya·po·see·*tee·*va

slow lento/a ⓜ/ⓕ *len·*to/a

slowly despacio des·*pa·*syo

small pequeño/a ⓜ/ⓕ pe·*ke·*nyo/a

smell olor ⓜ o·*lor*

smile sonreír son·re·*eer*

smoke fumar foo·*mar*

snack tentempié ⓜ ten·tem·*pye*

snail caracol ⓜ ka·ra·*kol*

snake serpiente ⓕ ser·*pyen*·te

snorkelling buceo ⓜ boo·*se*·o

snow nieve ⓕ *nye*·ve

snowboarding surf ⓜ sobre la nieve soorf *so*·bre la *nye*·ve

soap jabón ⓜ kha·*bon*

soap opera telenovela ⓕ te·le·no·*ve*·la

soccer fútbol ⓜ *foot*·bol

social welfare asistencia ⓕ social a·sees·*ten*·sya so·*syal*

socialist socialista so·sya·*lees*·ta

socks calcetines ⓜ pl kal·se·*tee*·nes

soft drink gaseosa ⓕ ga·se·o·sa

soldier soldado ⓜ sol·*da*·do

some algunos/as ⓜ/ⓕ pl al·*goo*·nos/as

someone alguien *al*·gyen

something algo *al*·go

sometimes de vez en cuando de ves en *kwan*·do

son hijo ⓜ *ee*·kho

song canción ⓕ kan·*syon*

soon pronto *pron*·to

sore dolorido/a ⓜ/ⓕ do·lo·*ree*·do/a

soup sopa ⓕ *so*·pa

sour cream crema ⓕ agria *kre*·ma *a*·grya

south sur ⓜ soor

South America Sudamérica ⓕ soo·da·*me*·ree·ka

South American sudamericano/a ⓜ/ⓕ soo·da·me·ree·*ka*·no/a

souvenir recuerdo ⓜ re·*kwer*·do

souvenir shop tienda ⓕ de recuerdos *tyen*·da de re·*kwer*·dos

soy milk leche ⓕ de soya *le*·che de *so*·ya

soy sauce salsa ⓕ de soya *sal*·sa de *so*·ya

space espacio ⓜ es·*pa*·syo

spade pala ⓕ *pa*·la

Spain España ⓕ es·*pa*·nya

speak hablar a·*blar*

special especial es·pe·*syal*

specialist especialista ⓜ&ⓕ es·pe·sya·*lees*·ta

speed velocidad ⓕ ve·lo·see·*da*

speed limit límite ⓜ de velocidad *lee*·mee·te de ve·lo·see·*da*

speedometer velocímetro ⓜ ve·lo·*see*·me·tro

spermicide espermicida ⓕ es·per·mee·*see*·da

spider araña ⓕ a·*ra*·nya

spinach espinacas ⓕ pl es·pee·*na*·kas

spoon cuchara ⓕ koo·*cha*·ra

sport deportes ⓜ pl de·*por*·tes

sports store tienda ⓕ deportiva *tyen*·da de·por·*tee*·va

sportsperson deportista ⓜ&ⓕ de·por·*tees*·ta

sprain torcedura ⓕ tor·se·*doo*·ra

spring (mechanical) muelle ⓜ *mwe*·ye

spring (season) primavera ⓕ pree·ma·*ve*·ra

square (shape) cuadrado ⓜ kwa·*dra*·do

square (town) plaza ⓕ *pla*·sa

stadium estadio ⓜ es·*ta*·dyo

stage escenario ⓜ e·se·*na*·ryo

stairway escalera ⓕ es·ka·*le*·ra

stamp sello ⓜ *se*·yo

standby ticket boleto ⓜ de lista de espera bo·*le*·to de *lees*·ta de es·*pe*·ra

stars estrellas ⓕ pl es·*tre*·yas

start comenzar ko·men·*sar*

station estación ⓕ es·ta·*syon*

statue estatua ⓕ es·*ta*·twa

stay (at a hotel) alojarse a·lo·*khar*·se

stay (remain) quedarse ke·*dar*·se

STD (sexually transmitted disease) enfermedad ⓕ de transmisión sexual en·fer·mee·*da* de trans·mee·*syon* sek·*swal*

steak (beef) bistec ⓜ bees·*tek*

steal robar ro·*bar*

steep escarpado/a ⓜ/ⓕ
es·kar·pa·do/a

step paso ⓜ pa·so

stereo equipo ⓜ estereofónico
e·kee·po es·te·re·o·fo·nee·ko

stingy tacaño/a ⓜ/ⓕ ta·ka·nyo/a

stockings medias ⓕ pl me·dyas

stomach estómago ⓜ es·to·ma·go

stomachache dolor ⓜ de estómago
do·lor de es·to·ma·go

stone piedra ⓕ pye·dra

stoned (drugged) volado/a ⓜ/ⓕ
vo·la·do/a

stop parada ⓕ pa·ra·da

stop parar pa·rar

storm tormenta ⓕ tor·men·ta

story cuento ⓜ kwen·to

stove estufa ⓕ es·too·fa

straight recto/a ⓜ/ⓕ rek·to/a

strange extraño/a ⓜ/ⓕ
ek·stra·nyo/a

stranger extraño/a ⓜ/ⓕ
ek·stra·nyo/a

strawberry frutilla ⓕ froo·tee·ya

stream arroyo ⓜ a·ro·yo

street calle ⓕ ka·ye

street market feria ⓕ fe·rya

string cuerda ⓕ kwer·da

strong fuerte fwer·te

stubborn testarudo/a ⓜ/ⓕ
tes·ta·roo·do/a

student estudiante ⓜ&ⓕ
es·too·dyan·te

studio estudio ⓜ es·too·dyo

stupid estúpido/a ⓜ/ⓕ
es·too·pee·do/a

style estilo ⓜ es·tee·lo

subtitles subtítulos ⓜ pl
soob·tee·too·los

suburb barrio ⓜ ba·ryo

subway subterráneo soob·te·ra·ne·o

sugar azúcar ⓜ a·soo·kar

sugar cane caña ⓕ de azúcar ka·nya
de a·soo·kar

suit traje ⓜ tra·khe

suitcase maleta ⓕ ma·le·ta

summer verano ⓜ ve·ra·no

sun sol ⓜ sol

sunblock crema ⓕ solar kre·ma
so·lar

sunburn quemadura ⓕ de sol
ke·ma·doo·ra de sol

sunglasses anteojos ⓕ pl de sol
an·te·o·khos de sol

sunny soleado/a ⓜ/ⓕ so·le·a·do/a

sunrise amanecer ⓜ a·ma·ne·ser

sunset puesta ⓕ del sol pwes·ta
del sol

sunstroke insolación ⓕ
een·so·la·syon

supermarket supermercado ⓜ
soo·per·mer·ka·do

superstition superstición ⓕ
soo·per·stee·syon

supporters hinchas ⓜ&ⓕ pl
een·chas

surf hacer surf a·ser soorf

surface mail por vía terrestre por
vee·a te·res·tre

surf hacer surfing ⓜ a·ser soorf·een

surfboard tabla ⓕ de surf ta·bla
de soorf

surname apellido ⓜ a·pe·yee·do

surprise sorpresa ⓕ sor·pre·sa

sweater (jumper) jersey ⓜ kher·say

sweet dulce dool·se

swim nadar na·dar

swimming pool piscina ⓕ
pee·see·na

swimsuit traje ⓜ de baño tra·khe
de ba·nyo

synagogue sinagoga ⓕ see·na·go·ga

synthetic sintético/a ⓜ/ⓕ
seen·te·tee·ko/a

syringe jeringa ⓕ khe·reen·ga

T

table mesa ⓕ me·sa

table tennis ping pong ⓜ peen pon

tablecloth mantel ⓜ man·tel

tail rabo ⓜ ra·bo

tailor sastre ⓜ sas·tre

take tomar to·*mar*

talk hablar a·*blar*

tall alto/a ⓜ/ⓕ *al*·to/a

tampons tampones ⓜ pl tam·*po*·nes

tanning lotion bronceador ⓜ bron·se·a·*dor*

tap (faucet) grifo ⓜ *gree*·fo

tapir danta ⓕ *dan*·ta

tasty sabroso/a ⓜ/ⓕ sa·*bro*·so/a

tax impuesto ⓜ eem·*pwes*·to

taxi stand parada ⓕ de taxis pa·*ra*·da de *tak*·sees

tea té ⓜ te

teacher profesor(a) ⓜ/ⓕ pro·fe·*sor*/pro·fe·*so*·ra

team equipo ⓜ e·*kee*·po

teaspoon cucharita ⓕ koo·cha·*ree*·ta

teeth dientes ⓜ pl *dyen*·tes

telegram telegrama ⓜ te·le·*gra*·ma

telephone teléfono ⓜ te·*le*·fo·no

telephone llamar (por teléfono) ya·*mar* (por te·*le*·fo·no)

telephone centre central ⓕ telefónica sen·*tral* te·le·fo·nee·ka

telephoto lens teleobjetivo ⓜ te·le·ob·khe·*tee*·vo

television televisión ⓕ te·le·vee·*syon*

tell decir de·*seer*

temperature (fever) fiebre ⓕ *fye*·bre

temperature (weather) temperatura ⓕ tem·pe·ra·*too*·ra

temple templo ⓜ *tem*·plo

tennis court cancha ⓕ de tenis *kan*·cha de te·nees

tent carpa ⓕ *kar*·pa

tent pegs estacas ⓕ de carpa es·*ta*·kas de *kar*·pa

terrible terible te·*ree*·ble

test prueba ⓕ *prwe*·ba

testimonial literature literatura ⓕ testimonial lee·te·ra·*too*·ra tes·tee·mo·*nyal*

thank dar gracias dar *gra*·syas

the Pill píldora ⓕ *peel*·do·ra

theatre teatro ⓜ te·a·tro

their su soo

they ellos/ellas ⓜ/ⓕ pl e·yos/e·yas

thief ladrón/ladrona ⓜ/ⓕ la·*dron*/la·*dro*·na

thin delgado/a ⓜ/ⓕ del·*ga*·do/a

think pensar pen·*sar*

third tercio ⓜ *ter*·syo

thirst sed ⓕ se

(be) thirsty tener sed ⓕ te·*ner* se

this éste/a ⓜ/ⓕ *es*·te/a

throat garganta ⓕ gar·*gan*·ta

thrush (medical) aftas ⓕ pl *af*·tas

ticket boleto ⓜ bo·*le*·to

ticket collector revisor(a) ⓜ/ⓕ re·vee·*sor*/re·vee·*so*·ra

ticket machine máquina ⓕ de boletos *ma*·kee·na de bo·*le*·tos

ticket office (theatre, cinema) taquilla ⓕ ta·*kee*·ya

ticket office (general) boletería ⓕ bo·le·te·*ree*·a

tide marea ⓕ ma·*re*·a

tight apretado/a ⓜ/ⓕ a·pre·*ta*·do/a

time (hour) hora ⓕ *o*·ra

time (period) tiempo ⓜ *tyem*·po

time difference diferencia ⓕ de horas dee·fe·*ren*·sya de o·ras

timetable horario ⓜ o·*ra*·ryo

tin (can) lata ⓕ *la*·ta

tin opener abrelatas ⓜ a·bre·*la*·tas

tiny pequeñito/a ⓜ/ⓕ pe·ke·*nyee*·to/a

tip (gratuity) propina ⓕ pro·*pee*·na

tired cansado/a ⓜ/ⓕ kan·*sa*·do/a

tissues pañuelos ⓜ pl de papel pa·*nywe*·los de pa·*pel*

toast tostada ⓕ tos·*ta*·da

toaster tostadora ⓕ tos·ta·*do*·ra

tobacco tabaco ⓜ ta·*ba*·ko

tobacconist estanquero ⓜ es·tan·*ke*·ro

tobogganing ir en tobogán eer en to·bo·*gan*

today hoy oy

toe dedo ⓜ del pie *de*·do del pye

together juntos/as ⓜ/ⓕ pl
*khoon·*tos/as

toilet baño ⓜ • servicio ⓜ *ba·*nyo •
ser·*vee·*syo

toilet paper papel ⓜ higiénico
pa·*pel* ee·*khye·*nee·ko

tomato tomate ⓜ to·*ma·*te

tomato sauce salsa ⓕ de tomate
sal·*sa* de to·*ma·*te

tomorrow mañana ⓕ ma·*nya·*na

tonight esta noche es·ta *no·*che

too (expensive) demasiado
(caro/a) ⓜ/ⓕ de·ma·*sya·*do (*ka·*ro/a)

tooth (back) muela ⓕ *mwe·*la

toothache dolor ⓜ de muelas do·*lor*
de *mwe·*las

toothbrush cepillo ⓜ de dientes
se·*pee·*yo de *dyen·*tes

toothpaste pasta ⓕ dentífrica
*pas·*ta den·*tee·*free·ka

toothpick palillo ⓜ pa·*lee·*yo

torch (flashlight) linterna ⓕ
leen·*ter·*na

touch tocar to·*kar*

tour excursión ⓕ ek·skoor·*syon*

tourist turista ⓜ&ⓕ too·*rees·*ta

tourist office oficina ⓕ de turismo
o·fee·*see·*na de too·*rees·*mo

towards hacia *a·*sya

towel toalla ⓕ to·*a·*ya

tower torre ⓕ *to·*re

toxic waste residuos ⓜ pl tóxicos
re·*see·*dwos *tok·*se·kos

toy shop juguetería ⓕ
khoo·ge·te·*ree·*a

track (path) camino ⓜ ka·*mee·*no

track (sports) pista ⓕ *pees·*ta

trade comercio ⓜ ko·*mer·*syo

traffic tráfico ⓜ *tra·*fee·ko

traffic lights semáforos ⓜ pl
se·*ma·*fo·ros

trail camino ⓜ ka·*mee·*no

train tren ⓜ tren

train station estación ⓕ de tren
es·ta·*syon* de tren

tram tranvía ⓜ tran·*vee·*a

transit lounge sala ⓕ de tránsito
*sa·*la de *tran·*see·to

translate traducir tra·doo·*seer*

transport transporte ⓜ trans·*por·*te

travel viajar vya·*khar*

travel agency agencia ⓕ de viajes
a·*khen·*sya de *vya·*khes

travel books libros ⓜ pl de viajes
*lee·*bros de *vya·*khes

travel sickness mareo ⓜ ma·*re·*o

travellers cheque cheque ⓜ de
viajero *che·*ke de vya·*khe·*ro

tree árbol ⓜ *ar·*bol

trip viaje ⓜ *vya·*khe

trousers pantalones ⓜ pl
pan·ta·*lo·*nes

truck camión ⓜ ka·*myon*

trust confianza ⓕ kon·*fyan·*sa

trust confiar kon·*fyar*

try (attempt) probar pro·*bar*

T-shirt camiseta ⓕ ka·mee·*se·*ta

tube (tyre) cámara ⓕ de aire
*ka·*ma·ra de *ai·*re

tuna atún ⓜ a·*toon*

tune melodía ⓕ me·lo·*dee·*a

turkey pavo ⓜ *pa·*vo

turn doblar do·*blar*

TV tele ⓕ *te·*le

tweezers pinzas ⓕ pl *peen·*sas

twice dos veces dos *ve·*ses

twin beds dos camas ⓕ pl dos
*ka·*mas

twins gemelos/as ⓜ/ⓕ pl
khe·*me·*los/as

type tipo ⓜ *tee·*po

typical típico/a ⓜ/ⓕ *tee·*pee·ko/a

tyre llanta ⓕ *yan·*ta

U

ultrasound ecografía ⓕ
e·ko·gra·*fee·*a

umbrella paraguas ⓜ pa·*ra·*gwas

umpire árbitro/a ⓜ/ⓕ ar·*bee·*tro/a

uncle tío ⓜ *tee·*o

uncomfortable incómodo/a ⓜ/ⓕ
een·*ko·*mo·do/a

V

underpants (men) calzoncillos ⓜ pl
kal·son·*see*·yos
underpants (women) bragas ⓕ pl
bra·gas
understand entender en·ten·*der*
underwater camera cámara ⓕ
submarina ka·ma·ra soob·ma·*ree*·na
underwear ropa ⓕ interior *ro*·pa
een·te·*ryor*
unemployed desempleado/a ⓜ/ⓕ
des·em·ple·*a*·do/a
unfair injusto/a ⓜ/ⓕ een·*khoos*·to/a
uniform uniforme ⓜ oo·nee·*for*·me
universe universo ⓜ oo·nee·*ver*·so
university universidad ⓕ
oo·nee·ver·*see*·da
unleaded sin plomo seen *plo*·mo
unsafe inseguro/a ⓜ/ⓕ
een·se·*goo*·ro/a
until hasta *as*·ta
unusual extraño/a ⓜ/ⓕ
ek·*stra*·nyo/a
up arriba a·*ree*·ba
uphill cuesta arriba kwes·ta a·*ree*·ba
urgent urgente oor·*khen*·te
Uruguay Uruguay ⓜ oo·roo·*gway*
USA Los Estados ⓜ pl Unidos los
es·*ta*·dos oo·*nee*·dos
useful útil oo·*teel*

V

vacant vacante va·*kan*·te
vacation vacaciones ⓕ pl
va·ka·*syo*·nes
vaccination vacuna ⓕ va·*koo*·na
vagina vagina ⓕ va·*khee*·na
vaginal discharge flujo ⓜ vaginal
floo·kho va·khee·*nal*
validate validar va·lee·*dar*
valley valle ⓜ *va*·ye
valuable valioso/a ⓜ/ⓕ va·*lyo*·so/a
value valor ⓜ va·*lor*
van caravana ⓕ ka·ra·*va*·na
veal ternera ⓕ ter·*ne*·ra
vegan vegetariano/a estricto/a ⓜ/ⓕ
ve·khe·ta·*rya*·no/a es·*treek*·to/a

vegetable verdura ⓕ ver·*doo*·ra
vegetable garden huerta ⓕ *wer*·ta
vegetarian vegetariano/a ⓜ/ⓕ
ve·khe·ta·*rya*·no/a
vein vena ⓕ *ve*·na
venereal disease enfermedad ⓕ
venérea en·fer·me·*da* ve·ne·*re*·a
Venezuela Venezuela ⓕ ve·ne·*swe*·la
venue local ⓜ lo·*kal*
very muy mooy
video tape cinta ⓕ de vídeo *seen*·ta
de *vee*·de·o
view vista ⓕ *vees*·ta
village pueblo ⓜ *pwe*·blo
vinegar vinagre ⓜ vee·*na*·gre
vineyard viñedo ⓜ vee·*nye*·do
virus virus ⓜ *vee*·roos
visa visado ⓜ vee·*sa*·do
visit visitar vee·see·*tar*
vitamins vitaminas ⓕ pl
vee·ta·*mee*·nas
voice voz ⓕ vos
vote votar vo·*tar*
vulture buitre ⓜ *bwee*·tre

W

wage sueldo ⓜ *swel*·do
wait esperar es·pe·*rar*
waiter camarero/a ⓜ/ⓕ
ka·ma·*re*·ro/a
waiting room sala ⓕ de espera *sa*·la
de es·*pe*·ra
wake up despertarse des·per·*tar*·se
walk caminar ka·mee·*nar*
wall (inside) pared ⓕ pa·*re*
wallet cartera ⓕ kar·*te*·ra
want querer ke·*rer*
war guerra ⓕ *ge*·ra
wardrobe vestuario ⓜ ves·*twa*·ryo
warm templado/a ⓜ/ⓕ
tem·*pla*·do/a
warn advertir ad·ver·*teer*
wash (oneself) lavarse la·*var*·se
wash (something) lavar la·*var*
wash cloth (flannel) toallita ⓕ
to·a·*yee*·ta

washing machine lavadora ⓕ
la·va·do·ra

watch reloj ⓜ de pulsera re·*lokh* de
pool·se·ra

watch mirar mee·*rar*

water agua ⓕ *a*·gwa

boiled water agua ⓕ hervida *a*·gwa
er·*vee*·da

still water agua ⓕsin gas *a*·gwa
seen gas

tap water agua ⓕ del grifo *a*·gwa
del *gree*·fo

water bottle cantimplora ⓕ
kan·teem·*plo*·ra

waterfall cascada ⓕ kas·*ka*·da

watermelon sandía ⓕ san·*dee*·a

waterproof impermeable
eem·per·me·*a*·ble

waterskiing esquí ⓜ acuático es·*kee*
a·*kwa*·tee·ko

water skis esquís ⓜ pl acuáticos
es·*kees* a·*kwa*·tee·kos

wave ola ⓕ o·la

way camino ⓜ ka·*mee*·no

we nosotros/as ⓜ/ⓕ no·so·tros/as

weak débil *de*·beel

wealthy rico/a ⓜ/ⓕ *ree*·ko/a

wear llevar ye·*var*

weather tiempo ⓜ *tyem*·po

wedding boda ⓕ *bo*·da

wedding cake tarta ⓕ nupcial *tar*·ta
noop·*syal*

wedding present regalo ⓜ de bodas
re·*ga*·lo de *bo*·das

week semana ⓕ se·*ma*·na

weekend fin ⓜ de semana feen de
se·*ma*·na

weight peso ⓜ *pe*·so

welcome dar la bienvenida dar la
byen·ve·*nee*·da

welfare bienestar ⓜ byen·es·*tar*

well bien byen

well (water) pozo ⓜ *po*·so

west oeste ⓜ o·es·te

wet mojado/a ⓜ/ⓕ mo·*kha*·do/a

what que ke

wheel rueda ⓕ *rwe*·da

wheelchair silla ⓕ de ruedas *see*·ya
de *rwe*·das

when cuando *kwan*·do

where donde *don*·de

white blanco/a ⓜ/ⓕ *blan*·ko/a

whiteboard pizarra ⓕ blanca
pee·*sa*·ra *blan*·ka

who quien kyen

why por qué por ke

wide ancho/a ⓜ/ⓕ *an*·cho/a

widow viuda ⓕ *vyoo*·da

widower viudo ⓜ *vyoo*·do

wife esposa ⓕ es·*po*·sa

win ganar ga·*nar*

wind viento ⓜ *vyen*·to

window ventana ⓕ ven·*ta*·na

window-shopping mirar
escaparates mee·*rar* es·ka·pa·*ra*·tes

windscreen parabrisas ⓜ
pa·ra·*bree*·sas

windsurfing hacer windsurfing a·*ser*
gween·soorf·een

wine vino ⓜ *vee*·no

red wine vino ⓜ tinto *vee*·no *teen*·to

sparkling wine vino ⓜ espumoso
vee·no es·poo·*mo*·so

white wine vino ⓜ blanco *vee*·no
blan·ko

winery bodega ⓕ bo·*de*·ga

wings alas ⓕ pl a·las

winner ganador(a) ⓜ/ⓕ ga·na·*dor*/
ga·na·*do*·ra

winter invierno ⓜ een·*vyer*·no

wire alambre ⓜ a·*lam*·bre

wish desear de·se·*ar*

with con kon

within (an hour) dentro de (una
hora) *den*·tro de (*oo*·na o·ra)

without sin seen

woman mujer ⓕ moo·*kher*

wonderful maravilloso/a ⓜ/ⓕ
ma·ra·vee·*yo*·so/a

wood madera ⓕ ma·*de*·ra

wool lana ⓕ *la*·na

word palabra ⓕ pa·*la*·bra

Y

work (occupation) trabajo ⓜ
tra·*ba*·kho
work (of art) obra ⓕ o·bra
work trabajar tra·ba·*khar*
work experience experiencia ⓕ
laboral ek·spe·*ryen*·sya la·bo·*ral*
work permit permiso ⓜ de trabajo
per·*mee*·so de tra·*ba*·kho
workout entreno ⓜ en·*tre*·no
workshop taller ⓜ ta·*yer*
world mundo ⓜ *moon*·do
World Cup La Copa ⓕ Mundial
la *ko*·pa moon·*dyal*
worried preocupado/a ⓜ/ⓕ
pre·o·koo·*pa*·do/a
worship (pray) rezar re·*sar*
wrist muñeca ⓕ moo·*nye*·ka
write escribir es·kree·*beer*
writer escritor(a) ⓜ/ⓕ es·kree·*tor*/
es·kree·*to*·ra
wrong equivocado/a ⓜ/ⓕ
e·kee·vo·*ka*·do/a

(this) year (este) año (*es*·te) *a*·nyo

Y

yellow amarillo/a ⓜ/ⓕ
a·ma·*ree*·yo/a
yellow fever fiebre ⓕ amarilla
fye·bre a·ma·*ree*·ya
yes sí see
(not) yet todavía (no) to·da·*vee*·a (no)
yesterday ayer a·*yer*
yogurt yogur ⓜ yo·*goor*
you sg inf tú too
you sg pol Usted oos·*te*
you pl Ustedes oos·*te*·des
young joven *kho*·ven
youth hostel albergue ⓜ juvenil
al·*ber*·ge khoo·ve·*neel*

Z

zodiac zodíaco ⓜ so·*dee*·a·ko
zoo zoológico ⓜ so·o·*lo*·khee·ko

A

Dictionary
SPANISH *to* ENGLISH
español – inglés

Nouns in the dictionary have their gender indicated by ⓜ or ⓕ. If it's a plural noun, you'll also see pl. When a word that could be either a noun or a verb has no gender indicated, it's a verb. For food terms, see the **menu decoder**.

A

a bordo *a bor*·do aboard
a larga distancia *a lar*·ga dees·tan·sya long-distance
a menudo *a* me·*noo*·do often
a tiempo *a tyem*·po on time
a través *a* tra·*ves* across
abajo *a*·ba·kho below
abarrotado/a ⓜ/ⓕ a·ba·ro·*ta*·do/a crowded
abeja ⓕ a·*be*·kha bee
abierto/a ⓜ/ⓕ a·*byer*·to/a open
abogado/a ⓜ/ⓕ a·bo·*ga*·do/a lawyer
aborto ⓜ a·*bor*·to abortion
— natural na·too·*ral* miscarriage
abrazo ⓜ a·*bra*·so hug
abrebotellas ⓜ a·bre·bo·*te*·yas bottle opener
abrelatas ⓜ a·bre·*la*·tas can opener • tin opener
abrigo ⓜ a·*bree*·go overcoat
abrir a·*breer* open
abuela ⓕ a·*bwe*·la grandmother
abuelo ⓜ a·*bwe*·lo grandfather
aburrido/a ⓜ/ⓕ a·boo·*ree*·do/a boring
acabar a·ka·*bar* end

acampar a·kam·*par* camp
acantilado ⓜ a·kan·tee·*la*·do cliff
accidente ⓜ ak·see·*den*·te accident
aceptar a·sep·*tar* accept
acera ⓕ a·*se*·ra footpath
acondicionador ⓜ a·kon·dee·syo·na·*dor* conditioner
aconsejar a·kon·se·*khar* advise
acoso ⓜ a·*ko*·so harassment
activista ⓜ&ⓕ ak·tee·*vees*·ta activist
actuación ⓕ ak·twa·*syon* gig • performance
acupuntura ⓕ a·koo·poon·*too*·ra acupuncture
adaptador ⓜ a·dap·ta·*dor* adaptor
addicto/a ⓜ/ⓕ a·*deek*·to/a addicted
adentro a·*den*·tro inside
adivinar a·dee·vee·*nar* guess
administración ⓕ ad·mee·nees·tra·*syon* administration
admitir ad·mee·*teer* accept • acknowledge • admit
aduana ⓕ a·*dwa*·na customs
adulto/a ⓜ/ⓕ a·*dool*·to/a adult
advertir ad·ver·*teer* warn
aerolínea ⓕ a·e·ro·*lee*·ne·a airline

aeropuerto ⓜ a·e·ro·*pwer*·to airport

afeitadora ⓕ a·fay·ta·*do*·ra razor

afeitarse a·fay·*tar*·se shave

afortunado/a ⓜ/ⓕ a·for·too·*na*·do/a lucky

agencia ⓕ **de viajes** a·*khen*·sya de *vya*·khes travel agency

agenda ⓕ a·*khen*·da diary

agresivo/a ⓜ/ⓕ a·gre·*see*·vo/a aggressive

agricultor(a) ⓜ/ⓕ a·gree·kool·*tor*/ a·gree·kool·*to*·ra farmer

agricultura ⓕ a·gree·kool·*too*·ra agriculture

aguja ⓕ a·*goo*·kha needle (sewing)

ahora a·*o*·ra now

aire ⓜ *ai*·re air

— acondicionado a·kon·dee·syo·*na*·do air-conditioning

ajedrez ⓜ a·khe·*dres* chess

al fondo de al *fon*·do de at the bottom

al lado de al *la*·do de next to

alambre ⓜ a·*lam*·bre wire

alas ⓕ p·*las* wings

albergue ⓜ **juvenil** al·*ber*·ge khoo·ve·*neel* youth hostel

alcalde ⓜ&ⓕ al·*kal*·de mayor

Alemania ⓕ a·le·*ma*·nya Germany

alergia ⓕ a·*ler*·khya allergy

alfarería ⓕ al·fa·re·*ree*·a pottery

alfombra ⓕ al·*fom*·bra rug

algo *al*·go something

algodón ⓜ al·go·*don* cotton

alguien *al*·gyen someone

algún al·*goon* some

alguno/a ⓜ/ⓕ sg al·*goo*·no/a any

algunos/as ⓜ/ⓕ pl al·*goo*·nos/as any

almacén ⓜ al·ma·*sen* general store

almohada ⓕ al·mo·*a*·da pillow

almuerzo ⓜ al·*mwer*·so lunch

alojamiento ⓜ a·lo·kha·*myen*·to accommodation

alojarse a·lo·*khar*·se stay (at a hotel)

alpinismo ⓜ al·pee·*nees*·mo mountaineering

alquilar al·kee·*lar* hire • rent

— un carro oon *ka*·ro hire a car

alquiler ⓜ al·kee·*ler* hire • rental

altar ⓜ al·*tar* altar

alto/a ⓜ/ⓕ *al*·to/a high • tall

altura ⓕ al·*too*·ra altitude

alucinar a·loo·see·*nar* hallucinate

ama ⓕ **de casa** a·ma de *ka*·sa homemaker

amable a·*ma*·ble kind

amanecer ⓜ a·ma·ne·*ser* sunrise

amante ⓜ&ⓕ a·*man*·te lover

amarillo/a ⓜ/ⓕ a·ma·*ree*·yo/a yellow

ambulancia ⓕ am·boo·*lan*·sya ambulance

amigo/a ⓜ/ⓕ a·*mee*·go/a friend

ampolla ⓕ am·*po*·ya blister

analgésicos ⓜ pl a·nal·*khe*·see·kos painkillers

análisis ⓜ **de sangre** a·*na*·lee·sees de *san*·gre blood test

anaranjado/a ⓜ/ⓕ a·na·ran·*kha*·do/a orange (colour)

anarquista ⓜ&ⓕ a·nar·*kees*·ta anarchist

ancho/a ⓜ/ⓕ *an*·cho/a wide

andar an·*dar* walk

— en bicicleta en bee·see·*kle*·ta cycle

anillo ⓜ a·*nee*·yo ring (on finger)

año *a*·nyo year

Año Nuevo ⓜ *a*·nyo *nwe*·vo New Year

anteayer an·te·a·*yer* day before yesterday

anteojos ⓜ pl an·te·o·*khos* glasses • goggles

— de sol de sol sunglasses

antes *an*·tes before

antibióticos ⓜ pl an·tee·*byo*·tee·kos antibiotics

anticonceptivo ⓜ an·tee·kon·sep·*tee*·vo contraceptive

B

antigüedad ① an·tee·gwe·*da* antique

antiguo/a ⓜ/① an·*tee*·gwo/a ancient

antihistaminicos ⓜ pl an·tee·ees·ta·*mee*·nee·kos antihistamines

antiséptico ⓜ an·tee·sep·tee·ko antiseptic

anuncio ⓜ a·*noon*·syo advertisement

apellido ⓜ a·pe·*yee*·do family name • surname

apéndice ⓜ a·*pen*·dee·se appendix

apodo ⓜ a·po·do nickname

aprender a·pren·*der* learn

apretado/a ⓜ/① a·pre·*ta*·do/a tight

apuesta ① a·*pwes*·ta bet

apuntar a·poon·*tar* point

aquí a·*kee* here

araña ① a·*ra*·nya spider

árbitro ⓜ *ar*·bee·tro referee

árbol ⓜ *ar*·bol tree

arena ① a·*re*·na sand

arenque ⓜ a·*ren*·ke herring

aretes ⓜ pl a·*re*·tes earrings

armadillo ⓜ ar·ma·*dee*·yo armadillo

armario ⓜ ar·*ma*·ryo cupboard

arqueológico/a ⓜ/① ar·ke·o·lo·*khee*·ko/a archaeological

arquitecto/a ⓜ/① ar·kee·*tek*·to/a architect

arquitectura ① ar·kee·tek·*too*·ra architecture

arrendar a·ren·*dar* hire • rent

arriba a·*ree*·ba above • up

arroyo ⓜ a·*ro*·yo stream

arte ⓜ *ar*·te art

artes ⓜ pl **marciales** *ar*·tes mar·*sya*·les martial arts

artesanía ① ar·te·sa·*nee*·a craft • handicraft

artista ⓜ&① ar·*tees*·ta artist

— callejero/a ⓜ/① ka·ye·*khe*·ro/a busker

ascensor ⓜ a·sen·*sor* elevator • lift

asiento ⓜ a·*syen*·to seat

asistencia ① **social** a·sees·*ten*·sya so·*syal* social welfare

asma ⓜ *as*·ma asthma

aspirina ① as·pee·*ree*·na aspirin

atascado/a ⓜ/① a·tas·*ka*·do/a blocked

atletismo ⓜ at·le·*tees*·mo athletics

atmósfera ① at·*mos*·fe·ra atmosphere

audífono ⓜ ow·*dee*·fo·no hearing aid

auto ⓜ *ow*·to car

autobús ⓜ ow·to·*boos* bus (city)

automatico/a ⓜ/① ow·to·ma·*tee*·ko/a automatic

autopista ① ow·to·*pees*·ta motorway

autoservicio ⓜ ow·to·ser·*vee*·syo self-service

avenida ① a·ve·*nee*·da avenue

avergonzado/a ⓜ/① a·ver·gon·*sa*·do/a embarrassed

averiado/a ⓜ/① a·ve·*rya*·do/a broken down (machine)

avión ⓜ a·*vyon* plane

ayer a·*yer* yesterday

ayudar a·yoo·*dar* help

azul a·*sool* blue

B

baile ⓜ *bai*·le dance

bailar bai·*lar* dance

bajo/a ⓜ/① *ba*·kho/a low • short (height)

balcón ⓜ bal·*kon* balcony

balde ⓜ *bal*·de bucket

bálsamo ⓜ **de labios** *bal*·sa·mo de *la*·byos lip balm

banco ⓜ *ban*·ko bank (money)

bandera ① ban·*de*·ra flag

baño ⓜ *ba*·nyo bath • bathroom • toilet

baños ⓜ pl *ba*·nyos toilets

barato/a ⓜ/① ba·*ra*·to/a cheap

barbero ⓜ bar·*be*·ro barber

C

barco ⓜ *bar*·ko boat • ship
— de vela de *ve*·la sailing boat
barrio ⓜ *ba*·ryo suburb
basquetbol ⓜ *bas*·ket·bol basketball
basura ⓕ ba·*soo*·ra rubbish
batería ⓕ ba·te·*ree*·a battery (car) • drums
bautizo ⓜ bow·*tee*·so baptism
bebé ⓜ&ⓕ be·*be* baby
bello/a ⓜ/ⓕ *be*·yo/a beautiful
beneficio ⓜ be·ne·*fee*·syo profit
besar be·*sar* kiss
beso ⓜ *be*·so kiss
biblia ⓕ *bee*·blya bible
biblioteca ⓕ bee·blyo·*te*·ka library
bicho ⓜ *bee*·cho bug
bici ⓕ *bee*·see bike
bicicleta ⓕ bee·see·*kle*·ta bicycle
— de carreras de ka·*re*·ras racing bike
— de montaña de mon·*ta*·nya mountain bike
bien byen well
bienestar ⓜ byen·es·*tar* welfare
billar ⓜ bee·*yar* pool (game)
billetes ⓜ pl **de banco** bee·*ye*·tes de *ban*·ko banknotes
biografía ⓕ byo·gra·*fee*·a biography
birome ⓕ bee·*ro*·me ballpoint pen
blanco y negro *blan*·ko ee *ne*·gro B&W (film)
blanco/a ⓜ/ⓕ *blan*·ko/a white
boca ⓕ *bo*·ka mouth
boda ⓕ *bo*·da wedding
bodega ⓕ bo·*de*·ga liquor store • winery
bol ⓜ bol bowl
bolas ⓕ pl **de algodón** *bo*·las de al·go·*don* cotton balls
boletería ⓕ bo·le·te·*ree*·a ticket office
boleto ⓜ bo·*le*·to ticket
— de ida y vuelta de *ee*·da ee *vwel*·ta return ticket
— de lista de espera de *lees*·ta de es·*pe*·ra standby ticket
— sencillo sen·*see*·yo one-way ticket

bolígrafo ⓜ bo·*lee*·gra·fo pen (ballpoint)
bolsa ⓕ **de compras** *bol*·sa de *kom*·pras shopping bag
bolsillo ⓜ bol·*see*·yo pocket
bolso ⓜ *bol*·so bag (general) • handbag
bomba ⓕ *bom*·ba bomb • pump
bombillo ⓜ bom·*bee*·yo light bulb
bondadoso/a ⓜ/ⓕ bon·da·*do*·so/a caring
bonito/a ⓜ/ⓕ bo·*nee*·to/a pretty
bosque ⓜ *bos*·ke forest
botas ⓕ pl *bo*·tas boots
— de montaña de mon·*ta*·nya hiking boots
botella ⓕ bo·*te*·ya bottle
botón ⓜ bo·*ton* button
boxeo ⓜ bok·*se*·o boxing
bragas ⓕ pl *bra*·gas underpants (women)
brazo ⓜ *bra*·so arm
brillante bree·*lyan*·te brilliant • glossy
broma ⓕ *bro*·ma joke
bronceador ⓜ bron·se·a·*dor* tanning lotion
bronquitis ⓜ bron·*kee*·tees bronchitis
brújula ⓕ *broo*·khoo·la compass
brumoso/a ⓜ/ⓕ broo·*mo*·so/a foggy
buceo ⓜ boo·*se*·o snorkelling
budista ⓜ&ⓕ boo·*dees*·ta Buddhist
bueno/a ⓜ/ⓕ *bwe*·no/a good • nice
bufanda ⓕ boo·*fan*·da scarf
bulto ⓜ *bool*·to lump
burro ⓜ *boo*·ro donkey
buscar boos·*kar* look for
buzón ⓜ boo·*son* mailbox

C

caballo ⓜ ka·*ba*·yo horse
cabaña ⓕ ka·*ba*·nya hut
cabeza ⓕ ka·*be*·sa head

cabina ① **telefónica** ka·bee·na te·le·fo·nee·ka phone box

cable ⓜ ka·ble cable

cables ⓜ pl **de arranque** ka·bles de a·ran·ke jumper leads

cabra ① ka·bra goat

cacharro ⓜ ka·cha·ro pot (ceramic)

cachorro ⓜ ka·cho·ro puppy

cacto ⓜ kak·to cactus

cada ka·da each

cadena ① ka·de·na chain

— de bici de bee·see bike chain

cafetería ① ka·fe·te·ree·a cafe

caída ① ka·ee·da fall (tumble)

caja ① ka·kha box

— fuerte fwer·te safe

— registradora re·khees·tra·do·ra cash register

cajero ⓜ **automático** ka·khe·ro ow·to·ma·tee·ko ATM

cajero/a ⓜ/① ka·khe·ro/a cashier

cajón ⓜ **con llave** ka·khon kon ya·ve locker

calcetines ⓜ pl kal·se·tee·nes socks

calculadora ① kal·koo·la·do·ra calculator

calefacción ① ka·le·fak·syon heating

— central sen·tral central heating

calendario ⓜ ka·len·da·ryo calendar

calidad ① ka·lee·da quality

caliente ka·lyen·te hot

calle ① ka·ye road

calor ⓜ ka·lor heat

calzoncillos ⓜ pl kal·son·see·yos underpants (men)

cama ① ka·ma bed

— de matrimonio de ma·tree·mo·nyo double bed

cámara ① **(fotográfica)** ka·ma·ra (fo·to·gra·fee·ka) camera

— de aire de ai·re tube (tyre)

— descartable des·kar·ta·ble disposable camera

— digital de·khee·tal digital camera

— submarina soob·ma·ree·na underwater camera

camarero/a ⓜ/① ka·ma·re·ro/a waiter

cambiar kam·byar change • exchange

cambio ⓜ kam·byo change (coins) • exchange

— de dinero de dee·ne·ro currency exchange

caminar ka·mee·nar walk

camino ⓜ ka·mee·no track • trail • way

— de bici de bee·see bike path

— rural roo·ral hiking route

camión ⓜ ka·myon truck

camisa ① ka·mee·sa shirt

camiseta ① ka·mee·se·ta singlet • T-shirt

cámping ⓜ kam·peen campsite

campo ⓜ kam·po countryside

caña ① **de azúcar** ka·nya de a·soo·kar sugar cane

canasta ① ka·nas·ta basket

cancelar kan·se·lar cancel

cáncer ⓜ kan·ser cancer

cancha ① **de golf** kan·cha de golf golf course

cancha ① **de tenis** kan·cha de te·nees tennis court

canción ① kan·syon song

candado ⓜ kan·da·do padlock

candidiasis ① kan·dee·dya·sees thrush (medical)

cansado/a ⓜ/① kan·sa·do/a tired

cantante ⓜ&① kan·tan·te singer

cantar kan·tar sing

cantidad ① kan·tee·da amount

cantimplora ① kan·teem·plo·ra water bottle

capa ① **de ozono** ka·pa de o·so·no ozone layer

capacidad ① **de SMS** ka·pa·see·da de e·se em·e·e·se SMS capability

capilla ① ka·pee·ya shrine

capote ⓜ ka·po·te cloak

cara ① ka·ra face

caramelos ⓜ pl ka·ra·me·los lollies

caravana ⓕ ka·ra·va·na caravan • van

cárcel ⓕ kar·sel jail • prison

caries ⓕ ka·ryes cavity (tooth)

carnet ⓜ kar·net drivers licence

carnicería ⓕ kar·nee·se·ree·a butcher's shop

caro/a ⓜ/ⓕ ka·ro/a expensive

carpa ⓕ kar·pa tent

carpintero ⓜ kar·peen·te·ro carpenter

carrera ⓕ ka·re·ra race (sport)

carro ⓜ ka·ro car

carta ⓕ kar·ta letter

cartas ⓕ pl kar·tas cards

cartera ⓕ kar·te·ra wallet

cartucho ⓜ **de gas** kar·too·cho de gas gas cartridge

casa ⓕ ka·sa home • house

casado/a ⓜ/ⓕ ka·sa·do/a married

casarse ka·sar·se marry

cascada ⓕ kas·ka·da waterfall

casco ⓜ kas·ko helmet

casi ka·see almost

castigar kas·tee·gar punish

castillo ⓜ kas·tee·yo castle

catedral ⓕ ka·te·dral cathedral

católico/a ⓜ/ⓕ ka·to·lee·ko/a Catholic

caza ⓕ ka·sa hunting

cédula ⓜ **de identidad** se·doo·la de ee·den·tee·da identification card (ID)

celebración ⓕ se·le·bra·syon celebration

celoso/a ⓜ/ⓕ se·lo·so/a jealous

cementerio ⓜ se·men·te·ryo cemetery

cena ⓕ se·na dinner

cenicero ⓜ se·nee·se·ro ashtray

centavo ⓜ sen·ta·vo cent

centímetro ⓜ sen·tee·me·tro centimetre

central ⓕ **telefónica** sen·tral te·le·fo·nee·ka telephone centre

centro ⓜ sen·tro centre

— comercial ko·mer·syal shopping centre

— de la ciudad de la syoo·da city centre

Centroamérica ⓕ sen·tro·a·me·ree·ka Central America

centroamericano/a ⓜ/ⓕ sen·tro·a·me·ree·ka·no/a Central American

cepillo ⓜ **de dientes** se·pee·yo de dyen·tes toothbrush

cerámica ⓕ se·ra·mee·ka ceramic

cerca ⓕ ser·ka fence

cerca ser·ka near • nearby

cerrado/a ⓜ/ⓕ se·ra·do/a closed • locked • shut

— con llave kon ya·ve locked

cerradura ⓕ se·ra·doo·ra lock (door)

cerrar se·rar close • lock • shut

certificado ⓜ ser·tee·fee·ka·do certificate

chaleco ⓜ **salvavidas** cha·le·ko sal·va·vee·das life jacket

champú ⓜ cham·poo shampoo

chaqueta ⓕ cha·ke·ta jacket

cheque ⓜ che·ke cheque

— de viajero de vya·khe·ro travellers cheque

chica ⓕ chee·ka girl

chicle ⓜ chee·kle chewing gum

chico ⓜ chee·ko boy

choque ⓜ cho·ke crash (accident)

chupete ⓜ choo·pe·te dummy • pacifier

cibercafé ⓜ see·ber·ka·fe internet cafe

ciclismo ⓜ see·klees·mo cycling

ciclista ⓜ&ⓕ see·klees·ta cyclist

ciego/a ⓜ/ⓕ sye·go/a blind

cielo ⓜ sye·lo sky

ciencia ⓕ syen·sya science

— ficción feek·syon science fiction

científico/a ⓜ/ⓕ syen·tee·fee·ko/a scientist

cigarillo ⓜ see·ga·ree·yo cigarette

cigarro m see·*ga*·ro cigar

cine m *see*·ne cinema

cinta f **de vídeo** *seen*·ta de *vee*·de·o video tape

cinturón m **de seguridad** seen·too·*ron* de se·goo·ree·*da* seatbelt

circo m *seer*·ko circus

cita f *see*·ta appointment • date

citología f see·to·lo·*khee*·a pap smear

ciudad f syoo·*da* city

ciudadanía f syoo·da·da·*nee*·a citizenship

claro/a m/f *kla*·ro/a light (colour)

clase f *kla*·se class

— preferente pre·fe·*ren*·te business class

— turística too·*rees*·tee·ka economy class

clásico/a m/f *kla*·see·ko/a classical

cliente/a m/f *klyen*·te/a client

cobrar (un cheque) ko·*brar* (oon *che*·ke) cash (a cheque)

coca f *ko*·ka coca plant • coke (drug)

cocaína f ko·ka·ee·na cocaine

coche m **cama** *ko*·che *ka*·ma sleeping car

cocina f ko·*see*·na cuisine • kitchen

cocinar ko·see·*nar* cook

cocinero/a m/f ko·see·ne·*ro*/a chef • cook

cocodrilo m ko·ko·*dree*·lo crocodile

codeína f ko·de·ee·na codeine

código m **postal** *ko*·dee·go pos·*tal* post code

coima f *koy*·ma bribe

coimear koy·me·*ar* bribe

cola f *ko*·la queue

colchón m kol·*chon* mattress

colega m&f ko·*le*·ga colleague

cólera f *ko*·le·ra cholera

colibrí m ko·lee·*bree* hummingbird

colina f ko·*lee*·na hill

color m ko·*lor* colour

comedia f ko·me·dya comedy

comenzar ko·men·*sar* begin • start

comer ko·*mer* eat

comerciante m&f ko·mer·*syan*·te business person

comercio m ko·*mer*·syo trade

comida f ko·mee·da food

— de bebé de be·*be* baby food

comisaría f ko·mee·sa·*ree*·a police station

como *ko*·mo how

cómodo/a m/f *ko*·mo·do/a comfortable

cómpact m *kom*·pak CD

compañero/a m/f kom·pa·*nye*·ro/a companion

compañía f kom·pa·*nyee*·a company

compartir kom·par·*teer* share (with)

comprar kom·*prar* buy

compresas f pl kom·*pre*·sas sanitary napkins

compromiso m kom·pro·mee·so engagement (marriage)

computadora f kom·poo·ta·*do*·ra computer

— portátil por·*ta*·teel laptop

comunión f ko·moo·*nyon* communion

comunista m&f ko·moo·*nees*·ta communist

con kon with

— filtro *feel*·tro filtered

concierto m kon·*syer*·to concert

condición f **cardíaca** kon·dee·*syon* kar·*dee*·a·ka heart condition

condón m kon·*don* condom

conducir kon·doo·*seer* drive

conejo m ko·ne·kho rabbit

conexión f ko·nek·*syon* connection

confesión f kon·fe·*syon* confession

confianza f kon·*fyan*·sa trust

confiar kon·*fyar* trust

confirmar kon·feer·*mar* confirm

C

congelación ⓕ kon·khe·la·*syon* frostbite

conocer ko·no·*ser* know (a person)

conocido/a ⓜ/ⓕ ko·no·*see*·do/a famous

consejo ⓜ kon·*se*·kho advice

conservador(a) ⓜ/ⓕ kon·ser·va·*dor*/kon·ser·va·*do*·ra conservative

consigna ⓕ kon·*see*·nya left-luggage office

— automática ow·to·ma·*tee*·ka luggage lockers

construir kon·stroo·*eer* build

consulado ⓜ kon·soo·*la*·do consulate

contaminación ⓕ kon·ta·mee·na·*syon* pollution

contar kon·*tar* count

contemporáneo/a ⓜ/ⓕ kon·tem·po·ra·ne·o/a contemporary

contrato ⓜ kon·*tra*·to contract

control ⓜ kon·*trol* checkpoint

convento ⓜ kon·*ven*·to convent

copa ⓕ *ko*·pa drink

corazón ⓜ ko·ra·*son* heart

cordillera ⓕ kor·dee·ye·ra mountain range

corpiño ⓜ kor·*pee*·nyo bra

correcto/a ⓜ/ⓕ ko·*rek*·to/a right (correct)

correo ⓜ ko·*re*·o mail

— aéreo a·e·re·o airmail

— certificado ser·tee·fee·*ka*·do registered mail

— urgente oor·*khen*·te express mail

correos ⓜ pl ko·*re*·os post office

corrida ⓕ ko·*ree*·da bullfight

corriente ko·*ryen*·te current

corriente ko·*ryen*·te ordinary

corrupto/a ⓜ/ⓕ ko·*roop*·to/a corrupt

cortar kor·*tar* cut

cortauñas ⓜ kor·ta·oo·nyas nail clippers

corte ⓜ **de pelo** *kor*·te de *pe*·lo haircut

corto/a ⓜ/ⓕ *kor*·to/a short (length)

cosecha ⓕ ko·se·cha crop • harvest

coser ko·*ser* sew

costa ⓕ *kos*·ta coast

costar kos·*tar* cost

crecer kre·*ser* grow

crema ⓕ *kre*·ma cream

— agria a·grya sour cream

— hidratante ee·dra·*tan*·te moisturiser

— solar so·*lar* sunblock

cristiano/a ⓜ/ⓕ krees·*tya*·no/a Christian

crítica ⓕ *kree*·tee·ka review

crudo/a ⓜ/ⓕ *kroo*·do/a raw

cuaderno ⓜ kwa·*der*·no notebook

cuadrado ⓜ kwa·*dra*·do square (place)

cuadro ⓜ *kwa*·dro painting (canvas)

cualificaciones ⓕ pl kwa·lee·fee·ka·*syo*·nes qualifications

cuando *kwan*·do when

cuanto *kwan*·to how much

cuarentena ⓕ kwa·ren·*te*·na quarantine

cuarto ⓜ *kwar*·to quarter

cubiertos ⓜ pl koo·*byer*·tos cutlery

cucaracha ⓕ koo·ka·*ra*·cha cockroach

cuchara ⓕ koo·*cha*·ra spoon

cucharita ⓕ koo·cha·*ree*·ta teaspoon

cuchillo ⓜ koo·*chee*·yo knife

cuenta ⓕ *kwen*·ta bill • check

— bancaria ban·*ka*·rya bank account

cuento ⓜ *kwen*·to short story • story

cuerda ⓕ *kwer*·da rope • string

— para tender la ropa *pa*·ra ten·*der* la *ro*·pa clothes line

cuero ⓜ *kwe*·ro leather

cuerpo ⓜ *kwer*·po body

cuervo ⓜ *kwer*·vo vulture

cuesta abajo *kwes*·ta a·*ba*·kho downhill

cuesta arriba *kwes*·ta a·*ree*·ba uphill

cueva ① *kwe·*va cave
cuidar kwee·*dar* care for • mind (an object)
culo ⓜ *koo·*lo bum (body)
culpa ① *kool·*pa (someone's) fault
culpable kool·*pa·*ble guilty
cumbre ① *koom·*bre peak
cumpleaños ⓜ koom·ple·*a·*nyos birthday
cupón ⓜ koo·*pon* coupon
curitas ① pl koo·*ree·*tas Band-Aids
currículum ⓜ koo·*ree·*koo·loom resume

D

dañar da·*nyar* hurt
danta ① *dan·*ta tapir
dar dar give
— gracias *gra·*syas thank
— la bienvenida la byen·ve·*nee·*da welcome
— una patada *oo·*na pa·*ta·*da kick
de de from
— cercanías ser·ka·*nee·*as local
— (cuatro) estrellas (*kwa·*tro) es·*tre·*yas (four-)star
— derecha de·*re·*cha right-wing
— izquierda ees·*kyer·*da left-wing
— lujo *loo·*kho luxurious
— menos *me·*nos less
— segunda mano se·*goon·*da *ma·*no second-hand
— vez en cuando ves en *kwan·*do sometimes
débil *de·*beel weak
decidir de·see·*deer* decide
decir de·*seer* say • tell
dedo ⓜ *de·*do finger
— del pie del pye toe
defectuoso/a ⓜ/① de·fek·*two·*so/a faulty
deforestación ① de·fo·res·ta·*syon* deforestation
dejar entrar de·*khar* en·*trar* admit (allow to enter)
delgado/a ⓜ/① del·*ga·*do/a thin

demasiado (caro/a) ⓜ/① de·ma·*sya·*do (*ka·*ro/a) too (expensive)
democracia ① de·mo·*kra·*see·a democracy
demora ① de·*mo·*ra delay
dentista ⓜ&① den·*tees·*ta dentist
dentro de (una hora) *den·*tro de (*oo·*na *o·*ra) within (an hour)
deportes ⓜ pl de·*por·*tes sport
deportista ⓜ&① de·por·*tees·*ta sportsperson
depósito ⓜ de·*po·*see·to deposit (bank)
derecha de·*re·*cha right (direction)
derechista de·re·*chees·*ta right-wing
derechos ⓜ pl de·*re·*chos rights
— civiles see·*vee·*les civil rights
— de animales de a·nee·*ma·*les animal rights
— humanos oo·*ma·*nos human rights
desayuno ⓜ de·sa·*yoo·*no breakfast
descansar des·kan·*sar* rest
descanso ⓜ des·*kan·*so intermission
descendiente ⓜ de·sen·*dyen·*te descendant
descomponerse des·kom·po·*ner·*se break down
descubrir des·koo·*breer* discover
descuento ⓜ des·*kwen·*to discount
desde *des·*de since (time)
desear de·se·*ar* wish
desempleado/a ⓜ/① des·em·ple·*a·*do/a unemployed
desierto ⓜ de·*syer·*to desert
desodorante ⓜ de·so·do·*ran·*te deodorant
despacio des·*pa·*syo slowly
despertador ⓜ des·per·ta·*dor* alarm clock
despertarse des·per·*tar·*se wake up
después de des·*pwes* de after
destino ⓜ des·*tee·*no destination
detallado/a ⓜ/① de·ta·*ya·*do/a itemised
detalle ⓜ de·*ta·*ye detail

detener de·te·*ner* arrest
detrás de de·*tras* de behind
día ⓜ *dee*·a day
— festivo fes·*tee*·vo holiday
diafragma ⓜ dya·*frag*·ma diaphragm
diapositiva ⓕ dya·po·see·*tee*·va slide (film)
diariamente dya·rya·*men*·te daily
diarrea ⓕ dya·*re*·a diarrhoea
dibujar dee·boo·*khar* draw
diccionario ⓜ deek·syo·*na*·ryo dictionary
dientes ⓜ pl *dyen*·tes teeth
diferencia ⓕ **de horas** dee·fe·*ren*·sya de o·ras time difference
diferente dee·fe·*ren*·te different
difícil dee·*fee*·seel difficult
dinero ⓜ dee·*ne*·ro money
— en efectivo en e·*fek*·tee·vo cash
dios dyos god (general)
dirección ⓕ dee·*rek*·syon address
direccionales ⓜ pl dee·rek·syo·*na*·les indicators (car)
directo/a ⓜ/ⓕ dee·*rek*·to/a direct
director(a) ⓜ/ⓕ dee·rek·*tor*/ dee·rek·*to*·ra director
disco ⓜ *dees*·ko disk
discoteca ⓕ dees·ko·*te*·ka disco
discriminación ⓕ dees·kree·mee·na·*syon* discrimination
discutir dees·koo·*teer* argue
diseño ⓜ dee·*se*·nyo design
disentería ⓕ dee·sen·te·*ree*·a dysentery
disparar dees·pa·*rar* shoot
DIU ⓜ de·ee·oo IUD (contraceptive device)
diversión ⓕ dee·ver·*syon* fun
divertirse dee·ver·*teer*·se enjoy (oneself)
doblar do·*blar* turn
doble *do*·ble double
docena ⓕ do·*se*·na dozen

dolor ⓜ do·*lor* pain
— de cabeza de ka·*be*·sa headache
— de estómago de es·*to*·ma·go stomachache
— de muelas de *mwe*·las toothache
— menstrual mens·*trwal* period pain
dolorido/a ⓜ/ⓕ do·lo·*ree*·do/a sore
doloroso/a ⓜ/ⓕ do·lo·*ro*·so/a painful
donde *don*·de where
dormir dor·*meer* sleep
dos ⓜ/ⓕ dos two
— camas ⓕ pl *ka*·mas twin beds
— copias ⓕ pl *ko*·pyas double copies (photos)
— veces *ve*·ses twice
droga ⓕ *dro*·ga drug (illegal)
drogadicción ⓕ dro·ga·deek·*syon* drug addiction
drogas ⓕ pl *dro*·gas drugs (illegal)
ducha ⓕ *doo*·cha shower
dueño/a ⓜ/ⓕ *dwe*·nyo/a owner
dulce *dool*·se candy • sweet
durante doo·*ran*·te during
duro/a ⓜ/ⓕ *doo*·ro/a hard (not soft)

E

ecografía ⓕ e·ko·gra·*fee*·a ultrasound
edad ⓕ e·*da* age
edificio ⓜ e·dee·*fee*·syo building
educación ⓕ e·doo·ka·*syon* education
egoísta ⓜ&ⓕ e·go·*ees*·ta selfish
ejemplo ⓜ e·*khem*·plo example
ejército ⓜ e·*kher*·see·to army
él el he
elecciones ⓕ pl e·lek·*syo*·nes elections
electricidad ⓕ e·lek·tree·see·*da* electricity
electricista ⓜ&ⓕ e·lek·tree·*sees*·ta electrician
ella *e*·ya she

E

ellos/ellas ⓜ/ⓕ pl e·*yos*/e·*yas* they

embajada ⓕ em·ba·*kha*·da embassy

embajador(a) ⓜ/ⓕ em·ba·kha·*dor*/ em·ba·kha·*do*·ra ambassador

embarazada ⓕ em·ba·ra·*sa*·da pregnant

embarcarse em·bar·*kar*·se board (plane, ship)

emborrachado/a ⓜ/ⓕ em·bo·ra·*cha*·do/a drunk

embrague ⓜ em·*bra*·ge clutch

emergencia ⓕ e·mer·*khen*·sya emergency

emocional e·mo·syo·*nal* emotional

empleado/a ⓜ/ⓕ em·ple·a·*do*/a employee

empujar em·poo·*khar* push

en en in • on

— el extranjero el ek·stran·*khe*·ro abroad

encaje ⓜ en·*ka*·khe lace

encantador(a) ⓜ/ⓕ en·kan·ta·*dor*/ en·kan·ta·*do*·ra charming

encendedor ⓜ en·sen·de·*dor* lighter

enchufe ⓜ en·*choo*·fe plug (electricity)

encía ⓕ en·*see*·a gum (mouth)

encontrar en·kon·*trar* meet • find

energía ⓕ **nuclear** e·ner·*khee*·a noo·kle·*ar* nuclear energy

enfadado/a ⓜ/ⓕ en·fa·*da*·do/a angry

enfermedad ⓕ en·fer·mee·*da* disease

— venérea ve·*ne*·re·a venereal disease

enfermero/a ⓜ/ⓕ en·fer·*me*·ro/a nurse

enfermo/a ⓜ/ⓕ en·*fer*·mo/a sick

enorme e·*nor*·me huge

entender en·ten·*der* understand

entrar en·*trar* enter

entre *en*·tre among • between

entregar en·tre·*gar* deliver

entrenador(a) ⓜ/ⓕ en·tre·na·*dor*/ en·tren·na·*do*·ra coach

entreno ⓜ en·*tre*·no workout

entrevista ⓕ en·tre·*vees*·ta interview

enviar en·*vyar* send

epilepsia ⓕ e·pee·*lep*·sya epilepsy

equipaje ⓜ e·kee·*pa*·khe luggage

equipo ⓜ e·*kee*·po equipment • team

— de inmersión de een·mer·*syon* diving equipment

— estereofónico es·te·re·o·*fo*·nee·ko stereo

equitación ⓕ e·kee·ta·*syon* horse riding

equivocado/a ⓜ/ⓕ e·kee·vo·*ka*·do/a wrong

error ⓜ e·*ror* mistake

escalada ⓕ es·ka·*la*·da rock climbing

escalera ⓕ es·ka·*le*·ra stairway

— electrica e·*lek*·tree·ka escalator

escape ⓜ es·*ka*·pe exhaust (car)

escarcha ⓕ es·*kar*·cha frost

escarpado/a ⓜ/ⓕ es·kar·*pa*·do/a steep

escasez ⓕ es·ka·*ses* shortage

escenario ⓜ e·se·*na*·ryo stage

escoger es·ko·*kher* choose

escribir es·kree·*beer* write

escritor(a) ⓜ/ⓕ es·kree·*tor*/ es·kree·*to*·ra writer

escuchar es·koo·*char* listen

escuela ⓕ es·*kwe*·la school

esgrima ⓕ es·*gree*·ma fencing (sport)

espacio ⓜ es·*pa*·syo space

espalda ⓕ es·*pal*·da back (body)

España ⓕ es·*pa*·nya Spain

especial es·pe·*syal* special

especialista ⓜ&ⓕ es·pe·sya·*lees*·ta specialist

espectáculo ⓜ es·pek·*ta*·koo·lo show

espejo ⓜ es·*pe*·kho mirror

esperar es·pe·*rar* wait

espermicida ⓕ es·per·mee·*see*·da spermicide

F

esposa ① es·*po*·sa wife
esposo ⓜ es·*po*·so husband
espuma ① **de afeitar** es·poo·ma de a·fay·*tar* shaving cream
esquí ⓜ es·*kee* skiing
— acuático a·kwa·tee·ko waterskiing
esquiar es·*kyar* ski
esquina ① es·*kee*·na corner
esquís ⓜ pl es·*kees* skis
— acuáticos a·kwa·tee·kos water skis
esta noche es·ta *no*·che tonight
estacas ① pl es·*ta*·kas pegs (tent)
estación ① es·ta·*syon* season • station
— de tren de tren railway station
— de autobuses de ow·to·*boo*·ses bus station (city)
— de ómnibuses de om·nee·boo·ses bus station (intercity)
— de subterráneo de soob·te·*ra*·ne·o metro station
estacionamiento ⓜ es·ta·syo·na·*myen*·to car park
estacionar es·ta·syo·*nar* park (car)
estadio ⓜ es·*ta*·dyo stadium
estado ⓜ **civil** es·*ta*·do see·*veel* marital status
estafa ① es·*ta*·fa rip-off
estanquero ⓜ es·tan·*ke*·ro tobacconist
estar es·*tar* be
— aburrido/a ⓜ/① a·boo·ree·do·a be bored
— de acuerdo de a·*kwer*·do agree
estatua ① es·*ta*·twa statue
este ⓜ es·te east
éste/a ⓜ/① es·te/a this
esterilla ① es·te·*ree*·ya mat
esteticista ⓜ&① es·te·tee·*sees*·ta beautician
estilo ⓜ es·*tee*·lo style
estómago ⓜ es·*to*·ma·go stomach
estrellas ① pl es·*tre*·yas stars
estreñimiento ⓜ es·tre·nyee·*myen*·to constipation

estudiante ⓜ&① es·too·*dyan*·te student
estudio ⓜ es·*too*·dyo studio
estufa ① es·*too*·fa heater • stove
estúpido/a ⓜ/① es·*too*·pee·do/a stupid
etiqueta ① **de equipaje** e·tee·*ke*·ta de e·kee·*pa*·khe luggage tag
exceso ⓜ **de equipaje** ek·*se*·so de e·kee·*pa*·khe excess baggage
excursión ① ek·skoor·*syon* tour
excursionismo ⓜ ek·skoor·syo·*nees*·mo hiking
experiencia ① ek·spe·*ryen*·sya experience
— laboral la·bo·*ral* work experience
explotación ① ek·splo·ta·*syon* exploitation
exposición ① ek·spo·see·*syon* exhibition
expreso/a ⓜ/① ek·*spre*·so/a express
exterior ⓜ ek·ste·*ryor* outside
extrañar ek·stra·*nyar* miss (feel absence of)
extranjero/a ⓜ/① ek·stran·*khe*·ro/a foreign • foreigner
extraño/a ⓜ/① ek·*stra*·nyo/a strange • stranger • unusual

F

fábrica ① *fa*·bree·ka factory
fácil *fa*·seel easy
facturación ① fak·too·ra·*syon* check-in (airport)
— de equipaje de e·kee·*pa*·khe check-in (luggage)
falda ① *fal*·da skirt
familia ① fa·*mee*·lya family
fantástico/a ⓜ/① fan·*tas*·tee·ko/a fantastic • great
farmacia ① far·*ma*·sya chemist • pharmacy
faros ⓜ pl *fa*·ros headlights
fastidiado/a ⓜ/① fas·tee·*dya*·do/a annoyed

fecha ① *fe*·cha date (day)
— **de nacimiento** de na·see·*myen*·to date of birth
feliz fe·*lees* happy
feria ① *fe*·rya street market
ferretería ① fe·re·te·*ree*·a a hardware store
ficción ① feek·*syon* fiction
fiebre ① *fye*·bre fever
— **amarilla** a·ma·*ree*·ya yellow fever
— **del dengue** del *den*·ge dengue fever
— **del heno** del e·no hay fever
— **glandular** glan·doo·*lar* glandular fever
fiesta ① *fyes*·ta party (celebration)
fin ⓜ feen end
— **de semana** de se·*ma*·na weekend
firma ① *feer*·ma signature
flamenco ⓜ fla·*men*·ko flamenco (dance) • flamingo
flor ① flor flower
florista ⓜ&① flo·*rees*·ta florist
flujo ⓜ **vaginal** *floo*·kho va·khee·*nal* vaginal discharge
foco ⓜ *fo*·ko lightbulb
footing foo·*teen* jogging
forma ① *for*·ma shape
fósforos ⓜ pl *fos*·fo·ros matches
fotocopiadora ①
fo·to·ko·pee·a·*do*·ra photocopier
fotografía ① fo·to·gra·*fee*·a photo • photography
fotógrafo/a ⓜ/① fo·to·*gra*·fo/a photographer
fotómetro ⓜ fo·*to*·me·tro light meter
frágil *fra*·kheel fragile
franqueo ⓜ fran·*ke*·o postage
frazada ① fra·*sa*·da blanket
freír fre·*eer* fry
freno ⓜ *fre*·no brake
frente a *fren*·te a opposite
frigorífico ⓜ free·go·*ree*·fee·ko fridge

frío/a ⓜ/① *free*·o/a cold
frontera ① fron·*te*·ra border (frontier)
fuego ⓜ *fwe*·go fire
fuerte *fwer*·te strong
fumar foo·*mar* smoke
funda ① **de almohada** *foon*·da de al·mo·*a*·da pillowcase
funeral ⓜ foo·ne·*ral* funeral
fútbol ⓜ *foot*·bol football • soccer
futuro ⓜ foo·*too*·ro future

G

ganador(a) ⓜ/① ga·na·*dor*/ ga·na·*do*·ra winner
ganar ga·*nar* earn • win
garage ⓜ ga·ra·*khe* garage (car shelter)
garganta ① gar·*gan*·ta throat
gas ⓜ gas gas (for cooking)
gasolina ① ga·so·*lee*·na gas • petrol
gasolinera ① ga·so·lee·*ne*·ra service station
gatito/a ⓜ/① ga·*tee*·to/a kitten
gato/a ⓜ/① *ga*·to/a cat
gemelos/as ⓜ/① pl khe·*me*·los/as twins
general khe·ne·*ral* general
gente ① *khen*·te people
gimnasia ① kheem·*na*·sya gymnastics
ginecólogo/a ⓜ/①
khe·ne·ko·lo·go/a gynaecologist
glorieta ① glo·*rye*·ta roundabout
gobierno ⓜ go·*byer*·no government
goma ① *go*·ma gum (chewing)
gordo/a ⓜ/① *gor*·do/a fat
gotas ① pl **para los ojos** *go*·tas pa·ra los o·khos eye drops
grabación ① gra·ba·*syon* recording
gracioso/a ⓜ/① gra·*syo*·so/a funny
gramos ⓜ pl *gra*·mos grams
grande *gran*·de big

H

grandes almacenes ⓜ pl *gran·des al·ma·se·nes* department store
granizo ⓜ *gra·nee·so* hail
granja ⓕ *gran·kha* farm
grifo ⓜ *gree·fo* faucet • tap
gripe ⓕ *gree·pe* influenza
gris grees grey
gritar *gree·tar* shout
grupo ⓜ *groo·po* band (music) • group
— de rock de rok rock group
— sanguíneo san·*gwee·ne·o* blood group
guantes ⓜ pl *gwan·tes* gloves
guardarropa ⓜ *gwar·da·ro·pa* cloakroom
guardería ⓕ *gwar·de·ree·a* child-minding service • creche
guerra ⓕ *ge·ra* war
guía ⓕ *gee·a* guidebook
— audio *ow·*dyo audio guide
— de espectaculos de es·pek·*ta·koo·los* entertainment guide
— telefónica te·le·*fo·nee·ka* phone book
guía ⓜ&ⓕ *gee·a* guide (person)
guitarra ⓕ *gee·ta·ra* guitar
gustar(le) *goos·tar*(le) like

H

habitación a·bee·ta·*syon* bedroom • room
— doble *do·*ble double room
— individual een·dee·vee·*dwal* single room
hablar a·*blar* speak • talk
hacer a·*ser* do • make
— dedo de·do hitchhike
— surf soorf surf
— windsurf *gween·*soorf windsurfing
hachís ⓜ a·*chees* hash
hacia a·sya towards
— abajo a·*ba·*kho down
hamaca ⓕ a·*ma·*ka hammock
hasta as·ta until

hecho/a ⓜ/ⓕ e·cho/a made
— a mano a *ma·*no handmade
— de (algodón) de (al·go·*don*) made of (cotton)
heladería ⓕ e·la·de·*ree·a* ice-cream parlour
helar e·*lar* freeze
herborista ⓜ&ⓕ er·bo·*rees·ta* herbalist
herida ⓕ e·*ree·*da injury
hermana ⓕ er·*ma·*na sister
hermano ⓜ er·*ma·*no brother
hermoso/a ⓜ/ⓕ er·*mo·*so/a handsome
heroína ⓕ e·ro·ee·na heroin
hielo ⓜ *ye·*lo ice
hierba ⓕ *yer·*ba grass
hígado ⓜ *ee·*ga·do liver
hija ⓕ *ee·*kha daughter
hijo ⓜ *ee·*kho son
hilo ⓜ *ee·*lo thread
— dental den·*tal* dental floss
hinchas ⓜ&ⓕ pl *een·*chas fans (supporters)
hindú ⓜ&ⓕ een·*doo* Hindu
historial ⓜ **profesional** ees·to·*ryal* pro·fe·syo·*nal* CV
histórico/a ⓜ/ⓕ ees·*to·*ree·ko/a historical
hoja ⓕ *o·*kha leaf
— de afeitar de a·*fay·*tar razor blade
Holanda ⓕ o·*lan·*da Netherlands
hombre ⓜ *om·*bre man
hombros ⓜ pl *om·*bros shoulders
hora ⓕ *o·*ra time
horario ⓜ o·*ra·*ryo timetable
horas ⓕ pl **de abrir** *o·*ras de a·*breer* opening hours
hormiga ⓕ or·*mee·*ga ant
horno ⓜ *or·*no oven
horóscopo ⓜ o·*ros·*ko·po horoscope
hospital ⓜ os·pee·*tal* hospital
hosteleria ⓕ os·te·le·*ree·a* hospitality
hotel ⓜ o·*tel* hotel
hoy oy today

huerta ① *wer*·ta vegetable garden

hueso ⓜ *we*·so bone

hurto ⓜ **en tiendas** *oor*·to en *tyen*·das shoplifting

I

identificación ①
ee·den·tee·fee·ka·*syon* identification

idioma ⓜ ee·*dyo*·ma language

idiota ⓜ&① ee·*dyo*·ta idiot

iglesia ① ee·*gle*·sya church

igual ee·*gwal* same

igualdad ① ee·gwal·*da* equality

ilegal ee·le·*gal* illegal

impermeable ⓜ eem·per·me·*a*·ble raincoat

impermeable eem·per·me·*a*·ble waterproof

importante eem·por·*tan*·te important

imposible eem·po·*see*·ble impossible

impuesto ⓜ eem·*pwes*·to tax
— sobre la renta *so*·bre la *ren*·ta income tax

incluido/a ⓜ/① een·kloo·ee·do/a included

incómodo/a ⓜ/① een·*ko*·mo·do/a uncomfortable

indigestion ① een·dee·khes·*tyon* indigestion

industria ① een·*doos*·trya industry

infección ① een·fek·*syon* infection

inflamación ① een·fla·ma·*syon* inflammation

información ① een·for·ma·*syon* information

informática ① een·for·*ma*·tee·ka IT

informativo ⓜ een·for·ma·*tee*·vo current affairs

ingeniería ① een·khe·nye·*ree*·a engineering

ingeniero/a ⓜ/① een·khe·nye·ro/a engineer

Inglaterra ① een·gla·*te*·ra England

inglés ⓜ een·*gles* English (language)

inglés/inglesa ⓜ/① een·*gles*/een·*gle*·sa English

ingrediente ⓜ een·gre·*dyen*·te ingredient

inhalador ⓜ een·a·la·*dor* inhaler

injusto/a ⓜ/① een·*khoos*·to/a unfair

inmigración ① een·mee·gra·*syon* immigration

inocente ee·no·*sen*·te innocent

inseguro/a ⓜ/① een·se·*goo*·ro/a unsafe

insolación ① een·so·la·*syon* sunstroke

instituto ⓜ een·stee·*too*·to high school

instructor(a) ⓜ/① een·strook·*tor*/een·strook·*to*·ra instructor

interesante een·te·re·*san*·te interesting

internacional een·ter·na·syo·*nal* international

intérprete ⓜ&① een·*ter*·pre·te interpreter

intoxicación ① **alimenticia** een·tok·see·ka·*syon* a·lee·men·*tee*·sya food poisoning

inundación ① ee·noon·da·*syon* flood

invierno ⓜ een·*vyer*·no winter

invitar een·vee·*tar* invite

inyección ① een·yek·*syon* injection

inyectarse een·yek·*tar*·se inject

ir eer go
— de compras de *kom*·pras shop
— de excursión de ek·skoor·*syon* hike
— en tobogán en to·bo·*gan* tobogganing

irritación ① ee·ree·ta·*syon* irritation • rash
— de pañal de pa·*nyal* nappy rash

isla ① *ees*·la island

itinerario ⓜ ee·tee·ne·*ra*·ryo itinerary

IVA ⓜ *ee*·va sales tax

izquierda ① ees·*kyer*·da left (direction)

J

jabón ⓜ kha·*bon* soap
jaguar ⓜ kha·*gwar* jaguar
jalar kha·*lar* pull
Japón ⓜ kha·*pon* Japan
jarabe ⓜ kha·*ra*·be cough medicine
jardín ⓜ khar·*deen* garden
— botánico bo·*ta*·nee·ko botanic garden
— de infantes de een·*fan*·tes kindergarten
jardinería ⓕ khar·dee·ne·*ree*·a gardening
jarra ⓕ *kha*·ra jar
jefe/a ⓜ/ⓕ *khe*·fe/a boss • leader • manager
jeringa ⓕ khe·*reen*·ga syringe
jersey ⓜ kher·*say* jumper • sweater
jockey ⓜ kho·*kay* jockey
joven kho·ven young
joyería ⓕ kho·ye·*ree*·a jewellery
jubilado/a ⓜ/ⓕ khoo·bee·*la*·do/a retired
judío/a ⓜ/ⓕ khoo·*dee*·o/a Jewish
juego ⓜ *khwe*·go game (play)
— de computadora de kom·poo·ta·*do*·ra computer game
juegos ⓜ pl **olímpicos** *khwe*·gos o·*leem*·pee·kos Olympic Games
juez ⓜ&ⓕ khwes judge
jugar khoo·*gar* play (a game)
— al tenis al te·nees play tennis
juguetería ⓕ khoo·ge·te·*ree*·a toy shop
juicioso/a ⓜ/ⓕ khwee·*syo*·so/a sensible
juntos/as ⓜ/ⓕ pl *khoon*·tos/as together

L

la píldora ⓕ la *peel*·do·ra the Pill
labios ⓜ pl *la*·byos lips
lado ⓜ *la*·do side
ladrón/ladrona ⓜ/ⓕ la·*dron*/la·*dro*·na thief

lagartija ⓕ la·gar·*tee*·kha lizard
lago ⓜ *la*·go lake
lana ⓕ *la*·na wool
lápiz ⓜ *la*·pees pencil
— de labios de *la*·byos lipstick
largo/a ⓜ/ⓕ *lar*·go/a long
lata ⓕ *la*·ta can • tin
Latinoamérica ⓕ la·tee·no·a·*me*·ree·ka Latin America
latinoamericano/a ⓜ/ⓕ la·tee·no·a·me·ree·*ka*·no/a Latin American
lavadora ⓕ la·va·*do*·ra washing machine
lavandería ⓕ la·van·de·*ree*·a laundrette • laundry
lavar la·*var* wash (something)
lavarse la·*var*·se wash (oneself)
laxantes ⓜ pl lak·*san*·tes laxatives
leer le·*er* read
legal le·*gal* legal
legislación ⓕ le·khees·la·*syon* legislation
lejos *le*·khos far
leña ⓕ *le*·nya firewood
lentes ⓜ pl *len*·tes lenses
— de contacto de kon·*tak*·to contact lenses
lento/a ⓜ/ⓕ *len*·to/a slow
lesbiana ⓕ les·*bya*·na lesbian
levantar le·van·*tar* lift
levantarse le·van·*tar*·se get up
ley ⓕ lay law
libra ⓕ *lee*·bra pound (money)
libre *lee*·bre free (not bound)
librería ⓕ lee·bre·*ree*·a bookshop
libro ⓜ *lee*·bro book
— de frases de *fra*·ses phrasebook
— de viajes de *vya*·khes travel book
ligar lee·*gar* chat up
ligero/a ⓜ/ⓕ lee·*khe*·ro/a light (not heavy)
lila *lee*·la purple

M

limite ⓜ *lee·mee·te* limit

— de equipaje de e·kee·*pa*·khe baggage allowance

— de velocidad de ve·lo·see·*da* speed limit

limpio/a ⓜ/ⓕ *leem*·pyo/a clean

línea ⓕ *lee*·ne·a line

linterna ⓕ leen·*ter*·na flashlight • torch

listo/a ⓜ/ⓕ *lees*·to/a ready

literatura ⓕ lee·te·ra·*too*·ra literature

— de ficción de feek·*syon* fiction

— no novelesca no no·ve·*les*·ka nonfiction

llamada ⓕ ya·*ma*·da phone call

— a cobro revertido a ko·bro re·ver·*tee*·do collect call

llamar ya·*mar* call

— por telefono por te·*le*·fo·no ring (by phone)

llano/a ⓜ/ⓕ *ya*·no/a flat

llanta ⓕ *yan*·ta tyre

llave ⓕ *ya*·ve key

llegadas ⓕ pl ye·*ga*·das arrivals

llegar ye·*gar* arrive

lleno/a ⓜ/ⓕ *ye*·no/a booked out • full

llevar ye·*var* carry • wear

lluvia ⓕ *yoo*·vya rain

local ⓜ lo·*kal* venue

loción ⓕ lo·*syon* lotion

— para después del afeitado *pa*·ra des·*pwes* del a·fay·*ta*·do aftershave

loco/a ⓜ/ⓕ *lo*·ko/a crazy

lodo ⓜ *lo*·do mud

loro ⓜ *lo*·ro parrot

Los Estados ⓜ pl **Unidos** los es·*ta*·dos oo·*nee*·dos the USA

los/las dos ⓜ/ⓕ pl los/las dos both

lubricante ⓜ loo·bree·*kan*·te lubricant

lucha ⓕ *loo*·cha fight

lugar ⓜ loo·*gar* place

— de nacimiento de na·see·*myen*·to place of birth

luna ⓕ *loo*·na moon

— llena *ye*·na full moon

— de miel de myel honeymoon

luz ⓕ loos light

M

madera ⓕ ma·*de*·ra wood

madre ⓕ *ma*·dre mother

madrugada ⓕ ma·droo·*ga*·da dawn

mago/a ⓜ/ⓕ *ma*·go/a magician

maleta ⓕ ma·*le*·ta suitcase

maletín ⓜ ma·le·*teen* briefcase

— de primeros auxilios de pree·*me*·ros ow·*ksee*·yos first-aid kit

malla ⓕ *ma*·ya bathing suit

malo/a ⓜ/ⓕ *ma*·lo/a bad

mamá ⓕ ma·*ma* mum

mamograma ⓜ ma·mo·*gra*·ma mammogram

mañana ⓕ ma·*nya*·na morning • tomorrow

mandíbula ⓕ man·*dee*·boo·la jaw

mando a distancia *man*·do a dees·*tan*·sya remote control

manifestación ⓕ ma·nee·fes·ta·*syon* demonstration (protest)

manillar ⓜ ma·nee·*yar* handlebar

mano ⓕ *ma*·no hand

mantel ⓜ man·*tel* tablecloth

mapa ⓜ *ma*·pa map

maquillaje ⓜ ma·kee·ya·khe make-up

máquina ⓕ *ma*·kee·na machine

— de boletos de bo·*le*·tos ticket machine

mar ⓜ mar sea

maravilloso/a ⓜ/ⓕ ma·ra·vee·*yo*·so/a wonderful

marcador ⓜ mar·ka·*dor* scoreboard

marcapasos ⓜ mar·ka·*pa*·sos pacemaker

marcar mar·*kar* score

marchas ⓕ pl *mar*·chas gears

marcos ⓜ pl *mar*·kos borders (photography)

marea ① ma·*re*·a tide
mareado/a ⓜ/① ma·re·a·do/a dizzy
mareo ⓜ ma·*re*·o seasickness •
travel sickness
mariposa ① ma·ree·*po*·sa butterfly
marrón ma·*ron* brown
martillo ⓜ mar·*tee*·yo hammer
más mas more • most
más cercano/a ⓜ/① mas ser·*ka*·no
nearest
masaje ⓜ ma·*sa*·khe massage
masajista ⓜ&① ma·sa·*khees*·ta
masseur/masseuse
matar ma·*tar* kill
mate *ma*·te matte (photos)
matrícula ① ma·*tree*·koo·la car
registration • license plate number
matrimonio ⓜ ma·tree·*mo*·nyo
marriage
mazo ⓜ *ma*·so mallet
mecánico/a ⓜ/① me·*ka*·nee·ko/a
mechanic
mechero ⓜ me·*che*·ro cigarette
lighter
medianoche ① me·dya·*no*·che
midnight
medias ① pl *me*·dyas pantyhose •
stockings
medicina ① me·dee·*see*·na drug
(medicinal) • medicine
medico/a ⓜ/① me·*dee*·ko/a doctor
medio ⓜ **ambiente** *me*·dyo
am·*byen*·te environment
medio/a ⓜ/① *me*·dyo/a half
mediodía ⓜ me·dyo·*dee*·a noon
medios ⓜ pl *me*·dyos resources
— de comunicación de
ko·moo·nee·ka·*syon* media
— de transporte de trans·*por*·te
transport
meditación ① me·dee·ta·*syon*
meditation
mejor me·*khor* best • better
melodía ① me·lo·*dee*·a tune
mendigo/a ⓜ/① men·*dee*·go/a
beggar

mensaje ⓜ men·*sa*·khe message
menstruación ① mens·*trwa*·syon
menstruation
mentiroso/a ⓜ/① men·tee·ro·so/a
liar
menú ⓜ me·*noo* menu
(a) menudo a me·*noo*·do often
mercado ⓜ mer·*ka*·do market
— de artesanía de ar·te·sa·*nee*·a
craft market
mes ⓜ mes month
mesa ① *me*·sa table
meseta ① me·*se*·ta plateau
metal ⓜ me·*tal* metal
metro ⓜ *me*·tro metre (distance)
mezclar mes·*klar* mix
mezquita ① mes·*kee*·ta mosque
microondas ⓜ mee·kro·*on*·das
microwave oven
miembro ⓜ&① *myem*·bro member
migraña ① mee·*gra*·nya migraine
milímetro ⓜ mee·*lee*·me·tro
millimetre
militares ⓜ pl mee·lee·*ta*·res
military
millón ⓜ mee·*yon* million
minusválido/a ⓜ/①
mee·noos·*va*·lee·do/a disabled
minuto ⓜ mee·*noo*·to minute
mirador ⓜ mee·ra·*dor* lookout
mirar mee·*rar* look • watch
— las vidrieras las vee·*drye*·ras
window-shopping
misa ① *mee*·sa mass (Catholic)
mochila ① mo·*chee*·la backpack
mojado/a ⓜ/① mo·*kha*·do/a wet
monasterio ⓜ mo·nas·*te*·ryo
monastery
monedas ① pl mo·*ne*·das coins
— sueltas *swel*·tas loose change
monitor(a) ⓜ/① mo·nee·*tor*/
mo·nee·*to*·ra (skiing) instructor
monja ① *mon*·kha nun
monopatinaje ⓜ
mo·no·pa·tee·na·khe skateboarding
montaña ① mon·*ta*·nya mountain

N

montar mon·tar ride
monumento ⓜ mo·noo·men·to monument
mordedura ⓕ mor·de·doo·ra bite
moretón ⓜ mo·re·ton bruise
morir mo·reer die
mosca ⓕ mos·ka fly
mosquitera ⓕ mos·kee·te·ra mosquito net
mosquito ⓜ mos·kee·to mosquito
mostrador ⓜ mos·tra·dor counter (shop)
mostrar mos·trar show
motocicleta ⓕ mo·to·see·kle·ta motorcycle
motor ⓜ mo·tor engine
motora ⓕ mo·to·ra motorboat
muchos/as ⓜ/ⓕ pl moo·chos/as many
mudo/a ⓜ/ⓕ moo·do/a mute
muebles ⓜ pl mwe·bles furniture
muela ⓕ mwe·la tooth (back)
muelle ⓜ mwe·ye spring
muerto/a ⓜ/ⓕ mwer·to/a dead
mujer ⓕ moo·kher woman
multa ⓕ mool·ta fine (payment)
mundo ⓜ moon·do world
muñeca ⓕ moo·nye·ka doll • wrist
músculo ⓜ moos·koo·lo muscle
museo ⓜ moo·se·o museum
— **de arte** de ar·te art gallery
música ⓕ moo·see·ka music
músico/a ⓜ/ⓕ moo·see·ko/a musician
musulmán/musulmana ⓜ/ⓕ moo·sool·man/moo·sool·ma·na Muslim
muy mooy very

N

nacional na·syo·nal national
nacionalidad ⓕ na·syo·na·lee·da nationality
nada na·da none • nothing
nadar na·dar swim
nariz ⓕ na·rees nose

naturaleza ⓕ na·too·ra·le·sa nature
naturopatia ⓕ na·too·ro·pa·tya naturopathy
náusea ⓕ now·se·a nausea
náuseas ⓕ pl **del embarazo** now·se·as del em·ba·ra·so morning sickness
navaja ⓕ na·va·kha penknife
necesario/a ⓜ/ⓕ ne·se·sa·ryo/a necessary
necesitar ne·se·see·tar need
negar(se) ne·gar·(se) refuse
negocio ⓜ ne·go·syo business
— **de artículos básicos** de ar·tee·koo·los ba·see·kos convenience store
negro/a ⓜ/ⓕ ne·gro/a black
nieto/a ⓜ/ⓕ nye·to/a grandchild
nieve ⓕ nye·ve snow
niño/a ⓜ/ⓕ nee·nyo/a child
no fumadores foo·ma·do·res nonsmoking
no incluido/a ⓜ/ⓕ een·kloo·ee·do/a excluded
noche ⓕ no·che evening • night
nombre ⓜ nom·bre name
norte ⓜ nor·te north
nosotros/as ⓜ/ⓕ no·so·tros/as we
noticias ⓕ pl no·tee·syas news
novela ⓕ no·ve·la novel
— **negra** ne·gra detective novel
— **rosa** ro·sa romance novel
novia ⓕ no·vya girlfriend
novio ⓜ no·vyo boyfriend
nube ⓕ noo·be cloud
nublado/a ⓜ/ⓕ noo·bla·do/a cloudy
nuestro/a ⓜ/ⓕ nwes·tro/a our
Nueva Zelandia ⓕ nwe·va se·lan·dya New Zealand
nuevo/a ⓜ/ⓕ nwe·vo/a new
número ⓜ noo·me·ro number
— **de habitación** de a·bee·ta·syon room number
— **de pasaporte** de pa·sa·por·te passport number
nunca noon·ka never

O

o o or

objetivo ⓜ ob·khe·*tee*·vo lens

obra ⓕ *o*·bra play (theatre) • work (of art)

obrero/a ⓜ/ⓕ o·*bre*·ro/a factory worker • labourer

océano ⓜ o·*se*·a·no ocean

ocupado/a ⓜ/ⓕ o·koo·*pa*·do/a busy

oeste ⓜ o·*es*·te west

oficina ⓕ o·fee·*see*·na office

— de objetos perdidos de ob·*khe*·tos per·*dee*·dos lost-property office

— de turismo de too·*rees*·mo tourist office

oficinista ⓜ&ⓕ o·fee·see·*nees*·ta office worker

oír o·*eer* hear

ojo ⓜ *o*·kho eye

ola ⓕ *o*·la saucepan • wave

olor ⓜ o·*lor* smell

olvidar ol·vee·*dar* forget

ómnibus ⓜ *om*·nee·boos bus (intercity)

ópera ⓕ *o*·pe·ra opera

operación ⓕ o·pe·ra·*syon* operation (medical)

operador(a) ⓜ/ⓕ o·pe·ra·*dor*/ o·pe·ra·*do*·ra operator

opinión ⓕ o·pee·*nyon* opinion

oportunidad ⓕ o·por·too·nee·*da* chance

oración ⓕ o·ra·*syon* prayer

orden ⓜ or·den order (placement)

orden ⓕ or·den order (command)

ordenar or·de·*nar* order (give command)

oreja ⓕ o·*re*·kha ear

orgasmo ⓜ or·*gas*·mo orgasm

original o·ree·khee·*nal* original

orilla ⓕ **del mar** o·*ree*·ya del mar seaside

oro ⓜ *o*·ro gold

orquesta ⓕ or·*kes*·ta orchestra

orquídea ⓕ or·*kee*·de·a orchid

oscuro/a ⓜ/ⓕ os·koo·ro/a dark

otoño ⓜ o·*to*·nyo autumn

otra vez o·tra ves again

otro/a ⓜ/ⓕ o·tro/a other

oxígeno ⓜ ok·*see*·khe·no oxygen

P

padre ⓜ *pa*·dre father

padres ⓜ pl *pa*·dres parents

pagar pa·*gar* pay

página ⓕ *pa*·khee·na page

pago ⓜ *pa*·go payment

país ⓜ pa·*ees* country (nation)

pájaro ⓜ *pa*·kha·ro bird

pala ⓕ *pa*·la spade

palabra ⓕ pa·*la*·bra word

palacio ⓜ pa·*la*·syo palace

palillo ⓜ pa·*lee*·yo toothpick

paloma ⓕ pa·*lo*·ma dove

palm ⓜ palm palm pilot

palma ⓕ **de coco** *pal*·ma de *ko*·ko coconut palm

panadería ⓕ pa·na·de·*ree*·a bakery

pañal ⓜ pa·*nyal* diaper • nappy

panorámico/a ⓜ/ⓕ pa·no·ra·mee·ko/a panoramic

pantalla ⓕ pan·*ta*·ya screen

pantalones ⓜ pl pan·ta·*lo*·nes pants • trousers

— cortos *kor*·tos shorts

pantera ⓕ pan·*te*·ra panther

pañuelo ⓜ pa·*nywe*·lo handkerchief

— de papel de pa·*pel* tissue

papá ⓜ pa·*pa* dad

papagayo ⓜ pa·pa·*ga*·yo macaw

papel ⓜ pa·*pel* paper

— higiénico ee·*khye*·nee·ko toilet paper

papeles ⓜ pl **del auto** pa·*pe*·les del ow·to car owner's title

paquete ⓜ pa·*ke*·te package • packet • parcel

para siempre pa·ra *syem*·pre forever

parabrisas ⓜ pa·ra·*bree*·sas windscreen

parada ⓕ pa·ra·da stop

— de autobús de ow·to·*boos* bus stop (city)

— de ómnibus de om·nee·boos bus stop (intercity)

— de subteráneo de soob·te·ra·ne·o metro stop

— de taxis de *tak*·sees taxi stand

paraguas ⓜ pa·ra·gwas umbrella

para *pa*·ra for

parar pa·*rar* stop

pared ⓕ pa·*re* wall (inside)

pareja ⓕ pa·re·kha pair (couple) • partner

parlamento ⓜ par·la·*men*·to parliament

parque ⓜ *par*·ke park

— nacional na·syo·*nal* national park

parte ⓕ *par*·te part

partida ⓕ **de nacimiento** par·tee·da de na·see·*myen*·to birth certificate

partido ⓜ par·tee·do match (sport) • party (politics)

partir par·*teer* leave

pasado ⓜ pa·sa·do past

— mañana ma·*nya*·na day after tomorrow

pasado/a ⓜ/ⓕ pa·*sa*·do/a off (spoiled)

pasajero/a ⓜ/ⓕ pa·sa·*khe*·ro/a passenger

pasaporte ⓜ pa·sa·*por*·te passport

pase ⓜ *pa*·se pass (permit)

paseo ⓜ pa·se·o ride • street

pasillo ⓜ pa·*see*·yo aisle (plane, train)

paso ⓜ *pa*·so pass (mountain) • step

pasta dentífrica *pas*·ta den·*tee*·free·ka toothpaste

pastelería ⓕ pas·te·le·*ree*·a cake shop

pastillas ⓕ pl pas·*tee*·yas pills

— antipalúdicas an·tee·pa·*loo*·dee·kas antimalarial tablets

— de menta de *men*·ta mints

— para dormir *pa*·ra dor·*meer* sleeping pills

patrón/patrona ⓜ/ⓕ pa·*tron*/ pa·*tro*·na employer

paz ⓕ pas peace

peatón ⓜ&ⓕ pe·a·ton pedestrian

pecho ⓜ pe·cho chest

pedal ⓜ pe·*dal* pedal

pedazo ⓜ pe·*da*·so piece

pedir pe·*deer* ask (for something) • borrow

peine ⓜ *pay*·ne comb

pelea ⓕ pe·*le*·a quarrel

película ⓕ pe·*lee*·koo·la film (for camera) • movie

peligroso/a ⓜ/ⓕ pe·lee·*gro*·so/a dangerous

pelo ⓜ *pe*·lo hair

pelota ⓕ pe·*lo*·ta ball

— de golf de golf golf ball

peluquero/a ⓜ/ⓕ pe·loo·*ke*·ro/a hairdresser

pene ⓜ *pe*·ne penis

penicilina ⓕ pe·nee·see·*lee*·na penicillin

pensar pen·*sar* think

pensión ⓕ pen·*syon* boarding house

pensionado/a ⓜ/ⓕ pen·syo·*na*·do/a pensioner

pequeñito/a ⓜ/ⓕ pe·ke·*nyee*·to/a tiny

pequeño/a ⓜ/ⓕ pe·*ke*·nyo/a small

perder per·*der* lose

perdido/a ⓜ/ⓕ per·*dee*·do/a lost

perdonar per·do·*nar* forgive

perezoso/a ⓜ/ⓕ pe·re·*so*·so/a lazy

perfume ⓜ per·*foo*·me perfume

periódico ⓜ pe·ryo·dee·ko newspaper

periodista ⓜ&ⓕ pe·ryo·*dees*·ta journalist

P

permiso ⓜ per·*mee*·so permission •
permit
— de trabajo de tra·*ba*·kho work
permit
permitir per·mee·*teer* allow
pero *pe*·ro but
perro/a ⓜ/ⓕ *pe*·ro/a dog
— guía *gee*·a a guide dog
persona ⓕ per·*so*·na person
pesado/a ⓜ/ⓕ pe·*sa*·do/a heavy
pesca ⓕ *pes*·ka fishing
pescadería ⓕ pes·ka·de·*ree*·a fish
shop
peso ⓜ *pe*·so weight
petición ⓕ pe·tee·*syon* petition
pez ⓜ pes fish
picadura ⓕ pee·ka·*doo*·ra bite
(insect)
picazón ⓜ pee·ka·*son* itch
pie ⓜ pye foot
piedra ⓕ *pye*·dra stone
piel ⓕ pyel skin
pierna ⓕ *pyer*·na leg (body)
pila ⓕ *pee*·la battery (small)
píldora ⓕ *peel*·do·ra pill • the Pill
pinchar peen·*char* puncture
pintar peen·*tar* paint
pintor(a) ⓜ/ⓕ peen·*tor*/peen·*to*·ra
painter
pintura ⓕ peen·*too*·ra painting (art)
pinzas ⓕ pl *peen*·sas tweezers
piojos ⓜ pl *pyo*·khos lice
piolet ⓜ pyo·*let* ice axe
piqueta ⓕ pee·*ke*·ta pickaxe
piscina ⓕ pee·*see*·na swimming
pool
piso ⓜ *pee*·so floor (storey)
pista ⓕ *pees*·ta sports track • tennis
court
pizarra ⓕ **blanca** pee·*sa*·ra *blan*·ka
whiteboard
plancha ⓕ *plan*·cha iron (clothes)
planeta ⓜ pla·*ne*·ta planet
planta ⓕ *plan*·ta plant
plástico ⓜ *plas*·tee·ko plastic
plata ⓕ *pla*·ta silver

plataforma ⓕ pla·ta·*for*·ma platform
plato ⓜ *pla*·to plate
playa ⓕ *pla*·ya beach
plaza ⓕ *pla*·sa square
— de toros de *to*·ros bullring
pobre *po*·bre poor
pobreza ⓕ po·*bre*·sa poverty
pocos/as ⓜ/ⓕ pl *po*·kos/as few
poder ⓜ po·*der* power
poder po·*der* can (be able)
poesía ⓕ po·e·*see*·a poetry
polen ⓜ *po*·len pollen
policía ⓕ po·lee·*see*·a police
política ⓕ po·*lee*·tee·ka policy •
politics
político/a ⓜ/ⓕ po·*lee*·tee·ko/a
politician
póliza ⓕ *po*·lee·sa policy (insurance)
poner po·*ner* put
popular po·poo·*lar* popular
por por for
por (día) por (*dee*·a) per (day)
por ciento por *syen*·to percent
por qué por ke why
por vía aérea por *vee*·a a·e·*re*·a by
airmail
por vía terrestre por *vee*·a te·*res*·tre
surface mail
porque *por*·ke because
posible po·*see*·ble possible
potable po·*ta*·ble drinkable
potro ⓜ *po*·tro pony
pozo ⓜ *po*·so well (water)
precio ⓜ *pre*·syo price
— de entrada de en·*tra*·da
admission price
— del cubierto del koo·*byer*·to cover
charge (restaurant)
preferir pre·fe·*reer* prefer
pregunta ⓕ pre·*goon*·ta question
preguntar pre·goon·*tar* ask (a
question)
preocupado/a ⓜ/ⓕ
pre·o·koo·*pa*·do/a worried
preocuparse por pre·o·koo·*par*·se
por care (about something)

preparar pre·pa·*rar* prepare
presentación ① pre·sen·ta·*syon* presentation
presidente/a ⓜ/① pre·see·*den*·te/a president
presión ① pre·*syon* pressure
— arterial ar·te·*ryal* blood pressure
presupuesto ⓜ pre·soo·*pwes*·to budget
prevenir pre·ve·*neer* prevent
primavera ① pree·ma·*ve*·ra spring (season)
primer ministro/a ⓜ/① pree·*mer* mee·*nees*·tro/a prime minister
primera clase ① pree·me·ra *kla*·se first class
primero/a ⓜ/① pree·me·ro/a first
primo/a ⓜ/① *pree*·mo/a cousin
principal preen·see·*pal* main
prisionero/a ⓜ/① pree·syo·ne·ro/a prisoner
privado/a ⓜ/① pree·*va*·do/a private
probar pro·*bar* try (attempt)
producir pro·doo·*seer* produce
productos ⓜ pl pro·*dook*·tos kon·khe·*la*·dos frozen foods
profesor(a) pro·fe·*sor*/pro·fe·so·ra lecturer • teacher
profundo/a ⓜ/① pro·*foon*·do/a deep • profound
programa ⓜ pro·*gra*·ma programme
prolongación ① pro·lon·ga·*syon* extension (visa)
promesa ① pro·me·sa promise
prometida ① pro·me·*tee*·da fiancee
prometido ⓜ pro·me·*tee*·do fiance
pronto *pron*·to soon
propietaria ① pro·pye·*ta*·rya landlady
propietario ⓜ pro·pye·*ta*·ryo landlord
propina ① pro·*pee*·na tip (gratuity)

proteger pro·te·*kher* protect
propuesta ① pro·*pwes*·ta proposal
protegido/a ⓜ/① pro·te·*khee*·do/a protected
protesta ① pro·*tes*·ta protest
protestar pro·tes·*tar* protest
provisiones ① pl pro·vee·*syo*·nes provisions
proximo/a ⓜ/① *prok*·see·mo/a next
proyector ⓜ pro·yek·*tor* projector
prueba ① *prwe*·ba test
— del embarazo del em·ba·*ra*·so pregnancy test kit
pruebas ① pl **nucleares** *prwe*·bas noo·kle·a·res nuclear testing
pueblo ⓜ *pwe*·blo village
puente ⓜ *pwen*·te bridge
puerta ① *pwer*·ta door
puerto ⓜ *pwer*·to harbour • port
puesta ① **del sol** *pwes*·ta del sol sunset
pulga ① *pool*·ga flea
pulmones ⓜ pl pool·*mo*·nes lungs
puntero ⓜ **láser** poon·*te*·ro *la*·ser laser pointer
punto ⓜ *poon*·to dot • full stop • point
puro/a ⓜ/① *poo*·ro/a pure

Q

que ke what
quedar ke·*dar* stay (remain)
quedarse ke·*dar*·se stay (remain)
quejarse ke·*khar*·se complain
quemadura ① ke·ma·*doo*·ra burn
— de sol de sol sunburn
quemar ke·*mar* burn
querer ke·*rer* love • want
quien *kyen* who
quincena ① keen·*se*·na fortnight
quiosco ⓜ kee·*os*·ko newsagency
quiste ⓜ **ovárico** *kees*·te o·va·ree·ko ovarian cyst
quizás kee·*sas* maybe

R

rabo ⓜ *ra*·bo tail

radiador ⓜ ra·dya·*dor* radiator

rana ⓕ *ra*·na frog

rápido/a ⓜ/ⓕ *ra*·pee·do/a fast

raqueta ⓕ ra·*ke*·ta racquet

raro/a ⓜ/ⓕ *ra*·ro/a rare

rata ⓕ *ra*·ta rat

ratón ⓜ ra·*ton* mouse

ratonero ⓜ ra·to·*ne*·ro buzzard

razón ⓕ ra·*son* reason

realista re·a·*lees*·ta realistic

recibir re·see·*beer* receive

recibo ⓜ re·*see*·bo receipt

reciclable re·see·*kla*·ble recyclable

reciclar re·see·*klar* recycle

recientemente re·syen·te·*men*·te recently

recogida ⓕ **de equipajes** re·ko·*khee*·da de e·kee·*pa*·khes baggage claim

recolección ⓕ **de fruta** re·ko·lek·*syon* de *froo*·ta fruit picking

recomendar re·ko·men·*dar* recommend

reconocer re·ko·no·*ser* acknowledge • recognise

recorrido ⓜ **guiado** re·ko·*ree*·do gee·*a*·do guided tour

recto/a ⓜ/ⓕ *rek*·to/a straight

recuerdo ⓜ re·*kwer*·do souvenir

recuerdos ⓜ pl re·*kwer*·dos memories

red ⓕ re net

redondo/a ⓜ/ⓕ re·*don*·do/a round

reembolso ⓜ re·em·*bol*·so refund

referencias ⓕ pl re·fe·*ren*·syas references (work)

refrigeradora ⓕ re·free·khe·ra·*do*·ra refrigerator

refugiado/a ⓜ/ⓕ re·foo·*khya*·do/a refugee

regalo ⓜ re·*ga*·lo gift

— de bodas de *bo*·das wedding present

régimen ⓜ *re*·khee·men diet

registrar re·khees·*trar* check-in (hotel)

reglas ⓕ pl *re*·glas rules

reina ⓕ *ray*·na queen

reírse re·*eer*·se laugh

relación ⓕ re·la·*syon* relationship

relajarse re·la·*khar*·se relax

religión ⓕ re·lee·*khyon* religion

religioso/a ⓜ/ⓕ re·lee·*khyo*·so/a religious

reliquia ⓕ re·*lee*·kya relic

reloj ⓜ re·*lokh* clock

— de pulsera de pool·*se*·ra watch

remo ⓜ *re*·mo rowing

remoto/a ⓜ/ⓕ re·*mo*·to/a remote

reparar re·pa·*rar* repair

reproductor ⓜ **de mp3** re·pro·dook·*tor* de e·me pe tres mp3 player

república ⓕ re·*poo*·blee·ka republic

reserva ⓕ re·*ser*·va reservation

reservar re·ser·*var* book (reserve)

residencia ⓕ **de estudiantes** re·see·*den*·sya de es·too·*dyan*·tes college

residuos ⓜ pl **tóxicos** re·see·dwos *tok*·see·kos toxic waste

respirar res·pee·*rar* breathe

respuesta ⓕ res·*pwes*·ta answer

restaurante ⓜ res·tow·*ran*·te restaurant

revisar re·vee·*sar* check

revisor(a) ⓜ/ⓕ re·vee·*sor*/ re·vee·*so*·ra ticket collector

revista ⓕ re·*vees*·ta magazine

rey ⓜ *ray* king

rezar re·*sar* worship (pray)

rico/a ⓜ/ⓕ *ree*·ko/a rich

riesgo ⓜ *ryes*·go risk

río ⓜ *ree*·o river

ritmo ⓜ *reet*·mo rhythm

robar ro·*bar* rob

roca ⓕ *ro*·ka rock (stone)

rodilla ⓕ ro·*dee*·ya knee

rojo/a ⓜ/ⓕ *ro*·kho/a red

romántico/a ⓜ/ⓕ ro·*man*·tee·ko/a romantic

romper rom·*per* break

ropa ⓕ *ro*·pa clothing

— de cama de *ka*·ma bedding

— interior een·te·*ryor* underwear

rosa *ro*·sa pink

roto/a ⓜ/ⓕ *ro*·to/a broken

rueda ⓕ *rwe*·da wheel

ruidoso/a ⓜ/ⓕ rwee·*do*·so/a loud

ruinas ⓕ pl *rwee*·nas ruins

ruta ⓕ *roo*·ta route

S

sábana ⓕ *sa*·ba·na sheet (bed)

saber sa·*ber* know (how to)

sabroso/a ⓜ/ⓕ sa·*bro*·so/a tasty

sacacorchos ⓜ sa·ka·*kor*·chos corkscrew

sacerdote ⓜ sa·ser·*do*·te priest

saco ⓜ *sa*·ko coat

— de dormir de dor·*meer* sleeping bag

sala ⓕ *sa*·la room

— de espera de es·*pe*·ra waiting room

— de tránsito de *tran*·see·to transit lounge

salario ⓜ sa·*la*·ryo salary

saldo ⓜ *sal*·do balance (account)

salida ⓕ sa·*lee*·da departure • exit

salir sa·*leer* go out (exit)

salir con sa·*leer* kon date (a person)

salir de sa·*leer* de depart

salón ⓜ **de belleza** sa·*lon* de be·*ye*·sa beauty salon

saltar sal·*tar* jump

salud ⓕ sa·*loo* health

salvaeslips ⓜ pl *sal*·va·e·sleeps panty liners

sandalias ⓕ pl san·*da*·lyas sandals

sangre ⓕ *san*·gre blood

santo/a ⓜ/ⓕ *san*·to/a saint

sarampión ⓜ sa·ram·*pyon* measles

sartén ⓕ sar·*ten* frying pan

sastre ⓜ *sas*·tre tailor

secar se·*kar* dry

seco/a ⓜ/ⓕ *se*·ko/a dry

secretario/a ⓜ/ⓕ se·kre·*ta*·ryo/a secretary

seda ⓕ *se*·da silk

seguir se·*geer* follow

segundo ⓜ se·*goon*·do second (time)

segundo/a ⓜ/ⓕ se·*goon*·do/a second (place)

seguro ⓜ se·*goo*·ro insurance

seguro/a ⓜ/ⓕ se·*goo*·ro/a safe

sello ⓜ *se*·yo stamp

semáforos ⓜ pl se·*ma*·fo·ros traffic lights

semana ⓕ se·*ma*·na week

sembrar sem·*brar* plant

semidirecto/a se·mee·dee·*rek*·to/a nondirect

señal ⓕ se·*nyal* sign

sencillo/a ⓜ/ⓕ sen·*see*·yo/a simple

sendero ⓜ sen·*de*·ro path

senos ⓜ pl *se*·nos breasts

sensibilidad ⓕ sen·see·bee·lee·*da* film speed • sensitivity

sensual sen·*swal* sensual

sentarse sen·*tar*·se sit

sentimientos ⓜ pl sen·tee·*myen*·tos feelings

sentir sen·*teer* feel

separado/a ⓜ/ⓕ se·pa·*ra*·do/a separate

separar se·pa·*rar* separate

ser ser be

serie ⓕ *se*·rye series

serio/a ⓜ/ⓕ *se*·ryo/a serious

seropositivo/a ⓜ/ⓕ se·ro·po·see·*tee*·vo/a HIV positive

serpiente ⓕ ser·*pyen*·te snake

servicio ⓜ ser·*vee*·syo service • service charge

— militar mee·lee·*tar* military service

— telefónico automático te·le·*fo*·nee·ko ow·to·*ma*·tee·ko direct-dial

T

servilleta ① ser·vee·*ye*·ta napkin
sexismo ⓜ sek·*sees*·mo sexism
sexo ⓜ *sek*·so sex
— seguro se·*goo*·ro safe sex
si see if
sí see yes
SIDA ① *see*·da AIDS
siempre *syem*·pre always
silla ① *see*·ya chair
— de ruedas de *rwe*·das wheelchair
sillín ⓜ see·*yeen* saddle
sillita ① see·*yee*·ta child seat
similar see·mee·*lar* similar
simpático/a ⓜ/① seem·*pa*·tee·ko/a
nice (person)
sin seen without
— plomo *plo*·mo unleaded
— techo *te*·cho homeless
sinagoga ① see·na·*go*·ga synagogue
sintético/a ⓜ/① seen·*te*·tee·ko/a
synthetic
sobre ⓜ *so*·bre envelope
sobre *so*·bre about • over (above)
sobredosis ① so·bre·*do*·sees
overdose
socialista ⓜ&① so·sya·*lees*·ta
socialist
sol ⓜ sol sun
soldado ⓜ sol·*da*·do soldier
soleado/a ⓜ/① so·le·*a*·do/a sunny
sólo *so*·lo only
solo/a ⓜ/① *so*·lo/a alone
soltero/a ⓜ/① sol·*te*·ro/a single
(unmarried)
sombra ① *som*·bra shade • shadow
sombrero ⓜ som·*bre*·ro hat
soñar so·*nyar* dream
sondeos ⓜ pl son·*de*·os polls
sonreír son·re·*eer* smile
sordo/a ⓜ/① *sor*·do/a deaf
soroche ⓜ so·*ro*·che altitude
sickness
sorpresa ① sor·*pre*·sa surprise
su soo her • his • their
sostén ⓜ sos·*ten* bra
subir soo·*beer* climb

submarinismo ⓜ
soob·ma·ree·*nees*·mo diving
subsidio ⓜ **de desempleo**
soob·*see*·dyo de des·em·*ple*·o dole
subterráneo ⓜ soob·te·*ra*·ne·o
metro • subway
subtítulos ⓜ pl soob·*tee*·too·los
subtitles
sucio/a ⓜ/① *soo*·syo/a dirty
Sudamérica ① sood·a·*me*·ree·ka
South America
sudamericano/a ⓜ/①
sood·a·me·ree·*ka*·no/a South
American
sudar soo·*dar* perspire
suegra ① *swe*·gra mother-in-law
suegro ⓜ *swe*·gro father-in-law
sueldo ⓜ *swel*·do wage
suelo ⓜ *swe*·lo floor (ground)
suerte ① *swer*·te luck
suéter ⓜ *swe*·ter jumper • sweater
suficiente soo·fee·*syen*·te enough
supermercado ⓜ soo·per·mer·*ka*·do
supermarket
superstición ① soo·per·stee·*syon*
superstition
sur ⓜ soor south
surf ⓜ soorf surfing
— sobre la nieve *so*·bre la *nye*·ve
snowboarding

T

tabaco ⓜ ta·*ba*·ko tobacco
tabla ① **de surf** *ta*·bla de soorf
surfboard
tacaño/a ⓜ/① ta·*ka*·nyo/a stingy
tajo ⓜ *ta*·kho chopping board
talco ⓜ *tal*·ko baby powder
talla ① *ta*·ya size (clothes)
taller ⓜ ta·*yer* garage (car repair) •
workshop
tamaño ⓜ ta·*ma*·nyo size (general)
también tam·*byen* also
tampoco tam·*po*·ko neither
tampones ⓜ pl tam·*po*·nes
tampons

tapón ⓜ ta·*pon* plug (bath)
tapones ⓟ pl **para los oídos**
ta·*po*·nes *pa*·ra los o·*ee*·dos earplugs
taquilla ⓕ ta·*kee*·ya ticket office
(cinema, theatre)
tarde *tar*·de late
tarjeta ⓕ tar·*khe*·ta card
— de crédito de *kre*·dee·to credit
card
— de embarque de em·*bar*·ke
boarding pass
— de teléfono de te·*le*·fo·no phone
card
— SIM seem SIM card
tarta ⓕ *ta*·sa **nupcial** tar·ta noop·*syal*
wedding cake
tasa ⓕ **del aeropuerto** *ta*·sa del
a·e·ro·*pwer*·to airport tax
taza ⓕ *ta*·sa cup
teatro ⓜ te·*a*·tro theatre
— de la ópera de la o·*pe*·ra opera
house
techo ⓜ *te*·cho roof
teclado ⓜ te·*kla*·do keyboard
tela ⓕ *te*·la fabric
tele ⓕ *te*·le TV
teleférico ⓜ te·le·*fe*·ree·ko cable car
teléfono ⓜ te·*le*·fo·no telephone
— móbil *mo*·bil mobile phone
— celular se·loo·*lar* cell phone
— público *poo*·blee·ko public
telephone
telegrama ⓜ te·le·*gra*·ma telegram
telenovela ⓕ te·le·no·*ve*·la soap
opera
teleobjetivo ⓜ te·le·ob·khe·*tee*·vo
telephoto lens
telesquí ⓜ te·le·*skee* ski lift
televisión ⓕ te·le·vee·*syon*
television
temperatura ⓕ tem·pe·ra·*too*·ra
temperature
templado/a ⓜ/ⓕ tem·*pla*·do/a
warm
templo ⓜ *tem*·plo temple
temprano tem·*pra*·no early

tenedor ⓜ te·ne·*dor* fork
tener te·*ner* have
— hambre *am*·bre be hungry
— prisa *pree*·sa be in a hurry
— resfriado res·*frya*·do have a cold
— sed se be thirsty
— sueño *swe*·nyo be sleepy
tensión ⓕ **premenstrual** ten·*syon*
pre·mens·*trwal* premenstrual tension
tentempié ⓜ ten·tem·*pye* snack
tercio ⓜ *ter*·syo third
terrible te·*ree*·ble terrible
terminar ter·mee·*nar* finish
terremoto ⓜ te·re·*mo*·to earthquake
testarudo/a ⓜ/ⓕ tes·ta·*roo*·do/a
stubborn
tía ⓕ *tee*·a aunt
tiempo ⓜ *tyem*·po time • weather
tienda ⓕ *tyen*·da shop
— de fotografía de fo·to·gra·*fee*·a
camera shop
— de provisiones de cámping de
pro·vee·*syo*·nes de *kam*·peen
camping store
— de recuerdos de re·*kwer*·dos
souvenir shop
— de ropa de *ro*·pa clothing store
— deportiva de·por·*tee*·va sports
store
Tierra ⓕ *tye*·ra Earth
tierra ⓕ *tye*·ra land
tijeras ⓕ pl tee·*khe*·ras scissors
tímido/a ⓜ/ⓕ *tee*·mee·do/a shy
tío ⓜ *tee*·o uncle
típico/a ⓜ/ⓕ *tee*·pee·ko/a typical
tipo ⓜ *tee*·po type
— de cambio de *kam*·byo exchange
rate
toalla ⓕ to·*a*·ya towel
toallita ⓕ to·a·*yee*·ta flannel •
wash cloth
tobillo ⓜ to·*bee*·yo ankle
tocar to·*kar* play (an instrument) •
touch
— la guitarra la gee·*ta*·ra play the
guitar

todavía (no) to·da·*vee*·a (no) (not) yet
todo *to*·do everything
todo/a ⓜ/ⓕ sg *to*·do/a all
todos/as ⓜ/ⓕ pl *to*·dos/as all
tomar to·*mar* drink • take
tono ⓜ *to*·no dial tone
torcedura ⓕ tor·se·*doo*·ra sprain
tormenta ⓕ tor·*men*·ta storm
toro ⓜ *to*·ro bull
torre ⓕ *to*·re tower
torta ⓕ *tor*·ta cake
tos ⓕ tos cough
tostadora ⓕ tos·ta·*do*·ra toaster
trabajar tra·ba·*khar* work
trabajo ⓜ tra·*ba*·kho work
(occupation)
— a tiempo parcial a *tyem*·po
par·*syal* part-time work
— a tiempo completo a *tyem*·po
kom·*ple*·to full-time work
— administrativo
ad·mee·nees·tra·*tee*·vo paperwork
— de limpieza de leem·*pye*·sa
cleaning
— eventual e·ven·*twal* casual work
traducir tra·doo·*seer* translate
traer tra·*er* bring
traficante ⓜ **de drogas**
tra·fee·*kan*·te de *dro*·gas drug dealer
tráfico ⓜ *tra*·fee·ko traffic
traje ⓜ *tra*·khe suit
— de baño de *ba*·nyo swimsuit
tramposo/a ⓜ/ⓕ tram·*po*·so/a
cheat
tranquilo/a ⓜ/ⓕ tran·*kee*·lo/a quiet
tranvía ⓜ tran·*vee*·a tram
tratar de ligar tra·*tar* de lee·*gar*
chat up
tren ⓜ tren train
trepar tre·*par* climb • scale
tribunal ⓜ tree·boo·*nal* court (legal)
triste *trees*·te sad
tú too you sg inf
tumba ⓕ *toom*·ba grave • tomb
tumbarse toom·*bar*·se lie (not stand)
turista ⓜ&ⓕ too·*rees*·ta tourist

U

uniforme ⓜ oo·nee·*for*·me
uniform
universidad ⓕ oo·nee·ver·*see*·da
university
universo ⓜ oo·nee·*ver*·so universe
urgente oor·*khen*·te urgent
Usted oos·*te* you sg pol
Ustedes oo·*ste*·des you pl
útil *oo*·teel useful

V

vaca ⓕ *va*·ka cow
vacaciones ⓕ pl va·ka·*syo*·nes
holidays • vacation
vacante va·*kan*·te vacant
vacío/a ⓜ/ⓕ va·*see*·o/a empty
vacuna ⓕ va·*koo*·na vaccination
vagina ⓕ va·*khee*·na vagina
vagón ⓜ va·*gon* train carriage
— restaurante res·tow·*ran*·te dining
car
validar va·lee·*dar* validate
valiente va·*lyen*·te brave
valioso/a ⓜ/ⓕ va·*lyo*·so/a valuable
valle ⓜ *va*·ye valley
valor ⓜ va·*lor* value
varios/as ⓜ/ⓕ pl *va*·ryos/as
several
vaso ⓜ *va*·so glass (drinking)
vegetariano/a ⓜ/ⓕ
ve·khe·ta·*rya*·no/a vegetarian
— estricto/a ⓜ/ⓕ vs·*treek*·to/a
vegan
vela ⓕ *ve*·la candle • sail
velocidad ⓕ ve·lo·see·*da* speed
velocímetro ⓜ ve·lo·*see*·me·tro
speedometer
vena ⓕ *ve*·na vein
vendaje ⓜ ven·*da*·khe bandage
vender ven·*der* sell
venenoso/a ⓜ/ⓕ ve·ne·*no*·so/a
poisonous
venir ve·*neer* come
ventana ⓕ ven·*ta*·na window

ventilador ⓜ ven·tee·la·*dor* fan (machine)

ver ver see

verano ⓜ ve·*ra*·no summer

verde *ver*·de green

verdulero/a ⓜ/ⓕ ver·doo·le·ro/a greengrocer

verja ⓕ *ver*·kha gate

vestíbulo ⓜ ves·*tee*·boo·lo foyer

vestido ⓜ ves·*tee*·do dress

vestuario ⓜ ves·*twa*·ryo changing room • wardrobe

vez ⓕ ves time (occasion)

viajar vya·*khar* travel

viaje ⓜ *vya*·khe trip

vida ⓕ *vee*·da life

— nocturna nok·*toor*·na night life

vidrio ⓜ *vee*·dryo glass (material)

viejo/a ⓜ/ⓕ *vye*·kho/a old

viento ⓜ *vyen*·to wind

viñedo ⓜ vee·*nye*·do vineyard

violar vyo·*lar* rape

visado ⓜ vee·*sa*·do visa

visitar vee·see·*tar* visit

vista ⓕ *vees*·ta view

vitaminas ⓕ pl vee·ta·*mee*·nas vitamins

viuda ⓕ *vyoo*·da widow

viudo ⓜ *vyoo*·do widower

víveres ⓜ pl *vee*·ve·res food supplies

vivir vee·*veer* live

volado/a ⓜ/ⓕ vo·*la*·do/a stoned (drugged)

volar vo·*lar* fly

volver vol·*ver* return

votar vo·*tar* vote

voz ⓕ vos voice

vuelo ⓜ *vwe*·lo flight

— doméstico do·*mes*·tee·ko domestic flight

Y

y ee and

ya ya already

yip ⓜ yeep jeep

yo yo I

Z

zapatería ⓕ sa·pa·te·*ree*·a shoe shop

zapatos ⓜ pl sa·*pa*·tos shoes

zodíaco ⓜ so·*dee*·a·ko zodiac

zoológico ⓜ so·o·*lo*·khee·ko zoo

Index

For topics that are covered in several sections of this book, we've indicated the most relevant page number in bold.

INDEX

10 Ways to Start a Sentence

| When's (the next flight)? | ¿Cuándo sale (el próximo vuelo)? | kwan·do sa·le (el prok·see·mo vwe·lo) |

| Where's the (station)? | ¿Dónde está (la estación)? | don·de es·ta (la es·ta·syon) |

| How much is (a room)? | ¿Cuánto cuesta (una habitación)? | kwan·to kwes·ta (oo·na a·bee·ta·syon) |

| I'm looking for (a hotel). | Estoy buscando (un hotel). | es·toy boos·kan·do (oon o·tel) |

| Do you have (a map)? | ¿Tiene (un mapa)? | tye·ne (oon ma·pa) |

| Is there (a toilet)? | ¿Hay (un baño)? | ai (oon ba·nyo) |

| I'd like (a coffee). | Quisiera (un café). | kee·sye·ra (oon ka·fe) |

| Can I (enter)? | ¿Se puede (entrar)? | se pwe·de (en·trar) |

| Could you please (help me)? | ¿Puede (ayudarme), por favor? | pwe·de (a·yoo·dar·me) por fa·vor |

| Do I have to (get a visa)? | ¿Necesito (obtener un visado)? | ne·se·see·to (ob·te·ner oon vee·sa·do) |